INTERNATIONAL COMMUNICATION

Essential Readings

Second Edition

Edited by Vandana Pednekar-Magal

Grand Valley State University

Bassim Hamadeh, CEO and Publisher
Michael Simpson, Vice President of Acquisitions
Jamie Giganti, Managing Editor
Jess Busch, Graphic Design Supervisor
Mark Combes, Acquisitions Editor
Brian Fahey, Licensing Associate
Sean Adams, Interior Design

Copyright © 2015 by Vandana Pednekar-Magal. All rights reserved. No part of this publication may be reprinted, reproduced, transmitted, or utilized in any form or by any electronic, mechanical, or other means, now known or hereafter invented, including photocopying, microfilming, and recording, or in any information retrieval system without the written permission of Cognella, Inc.

First published in the United States of America in 2015 by Cognella, Inc.

Trademark Notice: Product or corporate names may be trademarks or registered trademarks, and are used only for identification and explanation without intent to infringe.

Printed in the United States of America

ISBN: 978-1-62661-541-0 (pbk)/ 978-1-62661-542-7 (br)

www.cognella.com   800-200-3908

CONTENTS

INTRODUCTION VII

PART I—MAKING SENSE OF GLOBALIZATION

THE WORLD HORIZON OPENS UP: ON THE SOCIOLOGY
OF GLOBALIZATION 3
    By Ulrich Beck

DISJUNCTURE AND DIFFERENCE IN GLOBAL CULTURAL ECONOMY 35
    By Arjun Appadurai

PART II—GLOBALIZATION AND COMMUNICATION

DRAWING A BEAD ON GLOBAL COMMUNICATION THEORIES 55
    By John D. H. Downing

GLOBAL COMMUNICATION ORDERS 69
    By Oliver Boyd-Barrett

Part III—State Power and Communication

PUBLIC DIPLOMACY AND SOFT POWER 93
    By Joseph S. Nye, Jr.

MEDIA AND SOVEREIGNTY: THE GLOBAL INFORMATION
REVOLUTION AND ITS CHALLENGE TO STATE POWER 107
    By Monroe E. Price

Part IV—Diaspora and Communication

DIASPORAS AND CONTRA-FLOWS BEYOND NATION-CENTRISM 115
    By Myria Georgiou and Roger Silverstone

TRANSNATIONAL COMMUNITIES AND GLOBAL COMMUNICATION 131
    By Vandana Pednekar-Magal and Keith Oppenheim

BRAZIL AND THE GLOBALIZATION OF TELENOVELAS 145
    By Cacilda M. Rêgo and Antonio C. La Pastina

ISSUES IN WORLD CINEMA 163
    By Wimal Dissanayake

Part V—Discontents of Globalism and New Directions

GLOBALISM'S DISCONTENTS 177
    By Joseph Stiglitz

COUNTERHEGEMONIC GLOBALIZATION: TRANSNATIONAL SOCIAL MOVEMENTS IN THE CONTEMPORARY POLITICAL ECONOMY 189
    By Peter Evans

THE NEW PUBLIC SPHERE: GLOBAL CIVIL SOCIETY, COMMUNICATION NETWORKS, AND GLOBAL GOVERNANCE 197
    By Manuel Castells

Introduction

At the end of the 20th century, International Communication Studies began grappling with the rapidly moving landscape of media and communication and the course and intensity of globalization. Intensified cross-border transactions of global finance, contingencies of a deeply global economy involving global business and labor deployment, as well as new political realities triggered by new coalitions, conflict and strife between nations and people are the new determinants of global flows. Making sense of cross-border communication in this rapidly intensifying movement of money, people, information, cultural texts and goods across national borders is a challenge for students of International Communication Studies.

Early scholars of International Communication examined the global communications infrastructure and the asymmetrical media flows. They developed theories about impact of global media content on national cultures seen as perpetuating dependency akin to colonial structures.

International Communication research today is rooted in those sensibilities and yet has moved beyond those frames of inquiry. Recent debates study global and regional complexities and consider global media usage of content from new production centers. They consider the multi-directional flows between affluent, technologically advanced nations and culturally diverse, developing nations. Clearly, International Communication Studies has intensified in its scope and scholarship. A wealth of literature exists that has grappled with this multifarious discipline and contributed to our understanding of globalization and communication.

They examine reception of media texts floating across national cultural spaces; and how the readers of these texts situated in unique cultural contexts tend to derive pleasures, identities and meanings in complex and often contradictory ways. They point out other developments such as the rise of active global publics and emergence of a global public sphere on the new media infrastructure.

With this collection I have aimed at bringing together key texts that guide the reader in making sense of this rapidly expanding and shifting terrain of global communication. In their varying modes of explanations, the selections provide an interpretation and criticism of contemporary media communication in its global dimension. I have selected what I consider critical and engaging texts that will guide the student through this terrain of scholarship. The collection is designed to provide diverse perspectives to enable the reader to get a sense of multiple dimensions of contemporary International Communication as well as to become critically aware of recent debates and issues in the International Communication theory.

Part I

MAKING SENSE OF GLOBALIZATION

The two selections in this section explain the dynamics of globalization. The first chapter excerpted from Ulrich Beck's book addresses the question: What is globalization? Beck addresses this by defining "dimensions" of globalization: ecological, economic, work organization, culture and civil society. Earlier models of society were centered on the nation-state so that all social practices are seen as contained in a nation. Beck argues that globalization and globality have shaken this conceptualization. Beck sees contemporary social and political practices unfolding in transnational global spaces where communities and identities are formed and post-international politics are played out. Beck describes the world as globalized and polycentric where organizations, problems, events, communities and structures are increasingly transnational in nature.

Appadurai's essay explains globalization in terms of flows: movement of money, ideas, people—refugees, tourists, immigrants, and media images that intersect in communities in different and contradictory ways. While these global flows homogenize the world to an extent, they are also the source of cultural heterogenization, as forces from new societies become indigenized. Ultimately, he refutes the utility of center-periphery relations as a useful framework and sees flows or "scapes" are cornerstones of a world that is imagined by people and groups of people, often subverting the official minds of business and politics.

THE WORLD HORIZON OPENS UP

On the Sociology of Globalization

By Ulrich Beck

> The bourgeoisie has through its exploitation of the world market given a cosmopolitan character to production and consumption in every country. To the great chagrin of reactionists, it has drawn from under the feel of industry the national ground on which it stood. All old-established national industries have been destroyed or are daily being destroyed. They are dislodged by new industries, whose introduction becomes a life and death question for all civilized nations. [...] In place of the old local and national seclusion and self-sufficiency, we have intercourse in every direction, universal interdependence of nations. And as in material, so also in intellectual production. The intellectual creations of individual nations become common property. National one-sidedness and narrow-mindedness become more and more impossible, and from the numerous national and local literatures, there arises a world literature.[1]

This quotation is not from some neoliberal manifesto of 1996 but from the *Communist Manifesto* of Marx and Engels, first published in February 1848. It shows a number of things: first, that the authors of the *Communist Manifesto* already eulogized the revolutionary role of the 'bourgeoisie' in world history; second, that the debate on 'exploitation of the world market' goes back much further than the

---

Ulrich Beck, "The World Horizon Opens Up: On the Sociology of Globalization," *What is Globalization*, pp. 22-63. Copyright © 2000 by Polity Press. Reprinted with permission.

short-term memory of public discussions would care to admit; third, that ironically the neo-liberal and original Marxist positions share the same basic assumptions; and fourth, but not least, that the national vision which still holds the social sciences captive was already being questioned when it first emerged in the maelstrom of rising industrial capitalism.

SOCIOLOGY AS THE POWER TO CREATE INTELLECTUAL ORDER: THE CONTAINER THEORY OF SOCIETY

'Modern' sociology is defined in its typical textbooks as the 'modern' science of 'modern' society. This both conceals and helps to gain acceptance for a classificatory schema that we might call the *container theory of society*.

1. According to this theory, societies both politically and theoretically presuppose 'state control of space' (J. Agnew and S. Corbridge), so that sociology here aligns itself with the regulatory authority or power of the national state. This is expressed in a vision of societies as (by definition) subordinate to states, of societies as *state* societies, of social order as state order. Thus, both in everyday life and in scientific discourse, one speaks of 'French', 'American' or 'German' society.

    Furthermore, the concept of the political is associated not with society but with the state—which has not always been the case, as M. Viroli has shown.[2] Only in this conceptual and institutional framework do 'modern' societies become individual societies separate from one another. They really are held in the space controlled by national states *as in a container*. At the same time, it is part of the very concept of 'modern' societies that they are unpolitical, whereas political action is located only in the space controlled by the state.

2. This schema applies not only outwardly but also on the inside. The internal space of outwardly separable societies is subdivided into a number of totalities which, on the one hand, are conceptualized and analysed as *collective identities* (classes, status groups, religious and ethnic groups, male and female ways of living) and, on the other hand, are classified according to the organic 'social system' metaphor and theoretically inserted into the autonomous worlds of economics, politics, law, science, family, etc., each with its own distinctive 'logics' or 'codes'. Internal homogeneity is essentially a creation of state control. All kinds of social practices—production, culture, language, labour market, capital, education—are stamped and standardized, defined and rationalized, by the national state, but at least are labelled as national economy, national language, literature, public life, history, and so on. The state establishes a territorial unit as a 'container', in which statistics are systematically collected about economic and social processes and situations. In this way, the categories of the state's self-observation become the categories of empirical social science, so that sociological definitions of reality confirm those of bureaucracy.

3. This image of externally and internally differentiated societies, constituted by individual national states, goes together with the *evolutionary self-image* and self-consciousness of modern societies. To be modern means to be superior. This universalist pretension is expressed, in the basic rights and rules of democratic self-regulation, as a claim to 'human emancipation from the self-incurred dependence of a minor' (Kant). But the claim to bestow happiness condensed, first, in the violent history of European colonialism and imperialism, and then, after the Second World War, in so-called 'development politics' and the 'theory of developing countries'. It is no accident that the word 'modernization' made its debut in the early fifties, in a book entitled *The Modernization of Developing Countries*. The empirical political and social sciences, seeing themselves as policy doctors or engineers, then worked out 'social indicators' that seemed to make it possible to measure the stages and successes of modernization and, in the case of national states, to monitor and shape the process.

I do not want to make a name for myself by setting up Aunt Sallies. Debates of recent years have severely shaken the axioms of a sociology of the first modernity focused on the national state. But its programmed vision—most of all in organized research and a number of long-standing controversies—remains dominant particularly in Germany. And what this container theory of society permits, or indeed compels, is a return to the origins of sociology in the formative period of the nation-state in nineteenth- and early twentieth-century Europe. The association between sociology and nation-state was so extensive that the image of 'modern', organized individual societies—which became definitive with the national model of political organization—itself became an absolutely necessary concept in and through the founding work of the classical social scientists. Beyond all their differences, such theorists as Emile Durkheim, Max Weber and even Karl Marx shared a territorial definition of modern society;[3] and thus a model of society centred on the national state, which has today been shaken by globality and globalization. If a Spenglerian mood of decline can be felt everywhere in people's musings, it surely has something to do with the fact that both society and sociology are caught in the 'territorial trap' (Agnew and Corbridge) of equating society with the national state. But the world is not declining, because—as Max Weber argued against himself, as it were—the light of the great cultural problems moves on and scientists too are forced to revise their thinking, to reorient themselves conceptually in the non-integrated multiplicity of a world without frontiers.

To make this background assumption clear and conscious, nothing is as helpful as to develop and probe *alternatives*. The sociology of globalization may be thought of as involving a loose, motley collection of dissidents from the sociology of national states. In comparison with the mainstream, it has long been a question of theories and research projects or approaches, often indeed no more than promises, which have arisen in quite different cultural and thematic contexts (from research into migration, through international class analysis, international politics and the theory of democracy, to cultural studies and the sociology of big cities), which often contradict one another, yet which somehow or other break through the thought-barrier of the national state—and, we should stress, do so less through criticism than through the working out of alternative ways of thinking. In other words, the globalization debate in the social sciences may be understood and developed as a fruitful dispute about which basic assumptions and images of society, which units *for analysis*, can *replace* the axiomatics of the national state.

Thought and research that remain trapped in a vision of separate social worlds organized on a national basis can find no place for anything that falls between the inner and the outer. This intermediate category—the category of the ambivalent, the mobile, the volatile, the Here-and-There—first opens up in the context of migration research, in the beginnings of *transnational social spaces*. World-system theory then deepens this perspective to the point that all social action is seen as taking place within *one overarching* framework, the framework of the capitalist world-system, in which an advancing inequality and division of labour install themselves.

But this world-system view has in turn been nuanced by reference to what the political theorist James Rosenau calls 'the two worlds of world polities': that is, the idea that there is not a single global society but at least *two* competing ones: the society of (national) states, and the many different transnational organizations, players, groups and individuals who build and consolidate a tissue of social relationships.

In all the analyses mentioned so far, spaces of transnational action arise in one way or another because actors set out to achieve them. In the theory of *world risk society*, however, the category of unintended consequences appears in place of the basic unity of purposive action. It is global risks (their social and political construction), and thus various ecological crises (or definitions of crisis), which bring about new kinds of world disorder and turmoil.

In research associated with 'cultural theory', the linearity assumption and the Either-Or of national axiomatics are replaced by Both-And postulates: globalization *and* regionalization, linkage *and* fragmentation, centralization *and* decentralization, are dynamics that belong together as two sides of the same coin.

In considerations on *transnational civil society*, socio-cultural processes, experiences, conflicts and identities become visible which orient themselves by a 'one-world model' of transnational social movements, globalization 'from below', and a new world citizenship. Here the axiomatics that equates modernity with non-political individual societies breaks down. World society without a world state means a society that is *not politically organized,* where new opportunities for action and power arise for transnational actors that have no democratic legitimation. This means that a new transnational space of the moral and the subpolitical is opening up, as we may see in such phenomena as consumer boycotts but also in questions to do with cross-cultural communication and criticism.

These basic ideas associated with post-national or transnational images of society, and the units that they mark out for investigation, should now be briefly outlined. At the same time, 'development logics' will have to be contrasted with the dynamic of globalization, so that a complex picture (one which includes internal contradictions) is drawn of the globalization debate in the social sciences.

TRANSNATIONAL SOCIAL SPACES

The pill to be used against abstractness, including the abstractness of 'the global', is examples. What does 'transnational social space' mean?

Africa is not a Continent but a Concept

As Patricia Alleyne-Dettmers shows in her study 'Tribal Arts', Africa is not a fixed geographical magnitude, not a separate place on the globe, but a *transnational idea and the staging of that idea*.[4] This is intentionally organized at many different places in the world: in the Caribbean, in the ghettoes of Manhattan, in the Southern states of the USA, in the *favelas* of Brazil, but also at Europe's largest street carnival in London. Here the masks, music, costumes and dance are carefully selected and designed in accordance with two governing principles. Everything is drawn from the 'African' reservoir of cultural ideas anywhere in the world; and everything must also be adapted to the subcultural peculiarities of London's black districts.

Nothing in the whole of the African continent corresponds to the Africa that is staged on the streets of London. How could it? Where is Africa to be found in a world society with porous frontiers? In the ruins that the colonial masters have left behind in Africa? In the big-city shapes of an only half-modernized Africa? In the African four-star hotels? On organized safaris? In the 'back to the roots' hopes and illusions of Black Americans? In the books about Africa that are written in Western universities? In the Caribbean with its riotous profusion of forms? Or even in the struggle for a national identity in Britain's black subcultures?

In the eyes of those who design the dances and masks of Notting Hill's 'African carnival', Africa has lost its geographical location. For them 'Africa' is a vision, an idea, from which models can be derived for a *black aesthetic*. Not the least aim of this is to ground, create or renew an African national identity for blacks *in Britain*. This Africa, or counter-Africa, is in the strictest sense an 'imagined community'; it serves to break down and overcome the alienation of Afro-Caribbean groups in Britain. We could say that 'there is Africa' in Notting Hill.

Transnational 'communities' really are that paradoxical. What is 'discovered' here, but in reality *invented*, often contradicts what floats around as 'Africa' in the heads of each transnational 'African'. A large part of historical Africa was reduced to slavery and scattered around the world. Its cultures were broken up and destroyed. Hence those people who are called 'African' (often by others) have also shaken off that image of Africa. For many 'Africans', indeed, Africa and being African is the very identity they oppose and reject. Perhaps they grew up in a pot-pourri of cultures where any clarity about the matter had long been lost, and where the quality of being black had an especially negative value. At any event, the outcome is quite paradoxical. Blacks in the Caribbean and in English cities associate 'Africa' with non-identity and non-progress, with drums, dancing, superstition, naked, uneducated tribesmen, permanent hopelessness.

One can see in this the negative mirror image of a Eurocentric idea of Africa, which blacks have adopted in the Western metropolis. But this only makes the question sharper: what and where is 'Africa' within transnational social space?

American Mexicans and Mexican Americans

Transnational social spaces cancel the local associations of community that are contained in the national concept of society. The figure of thought at issue joins together what cannot be combined: to live and act both here and there. Ludger Pries has illustrated what this means from the field of migration research.[5]

In the imaginative and political world of individual societies organized as national states, migration is broken down into the stages and contexts of dissolution, travel, arrival and (not necessarily successful) integration, each of which requires separate causal investigation. By contrast, the approach centred on transnational social spaces maintains that something new is emerging: social contexts of life and action to which Here-and-There or Both-And applies. Between the separate, organized worlds, what Martin Albrow calls new 'social landscapes' combine and transmute places of departure *and* places of arrival.

In a study of transnational forms of community, life and politics stretching between Mexicans in North America and their places of origin, Robert Smith shows how this everyday link operates.

> For some communities of the *Mixteca Poblana,* support committees were organized in New York that collected money among migrant workers for the laying of drinking-water pipes in their community of origin, or for the restoration of churches and village squares. Major decisions and issues were sorted out in tele-conferences with officials in the community of origin. It was not uncommon for the sums of money collected in New York to be greater than the public spending on infrastructure in the Mexican community. One important aspect—and a serious argument for the stability and stabilization of *transnational social spaces*—is the fact that the Mexican state has now recognized not only the huge economic significance of the migrant workers, but also their political significance. Since the presidential elections of 1988, the critical voting power of the Mexican workers abroad (who voted in on above-average proportion for the ruling PRI party) has become especially apparent, and the Mexican government pursues an active policy of integrating them economically, politically and culturally. Thus, Mexican mayors sometimes travel to New York to put investment proposals for village development before migrant associations. And the Embassy actively supports migrants' sports associations, as well as the development of Guadalupe groups (which are supposed to organize the cult worship of the Virgin of Guadalupe, the main national holy figure in Mexico). At every level of Mexican politics, labour migration is no longer seen just as a (passive) safety-valve for employment problems, but as an important capital and human resource for the country's own economic and social development. As a result of this policy orientation, the Mexico-USA migration system increasingly involves institutional pillars that give a flanking stability to the emergent *transnational social spaces*. [...] The social and economic dovetailing between region of origin and region of arrival is not, however, just a matter of nostalgia or tradition (sticking to village festivals) or of care for an older generation that has stayed behind. Rather, what develop in the *Mixteca* are

economic activities that point far beyond purely transitory relations of a migratory character. In Greater New York, for example, there are a *Puebla Food Incorporation* and a clan of tortilla-producing families that has already made millions from the traditional Mexican food. Transnational production and marketing structures thus stretch between the *Mixteca* and New York—structures that imply dimension of 'cumulative causation'. Insofar as the dynamic of migration networks keeps the migratory flow moving, the demand increases for specifically Mexican foods and services, which in turn open up new opportunities for migration-related gain in the regions of origin and arrival.

In New York itself, for example, newly arriving migrant workers can turn not only to relatives and acquaintances, but also to a well-polished network of informal support groups, specialist services and solidarity organizations (legal advice bureaux, committees to help people from special ethnic groups or regions, etc.). Whole streets (e.g. the northern part of Amsterdam Street, or certain neighbourhoods in Queen's) bear witness to this by now very stable infrastructure, on which transnational migrants can build and which is at the same time reproduced by them. There are gainful activities and social groups (of Mexicans and US-Americans) which live entirely on the constant migration and *transmigrants*, and whose vital interest lies in further building up *transnational social spaces*. This also applies to the sports associations, where some of the migrant workers living in New York (perhaps *indocumentados*, without a work or residence permit) come together every Sunday. In the 1996 football season, sixty-five teams were registered for the Mexicans' own league. [...]

In the USA (so far more strongly in California than in New York, for example), various political groupings and organizations (e.g. the *Frente indígena oaxaqueña binacional* or the newspaper *La Mixteca Año 2000*) support the economic interests and human rights of the migrant workers. The political pressure these groups can exert within the USA, but above all on the Mexican side of the border, is quite often greater than the potential influence of local politicians. The director of the Mexican football league in New York put it like this: 'As simple Mexicans and migrant workers, we don't count for anything at all. But now we're suddenly being courted by high-up Mexican politicians.'[6]

To the best of my knowledge, no one has yet investigated whether—as one may suspect—similar transnational social spaces exist between Turkish Germans and German Turks.

Logics, Dimensions and Consequences of Globalization

As we have already intimated, a basic dispute runs like a red thread through the globalization literature.[7] The question of the impetus behind globalization finds two contrasting answers (each in turn taking a number of different forms). The first group of authors point to the existence of one dominant 'logic' of globalization, while others work with theories that suggest a phenomenon with a complex set of causes. This central theoretical controversy, by the way, entails that the word 'globalization' does not have a single horizon of meaning, that indeed often *contradictory* meanings are associated with it.

At the same time, we see the sociology of globalization repeating the historical divergence between Marx and Weber; that is, between a view of the dominance of the economic, and a theoretical pluralism involving economic, social and cultural approaches (and for which any analysis that operates with just a single logic therefore excludes a crucial dimension of globalization). The adding together of (apparently) mutually exclusive logics of globalization introduces, or slides into, a view in which different partial logics of globalization compete with one another.

First, we should consider approaches which hold one special dimension or logic of globalization to be central. Here the key authors are Wallerstein, Rosenau, Gilpin, Held, Robertson and Appadurai, in addition to Giddens as the common reference point. Wallerstein—one of the first in the seventies to confront the social sciences with the question of globalization—introduced the concept of a *world-system* and argued that capitalism was the engine of globalization. Rosenau, Gilpin and Held have concerned themselves more with international politics. They challenge the nation-state orthodoxy by stressing the importance both of technological globalization (the science and information society) and of political-military factors and viewpoints (power politics).

No doubt, the ecological crisis and—following the Rio conference in 1992—its worldwide recognition have had a lasting and devastating impact on ways of thinking and acting that focus on the national state. World society, accused of being a 'world *risk* society', has become conscious of itself as sharing a common ecological fate.

Robertson, Appadurai, Albrow, Featherstone, Lash, Urry and many others argue within the tradition of cultural theory. Strongly opposing the widespread notion of a 'McDonaldization' of the planet, they insist that *cultural* globalization does not mean the world is becoming culturally homogeneous. Rather, it involves a process of 'glocalization', which is highly contradictory both in content and in its multiple consequences. Two of the most problematic effects for the stratification of world society should be briefly examined: the problem of *global wealth, local poverty* (Bauman), and the problem of *capitalism without work*.

Each of the authors mentioned locates the origin and results of the globalization dynamic mainly in *one* sector of institutional action (whether the economy, technology, international politics, ecology, culture or world industry), or else in new social inequalities measured on a world scale. It is in the interplay of these perspectives that a plural sociology of globalization comes into view.

Capitalist World-system: Wallerstein

The conception of transnational social spaces is a medium-range theory. It breaks down the nation-state view of society and its 'container theory' of nationally separate social worlds, replacing them with *different* modes of life, transnationally integrated spaces of social action that circumvent or cross over postulated frontiers.

The metaphor of a space or area is here contradictory. For the dominant feature of the 'spaces' in question is that they *overcome* distance. 'Transnational' implies that forms of life and action emerge whose inner logic comes from the inventiveness with which people create and maintain social lifeworlds and action contexts where distance is not a factor. This raises a number of questions for sociological research. How are transnational lifeworlds transcending distance and frontiers *possible* in the first place? How can they be put together and cultivated at the level of individual action, often in the teeth of resistance from national state bureaucracies? Are they stateless, or perhaps even institutionless, early forms of transnational world societies? Which orientations, resources and institutions favour or hinder them? What political consequences (disintegration or transnational mobilization) are associated with them?

What is clear is that, in these transnational social landscapes, something is (often illegally) blended together which seriously hinders national states in their claim to exercise control and order. The spaces for living and acting which take shape here are '*impure*'. To analyse them, sociology must stop thinking in Either-Or terms and open itself to specific, *distinguishable* modes of Both-And living.

Wallerstein's radical move replaces the image of separate individual societies with one of a *world-system* in which *everything*—every society, every government, every company, every culture, every class, every household, every individual—must insert and assert itself within a single division of labour. This single world-system, which provides a framework for the measurement of social inequalities on a world scale, imposes itself with the rise of capitalism. For Wallerstein, then, the very logic of capitalism is necessarily global.

Once it had arisen in Europe in the sixteenth century, the capitalist dynamic took hold of, and thoroughly transformed, more and more 'continents', spaces and niches of social life. The whole planet operates within this regulatory mechanism of a *binding* and *constant* division of labour, which we call the capitalist world economy.'[8]

According to Wallerstein, a capitalist world economy has three basic elements. First, metaphorically speaking, it consists of a single market governed by the principle of profit maximization. Second, it has a series of state structures whose power varies both internally and externally; these state structures chiefly serve to '*hinder*' the '*free*' functioning of the capitalist market, in order to '*improve*' the prospective profits of one or more groups. Third, in a capitalist world economy, the appropriation of surplus labour takes place within a relationship of exploitation not between two classes but among three layers: the *central areas or heartlands*, the *semiperiphery* and the *peripheral countries and regions*. (The question of which countries or regions belong where, and by which criteria, triggers historical-empirical disputes that are hard to resolve.)

Thus, while European capitalism since the collapse of the Eastern bloc has been forming a universal economic space or world market, humanity has remained divided into national states and identities, each with its own conceptions of sovereignty and descendance. At the same time, conflicts are multiplying and intensifying within the world-system, because it produces not only fabulous riches but also terrible poverty. The patterns of global inequality follow the tripartite division of social space into centre, semiperiphery and periphery—a division that integrates the world-system upon a conflictual basis.

Periodically occurring crises lead, in Wallerstein's view, to restructuring which intensifies the division of power and inequality and increases the level of conflict within the world-system. The universalization and deepening of the capitalist logic engenders resistance on a world scale, which includes anti-Western, anti-modern, fundamentalist reactions, as well as the environmental movement or neo-nationalist currents. The inner logic of the capitalist world-system thus engenders both world integration and world decomposition. The question of whether there is a positive side to all this is given no answer. For Wallerstein, the world-system is in the end threatened with collapse.

This line of argument (which we have only been able to outline here) has two striking features: it is both monocausal and economic. Globalization is exclusively defined in terms of institutionalization of the world market.

However, at least three points may be made in criticism of this approach. First, there are obvious difficulties in specifying and testing the historical-empirical content of the theory. Second, globalization is said to have begun with Columbus's discovery and subjugation of the New World, and is thus anything but specific to the late twentieth century. This means that Wallerstein's proposed framework does not enable us to identify what is historically new about the transnational.

Third, for all the dialectics, Wallerstein's is a *linear* argument. It never really considers whether the world market, as Marx and Engels argued in the *Communist Manifesto*, inconspicuously and inadvertently produces *cosmopolitan* conflicts and identities.[9]

Post-international Politics: Rosenau, Gilpin, Held

Rosenau, too, breaks with nationally centred thinking. But he does not replace the anarchy of national states with a world system of the world market; instead, he distinguishes between two phases of international politics. In his schema, globalization means that humanity has left behind the age when national states dominated, or monopolized, the international scene. Now an age of *post*-international politics has begun, in which national players have to share the global arena and global power with international organizations, transnational concerns and transnational social and political movements. Empirically, this may be seen *inter alia* in the sheer number of international organizations, including NGOs such as Greenpeace, which is evidently still increasing.

Asked whether it was wrong to think that US foreign policy was striking out in new directions, Secretary of State Timothy Wirth replied:

> The maxim 'Think globally, act locally!' is clearly becoming a reality. We see how international institutions and resolutions are becoming more and more important. There is a growing feeling that nations can also be governed by international institutions, and not just at a national level, The foreign policy establishment is starting to think in different dimensions from those of military and economic power, rifle bullets and dollars. Now there are also

global problems such as worldwide human rights and refugee programmes, or containing corruption and environmental disasters. This globality changes our thinking.

And this is how he sees the role of citizens and action groups in relation to globalization:

> Alongside internationalization, the growing influence of grassroots initiatives is the second challenge to the previous conception of politics. There is huge pressure for a decentralization of politics, already coming from the new possibilities of communication. Fax and the Internet are more and more part of everyday life. Anyone can talk to anyone at lightning speed, all over the world, without having to rely on government channels or diplomats.'[10]

For Rosenau, then, the passage from the national to the postnational age has to do, first, with conditions within the international political system and, second, with the fact that the monocentric power structure of rival national states has been and is being replaced by a polycentric distribution of power in which a great variety of transnational and national actors compete or cooperate with one another.

There are thus two arenas of world society: a *community of states*, in which the rules of diplomacy and national power remain the key variables; and a world of *transnational subpolitics*, in which such diverse players as multinational corporations, Greenpeace and Amnesty International, but also the World Bank, NATO or the European Union, stride around.

Polycentric world politics

The opposition between world-system theory and this view of a *dual* world society is obvious enough. In place of a single world-market system 'governed' by economics, Rosenau postulates a *polycentric world politics* in which it is not only capital or national governments, nor even the UN, World Bank or Greenpeace, which have the only say, but *all* compete with one another to achieve their aims—even if they do not all have the same power opportunities.

Rosenau also differs from Wallerstein in seeing the *technological* dimension and dynamic of globalization as the root of the passage from a politics dominated by national states to a polycentric politics. His theoretical political studies have taught him again and again that international ties of dependence have acquired a new density and significance. The reason for this, in his view, is the enormous and still continuing upsurge of information and communications technology.

> It is technology that has so greatly diminished geographical and social distances through the jet-powered airliner, the computer, the orbiting satellite, and the many other inventions that now move people, ideas, and goods more rapidly and surely across space and rime than ever before. [...] It is technology, in short, that has fostered an interdependence of local, national, and international communities that is far greater than any previously experienced.[11]

Rosenau's argument thus combines two factors: the advent of the information and science society, and its overcoming of distance and frontiers as a result of the multiplication of transnational players and organizations. This *irreversibly polycentric world politics* defines a situation where:[12]

- *transnational organizations* such as the World Bank, the Catholic Church, the International Association of Sociologists, McDonald's, Volkswagen, drug cartels and the Italian mafia, as well as the new International of NGOs, act alongside, with or against one another;
- *transnational problems* such as climate change, drugs, AIDS, ethnic conflicts and currency crises determine the political agenda;
- *transnational events* such as the World Cup, the Gulf War, the American election campaign or the publication of a Salman Rushdie novel can lead via satellite television to turmoil in quite different countries and continents;
- *transnational 'communities'* develop, for example, around religion (Islam), knowledge (experts), lifestyles (pop, ecology), kinship (the family) or political orientations (environmental movement, consumer boycotts); and
- *transnational structures* such as various forms of work, production and cooperation, banks, financial flows, technical know ledge, and so on, create and stabilize across distances the contexts of action and crisis.

Gilpin's approach to globalization, on the other hand, remains sceptical about all the talk of novelty and takes a position close to the orthodox view of international politics, arguing, as it were, on the basis of its inner logic. Gilpin sees that national states are more than ever linked—not to say, shackled—to one another. Unlike Wallerstein and Rosenau, however, he stresses that globalization comes about only under certain conditions of international politics, that it is the product of a *'permissive'* global order. By this he means an order among states which alone makes it possible for dependence and relationship networks to be established and maintained beyond and among national authorities.

Globalization, understood as the expansion of transnational spaces and actors, is in this view paradoxically still dependent upon national authorities or, to be more precise, upon a *hegemonic power.* Globalization, so to speak, presupposes the tacit *consent* of national states. The openness, or 'permissiveness', which is necessary for the development of a world market, world churches, world corporations, world banks and worldwide NGOs can survive and spread only in the shadow of a matching concentration of state power.

In Gilpin's approach, then, which asserts the primacy of national politics over all other factors, globalization is necessarily *contingent* and under threat, in the sense that the emergence and development of transnational social spaces and players presupposes a hegemonic power structure and an international political regime. Only this can, if need be, guarantee the openness of the world order.

My position is that a hegemon is necessary to the existence of a liberal international economy. [...] historical experience suggests that, in the absence of a dominant liberal power, international economic cooperation has been extremely difficult to attain or sustain and conflict has been the norm. [...] The expansion and success of the market in integrating modern economic life could not have occurred without the favourable political environment provided by the liberal economic power.[13]

Sovereignty divided and shackled

Against the theory of a hegemonic power structure as the precondition of globalization, it can and must be objected that globalization is making obsolete the concept of political sovereignty upon which it is based. This is the argument put forward by David Held. He shows how—as a result of international treaties, the internationalization of political decision-making and the growing interdependence of security policy (including the now far-advanced internationalization of arms production), as well as through the arms trade and the international division of labour—national politics has been losing what used to be the core of its power: namely, its sovereignty. In the wake of globalization, Held writes,

the 'disjunctures' reveal a set of forces which combine to restrict the freedom of action of governments and states by blurring the boundaries of domestic politics, transforming the conditions of political decision-making, changing the institutional and organizational context of national polities, altering the legal framework and administrative practices of governments and obscuring the lines of responsibility and accountability of national states themselves. These processes alone warrant the statement that the operation of states in an ever more complex international system both limits their autonomy (in some spheres radically) and impinges increasingly upon their sovereignty. Any conception of sovereignty which interprets it as an illimitable and indivisible form of public power—entrenched securely in individual nation-states—is undermined. Sovereignty itself has to be conceived today as already divided among a number of agencies—national, regional and international—and limited by the very nature of this plurality.[14]

World Risk Society: Economic Globalization as Forced Politicization

Someone investigating the political implications of the new perception of ecological crisis will certainly encounter a wide range of answers. One of these will refer to a threat to civilization which cannot be attributed to any god, idols or nature but only to human decisions and the triumphs of industry, or indeed to the very claim of human civilization to shape and control the world. The other side of this is a sense of the *fragility* of civilization, which—to put it politically—can be produced by the experience of a common destiny. The word 'destiny' is appropriate here, because *everyone* may in principle be faced with the consequences of scientific-industrial decisions; but it is also inappropriate, because the impending threats are the result of human decision.

The ecological shock, then, has forcibly thrust upon people an experience which political theorists thought was the preserve of wars. However, there is a characteristic openness in this experience. The community of national history was always raised in the dialectic of enemy-images, and the awareness of ecological crisis may also vent itself in hysterical panic attacks directed against certain groups or things. Nevertheless, the fact that the threat knows no frontiers may mean that for the first time people will experience the common character of a destiny. Paradoxical as it may seem, it is arousing a *cosmopolitan* everyday consciousness which transcends even the borders between man, animal and plant. Threats create society, and global threats create global society. Nor is this all that justifies us in speaking of world risk society.[15]

The very different ways in which all the previously mentioned authors deploy the concept of a post-national social reality have one essential point in common: they all start from the premise that transnational social spaces emerge only as a result of deliberate action; or, to put it less strongly, they assume the existence of purposive actors and institutions. The theory of world risk society, by contrast, does not make this assumption. It maintains that it is no longer possible to externalize the side-effects and dangers of highly developed industrial societies; that the associated risk-conflicts place a question mark over the whole institutional structure. It will be further argued below that transnational social spaces also come about conflictually and mysteriously through unintended, *denied* or *'repressed'* threats, 'behind people's backs', as it were.

This view appears to run straight up against the objection that unintended consequences must be known if they are to have any political effect. This cannot be denied. Yet the political, economic and cultural turmoil of world risk society can be understood only if one recognizes that publicly discussed dangers constitute a kind of 'negative currency'. They are coins that no one wants, but which find their way in nevertheless, compel people's attention, confuse and subvert. They turn upside down precisely what appeared to be solidly anchored in everyday normality.

One has only to think of the tragicomedy of mad cow disease in Europe. In the summer of 1997 in Upper Bavaria—a region protected from the supposedly British source of the danger by several frontiers and promises of police action—a visitor could drop into a pub-restaurant, open the menu and see a smiling local farmer in cosy harmony with his cattle and children. This photograph, and the advice that the steak of one's fancy would come from the cow in the picture, were supposed to restore the confidence that the ubiquitous reports of 'British' mad cow disease had shattered.

Three kinds of global threat may be distinguished. First, there are conflicts over the 'bad' other side of various 'goods': that is, ecological destruction and technological-industrial dangers *caused by affluence* (the ozone hole and greenhouse effect, but also the unpredictable and incalculable consequences of genetic engineering and reproductive medicine).

Second, there are ecological destruction and technological-industrial dangers *caused by poverty*. The Brundtland Commission was the first to point out, in 1987, that environmental destruction was not only the dangerous shadow of modern growth but also its exact opposite, because it was closely correlated with poverty. 'Inequality is the earth's most important "environmental" problem,' it stated, 'as well as its most important "development" problem.' From an integrated analysis of population and nutrition, loss of species and genetic resources, energy, industry and human settlement, it follows that all these things are interrelated and cannot be treated separately from one another.

'However,' writes Michael Zürn,

> there is a crucial difference between environmental destruction as a result of prosperity and environmental destruction as a result of poverty. Whereas many ecological dangers caused by affluence are the result of an externalization of production costs, ecological destruction caused by poverty involves self-destruction of the poor that also has side-effects for the rich. In other words, environmental destruction caused by affluence is distributed evenly across the globe, whereas environmental destruction caused by poverty mainly occurs at a certain time and place and only becomes international in the form of medium-term side-effects.[16]

The best-known example of this is the depletion of the tropical rainforest, currently running at a rate of some 17 million hectares per annum. Other examples are toxic waste (including waste imported from other countries) and obsolete large-scale technologies (e.g. in the chemical or atomic industry), and in future also genetic engineering and related research. These dangers result from a context of modernization processes begun but not completed. Industries develop with the potential to endanger the environment and life, but individual countries lack the institutional and political means to ward off the threat of destruction.

The dangers caused by either affluence or poverty are what might be called dangers of 'normality', which are constantly brought into the world through a lack of adequate safety provisions. Another, *third* type of danger comes from *weapons of mass destruction* (ABC weapons)—that is, from their possible use in the exceptional situation of war, not just from their deterrent capacity. Even after the end of the East–West conflict, the dangers of regional or global self-destruction by nuclear, chemical or biological weapons have by no means disappeared; indeed, they have broken out of the control structure of a superpower 'atomic pact'.

The dangers of military confrontation between states are compounded by the newly emerging dangers of fundamentalist or private *terrorism*. Less and less can it be ruled out that weapons of mass destruction, available not only to states but also to private organizations as a means of exerting (political) threats, will become a new source of danger in world risk society.

These various global dangers can and will complement and intensify one another. We must therefore now consider the interaction between ecological destruction, wars and the effects of incomplete modernization.

In what ways does ecological destruction favour war—whether in the form of armed conflict over resources necessary to survival (water, for instance), or in the calls of ecological fundamentalists in the West for military intervention to halt such processes as the loss of tropical rainforest?

It is easy to imagine that a country living in ever greater poverty will exploit its environment to the hilt. In desperation (or as a way of politically concealing desperation), armed force may even be used to make a grab for resources that are necessary to another people's survival. Ecological devastation (for example, floods in Bangladesh) may trigger mass migration which then leads in turn to military conflict. Or else, states threatened with military defeat in a war may, as a 'last resort', try to destroy both their own and other countries' atomic or chemical installations, thereby threatening nearby regions and cities with destruction. There are no limits to the nightmare scenarios of how the various dangers could all come together. Zürn speaks of a 'spiral of destruction', through which all such phenomena could culminate in one huge, overarching crisis.

It is precisely this which the diagnosis of a world risk society is meant to address. The various global dangers cause cracks to appear in the pillars that have supported traditional security calculations. The potential damages are no longer limited in space and time: they are global and enduring; and it is hardly possible any longer to assign a clear-cut primary responsibility. Nor can loss or damage be financially compensated any longer, and there is no point in insuring oneself against the worst-case effects of the spiralling global dangers. There are not even any plans for aftercare, should the worst case actually come to pass.

In this light, it is already clear that there are no global dangers per se, that they are indistinguishably mixed in with the poverty, ethnicity and nationality conflicts which have afflicted the world especially since the end of the order bound up with the East-West conflict. Thus, in the post-Soviet republics, a blunt diagnosis of environmental destruction is linked to political criticism of the imperial use of natural resources. To talk of one's 'native soil' is thus to claim rights both to natural resources *and* to national sovereignty.

The concept of world risk society may tempt one to exaggerate the independence of ecological crises, within a monocausal and one-dimensional view of global society. It is all the more necessary, therefore, to stress the special kind of *involuntary politicization* that risk conflicts bring about in all fields of social activity.

Perceived dangers appear to prise open firmly bolted mechanisms of social decision-making. Things which used to be negotiated and decided by managers and academics, behind closed doors and with no attempt at justification, must now suddenly have their consequences justified in the biting wind of public debate. Whereas the execution of particular legislation once seemed to take place automatically, those responsible now appear in public and, when the pressure is on, may even admit to mistakes or mention the alternatives that were once rejected. In sum, the risk technocracy unintentionally produces a political antidote as a result of, and in opposition to, its own way of handling things. Dangers which become publicly known, even though the relevant authorities claim to have everything under control, create new leeway for political action.[17]

Why the Thesis of a McDonaldization of the World Is Wrong: Paradoxes of Cultural Globalization

Kevin Robins has argued that the development of the world market has far-reaching consequences for cultures, identities and lifestyles.[18] The globalization of economic activity is accompanied by waves of cultural transformation, by a process that is called 'cultural globalization'. Centrally involved here, of course, is also the manufacturing of cultural symbols—a process which, to be sure, has long been observable. Both in the social sciences and among the wider public, a number of writers have adopted what may be called the *convergence of global culture* thesis. The keyword here has become *McDonaldization.* According to this view, there is an ever greater uniformity of lifestyles, cultural symbols and transnational modes of behaviour. In the villages of Lower Bavaria, just as in Calcutta, Singapore or the *favelas* of Rio de Janeiro, people watch *Dallas* on TV, wear blue jeans and smoke Marlboro as a sign of 'free, untouched nature'. In short, a global culture industry increasingly signifies the *convergence* of cultural symbols and ways of life. The chairman of Euro-Disneyland puts it like this: 'Disney's characters are universal. You try and convince an Italian child that Topolino—the Italian name for Mickey Mouse—is American! Obviously you would stand no chance.'[19]

In this perspective, a negative Utopia lies at the root of world market discourse. As the last niches are integrated into the world market, what emerges is indeed *one world:* not as a recognition of multiplicity or mutual openness, where images both of oneself and of foreigners are pluralist and cosmopolitan, but on the contrary as *a single commodity-world* where local cultures and identities are uprooted and replaced with symbols from the publicity and image departments of multinational corporations.

People are what they buy, or are able to buy. According to the argument we are considering, this law of cultural globalization continues to apply even when purchasing power is close to zero. Where purchasing power ends so too does *social* humanity—and the threat of exclusion begins. Exclusion! This is the sentence passed on those who fall outside the 'being equals design' equation.

The giant corporations, which aim at market-governed production of universal cultural symbols, employ in their own way the open-frontier world of information technologies about which Rosenau, for instance, goes into such raptures. Satellites make it possible to overcome all national and class boundaries, to plant the carefully devised glitter of white America in the hearts of people all around the world. The logic of economic activity does the rest.

Globalization, understood and forced through as an economic process, minimizes costs and maximizes profits. Even small market segments, with their corresponding lifestyles and consumption habits, can expect to win the applause of Wall Street once the barriers of oceans and continents fall away. Transregional market planning is thus a magic formula in the publicity and management departments of global culture industries. Although costs rise in the production of universally serviceable symbols, globalization offers itself as a promising route to the profit-paradise just around the corner.

'A cultural and social revolution is taking place as a result of economic globalization,' says a CNN spokesman. 'Employees in America are as much affected by this as the man in the street in Moscow or a manager in Tokyo. This means that what we do in and for America goes for everywhere in the world. Our news is global news.'

No more free, non-conformist information? On the world information markets, a new gold-digging mood has been unleashing powerful movements of corporate concentration. Observers see in this the beginning of the end for free, non-conformist information. And who with eyes to see could simply brush this fear aside?

'A global information structure covers the earth like a spider's web,' writes Ignacio Ramonet.

> It uses the advantages of digitalization and fosters the networking of all communication services. In particular, it promotes the link-up of three fields of technology—computers, telephones and television—which come together in multimedia and the Internet. There are 1.26 billion television viewers around the world (more than 200 million connected to cable and some 60 million with digital television); there are 690 million telephone subscribers (including 80 million in mobile networks) and some 200 million computers (some 30 million of them connected to the Internet). It is predicted that by the year 2001 there will be more connections via the Internet than by telephone, that the number of Internet users will be between 600 million and one billion, and that the World Wide Web will comprise more than 100,000 commercial sites. The turnover of the communications industry, which in 1995 totalled roughly 1,000 billion dollars, might double in five years to account for some 10 per cent of the world economy. The computer, telephone and television giants know that in future profits will be made in the newly opened 'mines', where digital technology is being opened up before their fascinated, hungry eyes. At the same time, they realize that their territory will no longer be protected, that giants in neighbouring sectors are watching them with covetous glances. Ruthless warfare is the norm in the media sector. Those who used to specialize only in telephones now want to make television too, and vice versa. All companies involved in networking, especially those which maintain a supply network (electricity, telephone, water, gas, railways, motorways, etc.), are in a gold-digging mood and trying to secure their share of the multimedia cake. These rivals do battle with one another in every part of the globe. The names of these giant firms, the new world rulers, are: AT&T (the world-market leader in telephones), the duo formed by MCI (America's second-largest telephone network) and British Telecom, Sprint (the third-largest long-distance network inside the United States), Cable & Wireless (which controls Hong Kong Telecom, among others), Bell Atlantic, Nynex, US-West, TCI (the main cable television supplier), NTT (Japan's largest telephone company), Disney (which has now bought up ABC), Time Warner (which belongs to CNN), News Corp., IBM, Microsoft (the number one in software), Netscape, Intel, and so on. [...] The higher logic of this shift in capitalism is not a quest for allies but the takeover of other companies. The aim, in a market characterized by constant and

unpredictable technological acceleration and surprising consumer successes (such as the Internet boom), is to gain the know-how of those who have already established themselves in the market. [...] But if the newly acquired infrastructure is to be of real use to users, it must be possible for communications to circulate around the world without hindrance, as freely as the wind wafts over the oceans. This is the reason why the United States (the number-one producer of new technologies and the site of the major firms) has brought its full weight to bear in the pursuit of deregulation and economic globalization, so that as many countries as possible will open their borders to the 'free flow of information'—that is, to the giants of the US media and entertainment industry.[20]

Hawaii veal sausage: the new importance of the local And yet *Le Monde diplomatique,* from which this quotation is taken, is living proof against the pitch-black view that the media are threatened with a new, economically driven system of world rule. For that outspoken left-wing monthly also makes skilful use of the world information market: it now appears in several languages and—against the trend in the printed media—may have more than doubled its circulation over the past few years (even if the circulation of the French original has fallen to around 100,000 over the same period, with a resulting loss of advertising income).

The widespread view of a linear convergence of content and information driven by world-market concentration fails to appreciate the *paradoxes* and *ambivalences*—or, in old-fashioned terms, the *dialectic*—of globalization which cultural theory has theoretically identified and empirically investigated. Roland Robertson, one of the founders of cultural globalization theory and research, never tires of emphasizing that globalization always also involves a process of *localization.* Those working in the field of 'cultural studies' do reject the image of closed societies, each with its own cultural space, and think instead in terms of an immanent 'dialectical' process of cultural 'globalization', in which the opposite at the same time becomes both *possible* and *actual.* Their basic insight is that globalization does not mean globalization automatically, unilaterally or 'one-dimensionally'—which is one of the endless sources of misunderstanding in this debate. On the contrary, analyses that base themselves on the 'G-word' are everywhere giving rise to a *new emphasis on the local.*

That globalization does not only mean 'delocation' but also implies 'relocation' is already clear from the facts of economic calculation. In the literal sense of the word, no one can produce anything 'globally'. Firms which produce and market 'globally' must also develop *local* connections: that is, their production must be able to stand on local feet, and globally marketable symbols must be 'creamed' off local cultures (which therefore continue to remain lively and distinctive). 'Global', more mundanely translated, means 'in several places at once', or *translocal.*

It is no wonder, then, that this local-global nexus plays a central role in corporate calculation. Coca-Cola and Sony, for example, describe their strategy as 'global localization'. Their bosses and managers stress that the point of globalization is not to build factories everywhere in the world, but to become part of the respective culture. 'Localism' is what they call this strategy, which gains importance with the spread of globalization.

These inherent boundaries of linear cultural globalization, understood as uniform 'McDonaldization' of the world, may be visualized in the following extreme case. A single world culture pushed to its outer limits, where local cultures die out and everyone consumes, eats, sleeps, loves, dresses, argues and dreams in accordance with a single schema (however neatly divided by income group), would spell the end of the market, the end of profits. A world capitalism shaken by sales crises has a special need for local diversity and contrast, as a means of surviving competition through product and market innovation.

Nevertheless, delocation and relocation do not automatically mean renaissance of the local. To put it in terms familiar in Bavaria, we could say that the celebration of 'veal sausage', 'Löwenbrau beer' and 'lederhosen' does not offer salvation in the transition to the global era. For the revival of local colour suppresses the process of *'delocation'*. And relocation, which has already been through the infinitude of delocation, cannot be equated with a 'carry on as before' traditionalism and practised in a blinkered provincial spirit. The framework in which the meaning of the local has to establish itself has changed.

Delocation and relocation, taken together, certainly have a number of different consequences, but the most important is that local cultures can no longer be justified, shaped and renewed in seclusion from the rest of the world. In place of that knee-jerk defence of tradition by traditional means (which Anthony Giddens calls 'fundamentalism'), there is a compulsion to relocate detraditionalized traditions *within a* global *context* of exchange, dialogue and conflict.

In short, a non-traditionalist renaissance of the local occurs when local specificities are globally relocated and there conflictually renewed. To stay with the example of Bavaria, the 'veal sausage' may be redefined and represented as 'Hawaiian veal sausage'.

Glocalization: Roland Robertson

As we have seen, the workings of globalization usually lead to an *intensification of mutual dependence* beyond national boundaries. The model of separate worlds is thus, in a first stage, replaced with one of transnational interdependence. But Roland Robertson goes one crucial step further, by stressing how widely and deeply the 'awareness of the world as a single place' has become part of everyday reality.[21] For Robertson, then, globalization of the contemporary world and *conscious* globalization *reflected in the mass media* are two sides of the same process. The generation of this cultural symbolic reflexivity thus becomes the *key* question in the cultural sociology of globalization. The new human condition is a *conscious attention* to the globality and fragility of this human condition at the end of the twentieth century.

In this sense, globalization is not just a question of the 'objectivity of growing interdependence'. What must be investigated, rather, is how the world horizon opens up in the cross-cultural production of meaning and cultural symbols. Cultural globalization thwarts the equation of national state with national society, by generating cross-cultural (and conflicting) modes of life and communication, attributions, responsibilities, self-images of groups and individuals and images they have of others. Elisabeth Beck-Gernsheim illustrates this by the example of cross-cultural marriages and families.

Over and above all the various judgements, hopes and fears, one thing is certain: namely, that ethnic attributions—simply because of developments in society and the population structure—are becoming more and more complicated. For in the age of mobility, mass transport and economic linkage, there is a growing number of people who live and work with others beyond the radius of their own original group; who for various reasons (whether hunger or persecution, education or occupation, travel or curiosity) leave their home country for a short or long period of time, perhaps for ever; who keep crossing borders, perhaps being born in one state and brought up in another, and marrying and having children in yet another. In the United States, this might already be becoming something 'quite normal': 'The number of bicultural partnerships is growing, and so it is no longer rare, for example, to be both white and Asian or Arab and Jewish' (R. C. Schneider). In Germany such mixed relationships are less common, but here too there is an unmistakable trend towards more 'colourful' family patterns. Take weddings, for example. In 1960 nearly everyone who married in the Federal Republic was German. Only in one case out of twenty-five—to quote the official statistics— were 'foreigners involved': that is, at least one of the partners had a foreign passport. By 1994, however, the man or woman or both were foreign citizens in one out of every seven marriage ceremonies. Or take the example of births. In 1960 children born in the Federal Republic nearly always issued from a 'purely German liaison' (in terms of citizenship); only 1.3 per cent had a foreign father or a foreign mother or both. By 1994 18.8 per cent of live births had a foreign father or mother or both—that is, nearly every fifth child issued from a German-foreign or wholly foreign liaison. This fast-growing group of '*transculturals*' and their families poses the problem of social classification all the more sharply: where do they belong, to us, to the others, and to which others? What is involved here are variable, multifarious life-courses, which defy insertion into the established categories. This gives rise to complicated official procedures and discretionary issues, and obviously also to slips and mistakes in dealing with them.[22]

Some years ago, Jürgen Habermas was already speaking of a 'new obscurity', and Zygmunt Bauman speaks today of the 'end of clarity'. Local and global, Robertson argues, are not mutually exclusive.[23] On the contrary, the local must be understood as an *aspect* of the global. Globalization also means the drawing or coming together of local cultures, whose content has to be redefined in this 'clash of localities'. Robertson proposes replacing the concept of cultural globalization with that of '*glocalization*'—through a combination of the words 'global' and 'local'.

This new amalgam, 'glocalization', serves to underline the main claim of cultural theory: namely, that it is *absurd* to think we can understand the contemporary world, with all its breakdowns and new departures, without grasping what is expressed in the keywords 'politics of culture, cultural capital, cultural difference, cultural homogeneity, ethnicity, race and gender'.[24]

It is no exaggeration to say that this is precisely the dividing-line between old 'world-system' approaches and the new, culturally attuned 'sociology of globalization'.

The carefully polished axiom which separates the wheat from the chaff is as follows. 'Global culture' cannot be understood as a static phenomenon, but only as a *contingent* and *dialectical process* (which is *not* economistically reducible to some one-sided logic of capital), in accordance with a model of 'glocalization' in which contradictory elements are conceived and deciphered *in their unity*. It is in this sense that one may speak of paradoxes of 'glocal' cultures.

This axiom has an important methodological-pragmatic application. Globalization—which seems to be the super-dimension, appearing at the end from outside and overshadowing everything else—can be grasped in the small and concrete, in the spatially particular, in one's own life, in cultural symbols that all bear the signature of the 'glocal'.

This may also be explained by saying that the sociology of globalization becomes *empirically possible* and necessary only as a 'glocal' cultural investigation of industry, inequality, technology and politics.

But what is meant by this word 'dialectical' which, having been dismissed by all clear-headed thinkers, now suddenly returns to the fore in cultural theory? What does globalization signify when conceptualized and investigated as a 'flow'?[25]

Universalism and particularism

The growing worldwide uniformity of institutions, symbols and behaviour (McDonald's, blue jeans, democracy, information technology, banks, human rights, etc.) is not contradicted by the new emphasis on, the new discovery and defence of, local cultures and identities (Islamicization, renationalization, German pop and North African rai, Afro-Caribbean street carnival in London or Hawaiian veal sausage). Indeed, to take the example of human rights, they are presented in nearly every culture as universal rights, but at the same time they are interpreted and represented in often quite different ways according to the context.

Connection and fragmentation

Globalization generates (compels) bonding. It is necessary to stress this, since the discussion of globalization deprecates it and virtually equates it with fragmentation. There emerge transnational or transcontinental 'communities' (this word needs to be redefined) which divide what has often long been seen as an indissoluble unit: they create the basis for geographical and social coexistence and cooperation, but also for a new form of social bonding. This new logic of living and working together in separate places is practised both in transnational corporations (whose offices may be moved to Singapore while production is distributed all over Europe) and in transnational 'communities' (Mexican Americans, American Mexicans), 'families', 'ethnic subcultures' (an imagined Africa), and so on.

For the same reason, however, it is true that globalization *fragments:* not only does it undermine the control of individual states over information and taxes, and therefore their authority in general; it may also lead to the destruction of local communities. Under the conditions of global culture, it is quite possible in extreme cases that direct relations between neighbouring countries will be abandoned, while transnational 'neighbourhoods' flourish. It is possible, not by any means necessary.

Centralization and decentralization Many people see globalization quite one-sidedly as a process of concentration and centralization—in the dimensions of capital, power, information, knowledge, wealth, decision-making, etc.—and the reasons they give are often good. But this overlooks the fact that the same dynamic also generates decentralization. Local—or, to be more precise, translocal—communities acquire influence by shaping their social spaces, but they also do this in their respective local (that is, national) contexts.

National states may cut themselves off from the outside world. But they may just as well adopt an active orientation towards it, relocating and redefining their politics and identity' in the global context of mutual relationships, dialogue and conflict. The same is true of actors at all levels, including intermediate ones, of social existence—from trade unions through churches or consumer associations right down to individuals.

Conflict and balance

It is not difficult to imagine the glocal as a world disintegrating into conflicts. In a sense, even the vision of a 'war of cultures'—for all its peculiarly horrific content—remains stuck in the children's shoes of the national state. For glocalization also means that conflict appears in the place of local ties of communality, and that 'disflict' appears in the place of conflict (which always assumes at least a minimum of integration). One has only to think of a division of the world triggered by *exclusion* of those 'without purchasing power'—perhaps the future majority of mankind—and hence a *Brazilianization* of the world.[26]

But this eerie and far from groundless vision inevitably raises the question of why it *one-sidedly* emphasizes only this aspect of the future. For while these gloomy prospects must not be covered up or glossed over, it seems to have gone unnoticed that glocalization also produces new kinds of 'commonality'. These range from Mickey Mouse and Coca-Cola through the symbolism of poisoned dying creatures (images of oil-soaked seagulls and baby seals) to the first signs of a world public sphere which, funnily enough, manifested themselves in the transnational Shell boycott.

A little while back, Fukuyama was still announcing the 'end of history'. Howard Perlmutter was right to counter this by talking of the beginnings of a history of *global* civilization,[27] in which globalization becomes *reflexive* and thus gains a new historical quality that justifies the term 'world society'. For this presupposes *experiences of a common destiny*, which is expressed in the quite incredible proximity of the faraway within a world without frontiers.

Excursus: two modes of distinction In this connection (and also to clarify the concept of 'dialectics'), I would propose to distinguish in general between *exclusive* and *inclusive* modes of distinction. Exclusive distinctions follow the logic of Either-Or. They delineate the world as a coordination and subordination of separate worlds, in which identities and memberships are mutually exclusive. Anything falling in between [*jeder Zwischen-Fall*] is a passing incident [*Zwischenfall*]. It may confuse and scandalize, forcing repression or activities to restore order.

Inclusive distinctions, on the other hand, draw a quite different picture of 'order'. To fall between the categories is here not an exception but the rule. If this appears scandalous, it is only because the motley image of inclusive distinctions challenges the 'naturalness' of models of exclusive classification.

One advantage of inclusive distinctions is, of course, that they facilitate a different, more mobile and, if you like, cooperative concept of 'borders'. Here borders arise not through exclusion but through particularly solid forms of 'double inclusion'. Someone, for example, is part of a large number of circles and is circumscribed *by that*. (Sociologically speaking, it is quite obvious that, although this is not the only way in which borders can be conceived and lived, it may be an important way in the future.) In the framework of inclusive distinctions, therefore, borders are conceived and strengthened as mobile patterns that facilitate overlapping loyalties.

In the paradigm of exclusive distinction, globalization is no more than a limiting case that blows everything apart. Here, globalization must appear as the peak of a development that cancels all distinctions and establishes the undifferentiatable in their place. The methodological consequence is that a grand totality can perhaps suddenly be viewed again. But it is clear that this view will suffer from eye strain, and may even shatter as a result.

For the paradigm of inclusive distinction, by contrast, there is above all a pragmatic *research argument:* namely, that *it alone makes possible the sociological investigation of globality.* The new hybrid of world and ego that appears here has given sociology a new foundation, for without sociology it can be neither theoretically-empirically conceived and studied nor politically handled. The assumption of inclusive distinctions thus acquires the status of an *empirical working hypothesis*, one which, in the adventures of current research, must be driven out into the unknown world society in which we live. What is logically subordinate in Either-Or thinking—the 'inclusive' forms of life, biography, conflict, rule, inequality and state typical of world society—must at least be spelt out and thoroughly investigated. But inclusive distinctions, too, can and must be *clearly* drawn.[28] To adapt something that Gottfried Benn once said, woolly thinking and an inability to make distinctions do not add up to a theory of reflexive modernization.

The Power of Imagining Possible Lives: Arjun Appadurai

Robertson's analysis of 'glocal' cultures has been taken further by Arjun Appadurai, who affirms and theorizes the *relative autonomy* and distinctive logic of a glocal culture and economy. In this connection Appadurai speaks of *ethnoscapes* or 'landscapes of people' such as tourists, immigrants, refugees, exiles, *Gastarbeiter* and other groups on the move, which mark the unsettled, friable world in which we live. They and their physical restlessness set up major impulses toward a change in politics within and between nations; they are one aspect of the face of global culture. Alongside ethnoscapes, Appadurai also identifies and describes:

- *Tedmoscapes:* cross-border movements of new and old technologies, based on both machines and computers.

- *Financescapes:* huge sums of money moving between countries with incredible speed, by means of currency markets, national stock exchanges and speculative enterprises.
- *Mediascapes:* the distribution of opportunities for the production and dissemination of electronic images.
- *Ideoscapes:* the interlinking of images, often in connection with state or opposition ideologies and ideas which have their roots in the Enlightenment.[29]

As Appadurai shows, these flows of images and landscapes also call into question the traditional distinction between centre and periphery. They are cornerstones of *'imagined worlds'* that are provided with different meanings as they are exchanged and experienced by people and groups around the globe.

'On a political map,' writes K. Ohmae,

> the boundaries between countries are as clear as ever. [… But] of all the forces eating them away, perhaps the most persistent is the flow of information—information that governments previously monopolized. […] Their monopoly of knowledge about things happening around the world enabled them to fool, mislead, or control the people. […] Today […] people everywhere are more and more able to get the information they want directly from all corners of the world.

The emerging global cultures, adds A. D. Smith, .are 'tied to no place or period'. They are 'context-less, a true mélange of disparate components drawn from everywhere and nowhere, borne upon. the modern (postmodern) chariots of global communications systems'.[30]

What does this mean? Imagination gains a special kind of power in people's everyday lives, answers Appadurai.[31] More people in more parts of the world dream of and consider a greater range of 'possible' lives than they have ever done before. A central source of this are the mass media, which offer a wide and constantly changing supply of such 'possible lives'. In this way, an imaginary closeness to symbolic media figures is also created. The spectacles through which people perceive and evaluate their lives, hopes, setbacks and present situations are made up of the prisms of possible lives which 'tele-vision' constantly presents and celebrates.

Even people fixed to the most hopeless and brutal situations in life—child labourers, for example, or those who live by rummaging through city refuse—are nevertheless open to the sinister play of the imagination fabricated by the culture industry. Impoverishment is refracted, perhaps even duplicated, in the glittering, enticing commodity forms of possible life that lurid advertising everywhere proclaims.

This new power of global imagination industries means that local lifestyles are diluted and stirred around with 'models' whose social and spatial origins lie somewhere altogether different. People's own lives and possible lives thus enter at least into ironical conflict with each other. For, as we have seen, even impoverishment is placed under the market power of imaginary lives, remaining locked into the global circulation of images and models which (actively and passively) keeps the cultural economy going.

Global Wealth, Local Poverty: Zygmunt Bauman

Let us sum up. British and American observers of the global scenery who received a training in cultural theory have taken leave of what might be called the 'McDonaldizatian of the world' thesis. It is agreed that globalization does *not* necessarily bring about cultural uniformity, and that the mass production of cultural symbols and information does *not* lead to the emergence of anything like a 'global culture'. Rather, the developing glocal scenery should be seen as a blatantly ambivalent 'imagining of possible lives' that permits a multiplicity of combinations. Indeed, for the purposes of one's life and group identities, sharply varying and motley collections are put together out of that range of possibilities.

For Zygmunt Bauman, different kinds of identity are woven with the global thread of cultural symbols. The local self-differentiation industry is becoming one of the (globally determined) hallmarks of the late twentieth century. The global consumer goods and information markets make a selection of what is to be absorbed unavoidable—but the type and mode of the choice are decided locally or communally, so as to provide new symbolic characteristics for the reawakened, reinvented or so far merely postulated identities. Bauman concludes that the community, rediscovered by a new breed of Romantic admirers who see it threatened by dark forces of deracination and depersonalization, is not the antidote to globalization but one of its inevitable global consequences—product and precondition at one and the same time.

In order to complete this stage in the argument concerning the distinctive logic involved in a dimension of globalization, let us now look at some crucial and disturbing consequences of global inequalities. According to Bauman, the global-local nexus does not simply permit or enforce new analytical-empirical modes of considering translocal cultures and lifeworlds; it actually splits the approaching world society. Globalization and localization are thus not only two moments or aspects of the same thing. They are at once driving forces and expressions of a new *polarization and stratification of the world population into globalized rich and localized poor*.

For Bauman, then, globalization and localization may be two sides of the same coin, but the two sections of the world's population live on different sides and see only one of the sides—rather as people on earth see only one side of the moon. Some have the planet as their residence, while others are chained to the spot. 'Glocalization' is first and foremost a 'redistribution of privileges and deprivations, of wealth and poverty, of resources and impotence, of power and powerlessness, of freedom and constraint'.

Glocalization is

> the process of a *world-wide restratification*, in the course of which a new socio-cultural hierarchy, on a world-wide scale, is put together. The quasi-sovereignties, territorial divisions and segregations of identities which the globalization of markets and information promotes and renders 'a must', do not reflect diversity of equal partners. What is a free choice for some descends as cruel fate upon others. And since those 'others' tend to grow unstoppably in numbers and sink ever deeper into despair born of a prospectless existence, one will be

well advised to speak of *'glocalization'* [...] and to define it mostly as the process of the concentration of capital, finance and all other resources of choice and effective action, but also—perhaps above all of the *concentration of freedom* to move and to act.

According to what Bauman calls the 'folkloristic beliefs of the new generation of enlightened classes',

> freedom (of trade and capital mobility, first and foremost) is the hothouse in which wealth would grow faster than ever before; and once the wealth is multiplied, there will be more of it for everybody. The poor of the world—whether old or new, hereditary or computer-made—would hardly recognize their plight in this folkloristic fiction. [...] The old rich needed the poor to make and keep them rich. That dependency at all times mitigated the conflict of interest and prompted some effort, however tenuous, to care. The new rich do not need the poor any more. At long last the bliss of ultimate freedom is nigh.
>
> As a matter of fact, the worlds sedimented on the two poles, at the top and at the bottom of the emergent hierarchy of mobility, differ sharply; they also become increasingly incommunicado to each other. For the first world, the world of the globally mobile, the space has lost its constraining quality and is easily traversed in both its 'real' and 'virtual' renditions. For the second world, the world of the 'locally tied', of those barred from moving and thus bound to bear passively whatever change may be visited on the locality they are tied to, the real space is fast closing up. This is a kind of deprivation which is made yet more painful by the obtrusive media display of the space conquest and of the *'virtual* accessibility' of distances that stay stubbornly unreachable in non-virtual reality.
>
> The shrinking of space abolishes the flow of time. The inhabitants of the first world live in a perpetual present, going through a succession of episodes hygienically insulated from their past as well as their future. These people are constantly busy and perpetually 'short of time', since each moment of time is non-extensive an experience identical with that of time 'full to the brim'. People marooned in the opposite world are crushed under the burden of abundant, redundant and useless time they have nothing to fill with. In their time 'nothing ever happens'. They do not 'control' time—but neither are they controlled by it, unlike their clocking-in, clocking-out ancestors, subject to the faceless rhythm of factory time. They can only kill time, as they are slowly killed by it.
>
> Residents of the first world live in *time;* space does not matter for them, since spanning every distance is instantaneous. It is this experience which Jean Baudrillard encapsulated in his image of 'hyperreality', where the virtual and the real are no longer separable, since both share or miss in the same measure that 'objectivity', 'externality' and 'punishing power' which Emile Durkheim listed as the symptoms of all reality. Residents of the second world, on the contrary, live in *space:* heavy, resilient, untouchable, which ties down time and keeps it beyond the residents' control. Their time is void; in their time, 'nothing ever happens'. Only the virtual, TV time has a structure, a 'timetable'—the rest of time is monotonously

ticking away; it comes and goes, making no demands and apparently leaving no trace. Its sediments appear all of a sudden, unannounced and uninvited, immaterial and light-weight, ephemeral, with nothing to fill it with sense and so give it gravity, time has no power over that all-too-real space to which the residents of the second world are confined.

As far as the rich 'inhabitants of the first world' are concerned, the poor or the vagabonds whom they glimpse on their travels

> are not really able to afford the kind of sophisticated choices in which the consumers are expected to excel. [...] This fault makes their position in society precarious. They are useless, in the sole sense of 'use' one can think of in a society of consumers or society of tourists. And because they are useless, they are also unwanted.[32]

What is new in the global age is this loss of the nexus between poverty and wealth. For globalization splits the world's population into the globalized rich, who overcome space and never have enough time, and the localized poor, who are chained to the spot and can only 'kill' time.

Between these winners and losers of globalization, Bauman argues, there will in future be *no* unity and *no* ties of dependence. The most important result is that the master-slave dialectic breaks down. Or rather, the bond that made some kind of solidarity not only necessary but possible loosens and dissolves. The relationship of dependence, or at least sympathy, which has lain at the basis of all previous historical forms of inequality, falls away in the new Nowhere of world society. Consequently, even the term 'glocalization' is a euphemism. It hides the fact that conditions are being generated *beyond* unity and dependence for which we have no name and know no answer.

Capitalism Without Work

Two points qualify Bauman's important argument that globalization is leading to a polarization of rich and poor on a world scale. In a way, he may be said to overlook himself. For at least in *his* perspective as observer, he *binds together* what he depicts as irrevocably disintegrated in trans-state world society: namely, the framework, the *minima moralia*, which make the poor appear as *our* poor, and the rich as *our* rich.

But the formation of a 'cosmopolitan solidarity' (Habermas) cannot be ruled out, even if it would have a weaker bonding power than the citizenship solidarity which grew up in Europe in the course of one to two centuries. And world societies do not only undermine nationally structured and controlled communities; they also create a new closeness between seemingly separate worlds—not only 'out there' but also here and now, in people's own ordinary lives, in a crucial sense (to take up Appadurai, for example), it is even questionable whether in the second modernity the cultural production of 'possible lives'—which literally includes or 'locks in' the richest and poorest alike—allows any groups at all to be excluded.[33]

The first world is contained in the third and fourth worlds, just as the third and fourth are contained in the first. Neither centre nor periphery can be identified with separate continents; here *and* there, both conflict with each other in a variety of hybrid relationships. This new impossibility of excluding the poor can be seen in Rio, for example, where the homeless 'occupy' luxury streets at nightfall.

Bauman does not adequately explain why globalization destroys even a modicum of community between rich and poor. Therefore we will take this question up here and ask: is work disappearing from the work society?[34]

'The future of work looks like this at our company', said the boss of BMW. And then he drew a line beginning in 1970 and falling to zero by the year 2000.

> Of course that's an exaggeration, and we can't put it like that in public. But productivity is increasing to such an extent that we can produce more and more cars with less and less work. Just to keep the employment level stable, we would have to expand our markets enormously. Only if we sell BMWs in every corner of the world is there any chance at all of keeping existing jobs.

Capitalism is doing away with work. Unemployment is no longer a marginal fate: it affects everyone potentially, as well as the democratic way of life.[35] But in abrogating responsibility for employment and democracy, global capitalism undermines its own legitimacy. Before a new Marx shakes up the West, some long-overdue ideas and models for a different social contract will need to be taken up again. The future of democracy beyond the work society must be given a new foundation.

In Britain, for example, the country so much praised for its jobs record, only a third of people capable of gainful employment are fully employed in the classical sense of the term, against more than 60 per cent still in Germany. Twenty years ago, the figure in both countries was above 80 per cent. What is presented as a rescue remedy—the flexibilization of paid employment—has concealed and displaced, not cured, the disease of unemployment. Indeed everything is now rising: the numbers of unemployed and the grey area of part-time work, the insecurity of employment conditions, and the hidden reserves of labour. In other words, the quantity of paid labour is rapidly shrinking. We are approaching a capitalism without work, in all the post-industrial countries of the world.

Three myths screen public debate from the reality of the situation: first, everything is much too complicated anyway (the unfathomability myth); second, the coming upturn in the service sector will save the work society (the services myth); and third, we have only to drive down wage-costs and the problem of unemployment will vanish (the costs myth).

That everything is connected (however weakly) to everything else, and is to that extent unfathomable, certainly applies to the development of the labour market under conditions of globalization. But this does not preclude statements about secular trends, such as the internationally comparable longitudinal sections commissioned or compiled by the German

Commission for Issues of the Future.[36] According to its recent report, the value of the labour factor was constantly increasing over a number of generations, until a break occurred in the middle of the seventies. Since then, the amount of paid employment has everywhere been declining either directly in the form of unemployment (as in Germany), or indirectly through the exponential growth of 'hybrid forms of employment' (as in the United States or Britain). Demand for labour has been decreasing, while the supply of labour has been increasing (also as a result of globalization). The two indicators of a decline in gainful employment—joblessness and unregulated labour—have set the alarm bells ringing.

For a long time now it has been a question not of redistributing work but of *redistributing unemployment*—including in the new hybrids of employment and unemployment (short-term contracts, 'junk jobs', part-time work, etc.), which are officially counted in the category of 'full employment'. This is true especially in the employment paradises of the USA and Britain, where a majority have for some time been living in the grey area between work and non-work, often having to make do with starvation wages.

Yet there are many who close their eyes to the fact that the soup of the work society is getting thinner with every fresh crisis, and that ever larger sections of the population have only insecure 'little jobs' which can hardly be said to provide a stable existence.

Politicians, institutions and indeed we ourselves think in the fictitious terms of a world of full employment. Even building societies and insurance companies conclude their deals on the assumption that 'employed' people will continue to have a stable income. The rapidly spreading category of the Neither-Nor—neither unemployed nor income-secure—does not fit into that stereotype.

Mothers give up their job when they have children. But the three-phase model in terms of which they operate is no longer applicable. The third phase—a return to their previous work after the children have left home—is based upon the illusion of full employment. We complain about 'mass unemployment', but at the same time we assume that a full-time job is an adult's natural state right up to the age of retirement. In this emphatic sense, the GDR too was a work society. Now it is necessary to dwell on the extensive unemployment in the new federal *Länder* of Eastern Germany.

Many think, hope and pray that the service society can save us from the evil dragon of unemployment. This is the *services myth*. The rival calculations still have to be put to the test. It is certainly true that new jobs will come into being. But first, on the contrary, the traditionally secure core of employment in the service sector will be sacrificed to a wave of automation that is only just beginning. For example, telebanking will lead to the closure of high-street banks; telecommunications will shed some 60,000 jobs through a process of consolidation; and whole occupational categories, such as typists, may simply disappear.

Even if new jobs do emerge, in this computer age they can easily be transferred anywhere in the world. Many firms—American Express being the most recent example—are switching whole sections of their administration to low-wage countries (in this case, southern India).

Contrary to the prophets of the information society, who predict an abundance of highly paid jobs even for people with only basic education, the sobering truth is that numerous jobs even in data-processing will be poorly paid routine activities. The foot-soldiers of the information economy—according to Clinton's former labour minister, the economist Robert Reich—are hordes of data-processors sitting at back-room computer terminals linked to worldwide databases.

The key illusion in current debate, however, is the *costs myth*. More and more people are infected with the (often very militant) conviction that only a radical lowering of labour costs will lead us out of the vale of unemployment. Here the 'American way' is held up as our beacon, yet it is clearly one that involves deep division. According to OECD statistics published in April 1996, jobs for the highly skilled (which are still secure and well paid) have been appearing just as rarely or as often in the United States as they have in high-wage Germany—by an extra 2.6 per cent a year. The real difference between the two countries is in the growth of low-paid unskilled jobs. What characterizes the 'American miracle' is the rise of *minor services*, but it must be emphasized that this presupposes an open immigration policy. In future, admittedly, an unemployed graduate in Munich may find himself compelled to pick asparagus in the villages of Lower Bavaria. Both the asparagus and the asparagus-growers will have cause to regret this, however, because he will have neither the skills nor the motivation that a Polish agricultural labourer would bring to what he would see as a generally better job.

The negative aspects of the American jobs miracle are the following. From 1979 to 1989, workers' incomes on the bottom tenth of the jobs ladder fell by a further 16 per cent. Even in middle grades real incomes fell by 2 per cent, and only at the top did they actually rise—by 5 per cent. This downward trend may, it is true, have been halted for the 'working poor' in the period between 1989 and 1997—after all, those who already receive the rock-bottom wage for their work can hardly take another cut. For the majority of middle-grade American workers, however, average incomes have fallen since 1989 by a further 5 per cent. For the first time, we are dealing with an upturn in the economy in which 'full employment' is *accompanied* by declining real incomes in the middle levels of society.[37] 'Great,' one said, 'Bill Clinton has created millions of new jobs.'—'Yes,' answered another, 'I've got three of them and I can't keep my family.' In Germany, by contrast, it is still (!) thought a problem that people who work all day for, say, 7 marks an hour should sleep at night in cardboard boxes.

Furthermore, even a comparison of labour productivity takes the gloss off the American 'solution'. Over the past twenty years, average productivity in the United States has risen by no more than 25 per cent, as opposed to 100 per cent in Germany. 'Just how do the Germans manage that?' an American colleague asked me recently. 'They work less and produce more.'

This is precisely where the new law of productivity of global capitalism makes itself apparent in the information age. A smaller and smaller number of well-educated, globally interchangeable people can produce more and more goods and services. Economic growth, then, no longer triggers a reduction in unemployment but, on the contrary, presupposes a reduction in the number of jobs—what has been called 'jobless growth'.

Let there be no mistake. An owner-capitalism which aims only to increase profits, taking no account of employees, the welfare state and democracy, undermines its own legitimacy. While globally active enterprises secure higher profit margins, they withdraw both jobs and fiscal revenue from more expensive countries and burden others with the costs of unemployment and developed civilization. Two chronic seats of poverty—the public purse and the private purse of those still in employment—are alone supposed to finance what the rich also enjoy by way of the 'luxuries' of the second modernity: high-quality schools and universities, a smoothly functioning transport system, protection of the countryside, safe streets, all the colour and variety of urban life.

If global capitalism in the highly developed countries of the West dissolves the core values of the work society, a historical link between capitalism, welfare state and democracy will break apart. Democracy in Europe and North America came into the world as 'labour democracy', in the sense that it rested upon participation in gainful employment. Citizens had to earn their money in one way or another, in order to breathe life into political rights and freedoms. Paid labour has always underpinned not only private but also political existence. What is at issue today, then, is not 'only' the millions of unemployed, nor only the future of the welfare state, the struggle against poverty, or the possibility of greater social justice. Everything we have is at stake. Political freedom and democracy in Europe are at stake.

The Western association of capitalism with basic political, social and economic rights is not some 'social favour' to be dispensed with when money gets tight. Rather, socially buffered capitalism was a gain that answered the experience of fascism and the challenge of communism. As an applied form of Enlightenment, it rests upon the realization that only people who have a home and a secure job, and therefore a material future, are or can become citizens for whom democracy is a living reality of their own making. The simple truth is that without material security there is no political freedom and no democracy, only a threat to everyone from new and old totalitarian regimes and ideologies.

Thus, it is not the fact that capitalism produces more and more with less and less labour, but the fact that it blocks any initiative towards a new social contract, which is robbing it of legitimacy. Anyone today who thinks about unemployment should not remain a prisoner of old concepts by arguing over the 'second labour market', the 'part-time offensive', the so-called 'benefits not covered by insurance' or the payment of wages in case of sickness. What should be asked instead is how democracy will be ending and decay must be interpreted in a different light, at a time when new ideas and models are being laid for the state, economy and society of the twenty-first century.[38]

DISJUNCTURE AND DIFFERENCE IN GLOBAL CULTURAL ECONOMY

By Arjun Appadurai

It takes only the merest acquaintance with the facts of the modern world to note that it is now an interactive system in a sense that is strikingly new. Historians and sociologists, especially those concerned with translocal processes (Hodgson 1974) and the world systems associated with capitalism (Abu-Lughod 1989; Braudel 1981–84; Curtin 1984; Wallerstein 1974; Wolf 1982), have long been aware that the world has been a congeries of large-scale interactions for many centuries. Yet today's world involves interactions of a new order and intensity. Cultural transactions between social groups in the past have generally been restricted, sometimes by the facts of geography and ecology, and at other times by active resistance to interactions with the Other (as in China for much of its history and in Japan before the Meiji Restoration). Where there have been sustained cultural transactions across large parts of the globe, they have usually involved the long-distance journey of commodities (and of the merchants most concerned with them] and of travelers and explorers of every type (Helms 1988; Schafer 1963). The two main forces for sustained cultural interaction before this century have been warfare (and the large-scale political systems sometimes generated by it) and religions of conversion, which have sometimes, as in the case of Islam, taken warfare as one of the legitimate instruments of their

Arjun Appadurai, "Disjuncture and Difference in Global Cultural Economy," *Public Culture*, vol. 2, no. 2, pp. 1-24. Copyright © 1990 by Duke University Press. Reprinted with permission.

expansion. Thus, between travelers and merchants, pilgrims and conquerors, the world has seen much long-distance (and long-term) cultural traffic. This much seems self-evident.

But few will deny that given the problems of time, distance, and limited technologies for the command of resources across vast spaces, cultural dealings between socially and spatially separated groups have, until the past few centuries, been bridged at great cost and sustained over time only with great effort. The forces of cultural gravity seemed always to pull away from the formation of large-scale ecumenes, whether religious, commercial, or political, toward smaller-scale accretions of intimacy and interest.

Sometime in the past few centuries, the nature of this gravitational field seems to have changed. Partly because of the spirit of the expansion of Western maritime interests after 1500, and partly because of the relatively autonomous developments of large and aggressive social formations in the Americas (such as the Aztecs and the Incas), in Eurasia (such as the Mongols and their descendants, the Mughals and Ottomans), in island Southeast Asia (such as the Buginese), and in the kingdoms of precolonial Africa (such as Dahomey), an overlapping set of ecumenes began to emerge, in which congeries of money, commerce, conquest, and migration began to create durable cross-societal bonds. This process was accelerated by the technology transfers and innovations of the late eighteenth and nineteenth centuries (e.g., Bayly 1989), which created complex colonial orders centered on European capitals and spread throughout the non-European world. This intricate and overlapping set of Eurocolonial worlds (first Spanish and Portuguese, later principally English, French, and Dutch) set the basis for a permanent traffic in ideas of peoplehood and selfhood, which created the imagined communities (Anderson 1983) of recent nationalisms throughout the world.

With what Benedict Anderson has called "print capitalism," a new power was unleashed in the world, the power of mass literacy and its attendant large-scale production of projects of ethnic affinity that were remarkably bee of the need for face-to-face communication or even of indirect communication between persons and groups. The act of reading things together set the stage for movements based on a paradox—the paradox of constructed primordialism. There is, of course, a great deal else that is involved in the story of colonialism and its dialectically generated nationalisms (Chatterjee 1986), but the issue of constructed ethnicities is surely a crucial strand in this tale.

But the revolution of print capitalism and the cultural affinities and dialogues unleashed by it were only modest precursors to the world we live in now. For in the past century, there has been a technological explosion, largely in the domain of transportation and information, that makes the interactions of a print-dominated world seem as hard-won and as easily erased as the print revolution made earlier forms of cultural traffic appear. For with the advent of the steamship, the automobile, the airplane, the camera, the computer, and the telephone, we have entered into an altogether new condition of neighborliness, even with those most distant from ourselves. Marshall McLuhan, among others, sought to theorize about this world as a "global village," but theories such as McLuhan's appear to have overestimated the communitarian implications of the new media order (McLuhan and Powers 1989). We are now aware that with media, each time we are tempted to speak of the global village, we must be reminded that media create communities with "no sense of place" (Meyrowitz 1985). The world we live in now seems rhizomic (Deleuze and Guattari 1987), even schizophrenic, calling for theories of rootlessness, alienation, and psychological distance between individuals and groups on the one hand, and fantasies (or nightmares) of electronic propinquity on the other. Here, we are close to the central problematic of cultural processes in today's world.

Thus, the curiosity that recently drove Pico Iyer to Asia (1988) is in some ways the product of a confusion between some ineffable McDonaldization of the world and the much subtler play of indigenous trajectories of desire and fear with global flows of people and things. Indeed, Iyer's own impressions are testimony to the fact that, if *a* global cultural system is emerging, it is filled with ironies and resistances, sometimes camouflaged as passivity and a bottomless appetite in the Asian world for things Western.

Iyer's own account of the uncanny Philippine affinity for American popular music is rich testimony to the global culture of the hypeneal, for somehow Philippine renditions of American popular songs are both more widespread in the Philippines, and more disturbingly faithful to their originals, than they are in the United States today. An entire nation seems to have learned to mimic Kenny Rogers and the Lennon sisters, like a vast Asian Motown chorus. But *Americanization* is certainly a pallid term to apply to such a situation, for not only are there more Filipinos singing perfect renditions of some American songs (often from the American past) than there are Americans doing so, there is also, of course, the fact that the rest of their lives is not in complete synchrony with the referential world that first gave birth to these songs.

In a further globalizing twist on what Fredric Jameson has recently called "nostalgia for the present" (1989), these Filipinos look back to a world they have never lost. This is one of the central ironies of the politics of global cultural flows, especially in the arena of entertainment and leisure. It plays havoc with the hegemony of Eurochronology. American nostalgia feeds on Filipino desire represented as a hypercompetent reproduction. Here, we have nostalgia without memory. The paradox, of course, has its explanations, and they are historical, unpacked, they lay bare the story of the American missionization and political rape of the Philippines, one result of which has been the creation of a nation of make-believe Americans, who tolerated for so long a leading lady who played the piano while the slums of Manila expanded and decayed. Perhaps the most radical postmodernists would argue that this is hardly surprising because in the peculiar chronicities of late capitalism, pastiche and nostalgia are central modes of image production and reception. Americans themselves are hardly in the present anymore as they stumble into the megatechnologies of the twenty-first century garbed in the film-noir scenarios of sixties chills, fifties diners, forties' clothing, thirties houses, twenties dances, and so on ad infinitum.

As far as the United States is concerned, one might suggest that the issue is no longer one of nostalgia but of a social *imaginaire* built largely around reruns. Jameson was bold to link the politics of nostalgia to the postmodern commodity sensibility, and surely he was right (1983). The drug wars in Colombia recapitulate the tropical sweat of Vietnam, with Ollie North and his succession of masks—Jimmy Stewart concealing John Wayne concealing Spiro Agnew and all of them transmogrifying into Sylvester Stallone, who wins in Afghanistan—thus simultaneously fulfilling the secret American envy of Soviet imperialism and the rerun (this time with a happy ending) of the Vietnam War. The Rolling Stones, approaching their fifties, gyrate before eighteen-year-olds who do not appear to need the machinery of nostalgia to be sold on their parents heroes. Paul McCartney is selling the Beatles to a new audience by hitching his oblique nostalgia to their desire for the new that smacks of the old. *Dragnet* is back in nineties' drag, and so is *Adam*-12 not to speak of *Batman* and *Mission Impossible*, all dressed up technologically but remarkably faithful to the atmospherics of their originals.

The past is now not a land to return to in a simple politics of memory. It has become a synchronic warehouse of cultural scenarios, a kind of temporal central casting, to which recourse can be taken as appropriate, depending on the movie to be made, the scene to be enacted, the hostages to be rescued. All this is par for the course, if you follow Jean Baudrillard or Jean-François Lyotard into a world of signs wholly unmoored from their social signifiers (all the worlds a Disneyland). But I would like to suggest that the apparent increasing substitutability of whole periods and postures for one another, in the cultural styles of advanced capitalism, is tied to larger global forces, which have done much to show Americans that the past is usually another country. If your present is their future (as in much modernization theory and in many self-satisfied tourist fantasies), and their future is your past (as in the case of the Filipino virtuosos of American popular music), then your own past can be made to appear as simply a normalized modality of your present. Thus, although some anthropologists may continue to relegate their Others to temporal spaces that they do not themselves occupy (Fabian 1983), postindustrial cultural productions have entered a postnostalgic phase.

The crucial point, however, is that the United States is no longer the puppeteer of a world system of images but is only one node of a complex transnational construction of imaginary landscapes. The world we live in today is characterized by a new role for the imagination in social life. To grasp this new role, we need to bring together the old idea of images, especially mechanically produced images (in the Frankfurt School sense); the idea of the imagined community (in Anderson's sense); and the French idea of the imaginary (*imaginaire*) as a constructed landscape of collective aspirations, which is no more and no less real than the collective representations of Émile Durkheim, now mediated through the complex prism of modem media.

The image, the imagined, the imaginary—these are all terms that direct us to something critical and new in global cultural processes: the *imagination as a social practice.* No longer mere fantasy (opium for the masses whose real work is elsewhere), no longer simple escape (from a world defined principally by more concrete purposes and structures), no longer elite pastime (thus not relevant to the lives of ordinary people), and no longer mere contemplation (irrelevant for new forms of desire and subjectivity), the imagination has become an organized field of social practices, a form of work (in the sense of both labor and culturally organized practice), and a form of negotiation between sites of agency (individuals) and globally defined fields of possibility. This unleashing of the imagination links the play of pastiche (in some setting) to the terror and coercion of states and their competitors. The imagination is now central to all forms of agency, is itself a social fact, and is the key component of the new global order. But to make this claim meaningful, we must address some other issues.

Homogenization and Heterogenization

The central problem of today's global interactions is the tension between cultural homogenization and cultural heterogenization. A vast array of empirical facts could be brought to bear on the side of the homogenization argument, and much of it has come from the left end of the spectrum of media studies (Hamelink 1983; Mattelart 1983; Schiller 1976), and some from other perspectives (Cans 1985; Iyer 1988). Most often, the homogenization argument subspeciates into either an argument about Americanization or an argument about commoditization, and very often the two arguments are closely linked. What these arguments fail to consider is that at least as rapidly as forces from various metropolises are brought into new societies they tend to become indigenized in one or another way: this is true of music and housing styles as much as it is true of science and terrorism, spectacles and constitutions. The dynamics of such indigenization have just begun to be explored systemically (Barber 1987; Feld 1988; Hannerz 1987, 1989; Ivy 1988; Nicoll 1989; Yoshimoto 1989), and much more needs to be done. But it is worth noticing that for the people of Irian Jaya, Indonesianization may be more worrisome than Americanization, as Japanization may be for Koreans, Indianization for Sri Lankans, Vietnamization for the Cambodians, and Russianization for the people of Soviet Armenia and the Baltic republics. Such a list of alternative fears to Americanization could be greatly expanded, but it is not a shapeless inventory: for polities of smaller scale, there is always a fear of cultural absorption by polities of larger scale, especially those that are nearby. One man's imagined community is another man's political prison.

This scalar dynamic, which has widespread global manifestations, is also tied to the relationship between nations and states, to which I shall return later. For the moment let us note that the simplification of these many forces (and fears) of homogenization can also be exploited by nation-states in relation to their own minorities, by posing global commoditization (or capitalism, or some other such external enemy) as more real than the threat of its own hegemonic strategies.

The new global cultural economy has to be seen as a complex, overlapping, disjunctive order that cannot any longer be understood in terms of existing center-periphery models (even those that might account for multiple centers and peripheries). Nor is it susceptible to simple models of push and pull (in terms of migration theory), or of surpluses and deficits (as in traditional models of balance of trade), or of consumers and producers (as in most neo-Marxist theories of development). Even the most complex and flexible theories of global development that have come out of the Marxist tradition (Amin 1980; Mandel 1978; Wallerstein

1974; Wolf 1982) are inadequately quirky and have failed to come to terms with what Scott Lash and John Urry have called disorganized capitalism (1987). The complexity of the current global economy has to do with certain fundamental disjunctures between economy, culture, and politics that we have only begun to theorize.[1]

I propose that an elementary framework for exploring such disjunctures is to look at the relationship among five dimensions of global cultural flows that can be termed (a) *ethnoscapes*, (b) *mediascapes*, (c) *technoscapes*, (d) *financescapes*, and (e) *ideoscapes*.[2] The suffix *-scape* allows us to point to the fluid, irregular shapes of these landscapes, shapes that characterize international capital as deeply as they do international clothing styles. These terms with the common suffix *-scape* also indicate that these are not objectively given relations that look the same from every angle of vision but, rather, that they are deeply perspectival constructs, inflected by the historical, linguistic, and political situatedness of different sorts of actors: nation-states, multinationals, diasporic communities, as well as subnational groupings and movements (whether religious, political, or economic), and even intimate face-to-face groups, such as villages, neighborhoods, and families. Indeed, the individual actor is the last locus of this perspectival set of landscapes, for these landscapes are eventually navigated by agents who both experience and constitute larger formations, in part from their own sense of what these landscapes offer.

These landscapes thus are the building blocks of what (extending Benedict Anderson) I would like to call *imagined worlds*, that is, the multiple worlds that are constituted by the historically situated imaginations of persons and groups spread around the globe (chap. 1). An important fact of the world we live in today is that many persons on the globe live in such imagined worlds (and not just in imagined communities) and thus are able to contest and sometimes even subvert the imagined worlds of the official mind and of the entrepreneurial mentality that surround them.

By *ethnoscape*, I mean the landscape of persons who constitute the shifting world in which we live: tourists, immigrants, refugees, exiles, guest workers, and other moving groups and individuals constitute an essential feature of the world and appear to affect the politics of (and between) nations to a hitherto unprecedented degree. This is not to say that there are no relatively stable communities and networks of kinship, friendship, work, and leisure, as well as of birth, residence, and other filial forms. But it is to say that the warp of these stabilities is everywhere shot through with the woof of human motion, as more persons and groups deal with the realities of having to move or the fantasies of wanting to move. What is more, both these realities and fantasies now function on larger scales, as men and women from villages in India think not just of moving to Poona or Madras but of moving to Dubai and Houston, and refugees from Sri Lanka find themselves in South India as well as in Switzerland, just as the Hmong are driven to London as well as to Philadelphia. And as international capital shifts its needs, as production and technology generate different needs, as nation-states shift their policies on refugee populations, these moving groups can never afford to let their imaginations rest too long, even if they wish to.

By *technoscape*, I mean the global configuration, also ever fluid, of technology and the fact that technology, both high and low, both mechanical and informational, now moves at high speeds across various kinds of previously impervious boundaries. Many countries now are the roots of multinational enterprise: a huge steel complex in Libya may involve interests from India, China, Russia, and Japan, providing different components of new technological configurations. The odd distribution of technologies, and thus the peculiarities of these technoscapes, are increasingly driven not by any obvious economies of scale, of political control, or of market rationality but by increasingly complex relationships among money flows, political possibilities, and the availability of both un- and highly-skilled labor. So, while India exports waiters and chauffeurs to Dubai and Sharjah, it also exports software engineers to the United States—indentured briefly to Tata-Burroughs or the World Bank, then laundered through the State Department to become wealthy resident aliens, who are in turn objects of seductive messages to invest their money and know-how in federal and state projects in India.

The global economy can still be described in terms of traditional indicators (as the World Bank continues to do) and studied in terms of traditional comparisons (as in Project Link at the University of Pennsylvania), but the complicated technoscapes (and the shifting ethnoscapes) that underlie these indicators and comparisons are further out of the reach of the queen of social sciences than ever before. How is one to make a meaningful comparison of wages in Japan and the United States or of real-estate costs in New York and Tokyo, without taking sophisticated account of the very complex fiscal and investment flows that link the two economies through a global grid of currency speculation and capital transfer?

Thus it is useful to speak as well of *financescapes*, as the disposition of global capital is now a more mysterious, rapid, and difficult landscape to follow than ever before, as currency markets, national stock exchanges, and commodity speculations move megamonies through national turnstiles at blinding speed, with vast, absolute implications for small differences in percentage points and time units. But the critical point is that the global relationship among ethnoscapes, technoscapes, and financescapes is deeply disjunctive and profoundly unpredictable because each of these landscapes is subject to its own constraints and incentives (some political, some informational, and some technoenvironmental), at the same time as each acts as a constraint and a parameter for movements in the others. Thus, even an elementary model of global political economy must take into account the deeply disjunctive relationships among human movement, technological flow, and financial transfers.

Further refracting these disjunctures (which hardly form a simple, mechanical global infrastructure in any case) are what I call *mediascapes* and *ideoscapes*, which are closely related landscapes of images. *Mediascapes* refer both to the distribution of the electronic capabilities to produce and disseminate information (newspapers, magazines, television stations, and film-production studios), which are now available to a growing number of private and public interests throughout the world, and to the images of the world created by these media. These images involve many complicated inflections, depending on their mode (documentary or entertainment), their hardware (electronic or preelectronic), their audiences (local, national, or transnational), and the interests of those who own and control them. What is most important about these mediascapes is that they provide (especially in their television, film, and cassette forms) large and complex repertoires of images, narratives, and ethnoscapes to viewers throughout the world, in which the world of commodities and the world of news and politics are profoundly mixed. What this means is that many audiences around the world experience the media themselves as a complicated and interconnected repertoire of print, celluloid, electronic screens, and billboards. The lines between the realistic and the fictional landscapes they see are blurred, so that the farther away these audiences are from the direct experiences of metropolitan life, the more likely they are to construct imagined worlds that are chimerical, aesthetic, even fantastic objects, particularly if assessed by the criteria of some other perspective, some other imagined world.

Mediascapes, whether produced by private or state interests, tend to be image-centered, narrative-based accounts of strips of reality, and what they offer to those who experience and transform them is a series of elements (such as characters, plots, and textual forms) out of which scripts can be formed of imagined lives, their own as well as those of others living in other places. These scripts can and do get disaggregated into complex sets of metaphors by which people live (Lakoff and Johnson 1980) as they help to constitute narratives of the Other and protonarratives of possible lives, fantasies that could become prolegomena to the desire for acquisition and movement.

Ideoscapes are also concatenations of images, but they are often directly political and frequently have to do with the ideologies of states and the counterideologies of movements explicitly oriented to capturing state power or a piece of it. These ideoscapes are composed of elements of the Enlightenment worldview, which consists of a chain of ideas, terms, and images, including *freedom, welfare, rights, sovereignty, representation,* and the master term *democracy.* The master narrative of the Enlightenment (and its many variants in Britain, France, and the United States) was constructed with a certain internal logic and presupposed a certain relationship between reading, representation, and the public sphere. (For the dynamics of this process in the early history of the United States, see Warner 1990.) But the diaspora of these terms and images across the world, especially since the nineteenth century, has loosened the internal coherence that held them together in a Euro-American master narrative and provided instead a loosely structured synopticon of politics, in which different nation-states, as part of their evolution, have organized their political cultures around different keywords (e.g., Williams 1976).

As a result of the differential diaspora of these keywords, the political narratives that govern communication between elites and followers in different parts of the world involve problems of both a semantic and pragmatic nature: semantic to the extent that words (and their lexical equivalents) require careful translation from context to context in their global movements, and pragmatic to the extent that the use of these words by political actors and their audiences may be subject to very different sets of contextual conventions that mediate their translation into public politics. Such conventions are not only matters of the nature of political rhetoric: for example, what does the aging Chinese leadership mean when it refers to the dangers of hooliganism: What does the South Korean leadership mean when it speaks of discipline as the key to democratic industrial growth?

These conventions also involve the far more subtle question of what sets of communicative genres are valued in what way (newspapers versus cinema, for example) and what sorts of pragmatic genre conventions govern the collective readings of different kinds of text. So, while an Indian audience may be attentive to the resonances of a political speech in terms of some keywords and phrases reminiscent of Hindi cinema, a Korean audience may respond to the subtle codings of Buddhist or neo-Confucian rhetoric encoded in a political document. The very relationship of reading to hearing and seeing may vary in important ways that determine the morphology of these different ideoscapes as they shape themselves in different national and transnational contexts. This globally variable synaesthesia has hardly even been noted, but it demands urgent analysis. Thus *democracy* has clearly become a master term, with powerful echoes from Haiti and Poland to the former Soviet Union and China, but it sits at the center of a variety of ideoscapes, composed of distinctive pragmatic configurations of rough translations of other central terms from the vocabulary of the Enlightenment. This creates ever new terminological kaleidoscopes, as states (and the groups that seek to capture them) seek to pacify populations whose own ethnoscapes are in motion and whose mediascapes may create severe problems for the ideoscapes with which they are presented. The fluidity of ideoscapes is complicated in particular by the growing diasporas (both voluntary and involuntary) of intellectuals who continuously inject new meaning-streams into the discourse of democracy in different parts of the world.

This extended terminological discussion of the five terms I have coined sets the basis for a tentative formulation about the conditions under which current global flows occur: they occur in and through the growing disjunctures among ethnoscapes, technoscapes, financescapes, mediascapes, and ideoscapes. This formulation, the core of my model of global cultural flow, needs some explanation. First, people, machinery, money, images, and ideas now follow increasingly nonisomorphic paths; of course, at all periods in human history, there have been some disjunctures in the flows of these things, but the sheer speed, scale, and volume of each of these flows are now so great that the disjunctures have become central to the politics of global culture. The Japanese are notoriously hospitable to ideas and are stereotyped as inclined to export (all) and import (some) goods, but they are also notoriously closed to immigration, like the Swiss, the Swedes, and the Saudis. Yet the Swiss and the Saudis accept populations of guest workers, thus creating labor diasporas of Turks, Italians, and other circum-Mediterranean groups. Some such guest-worker groups maintain continuous contact with their home nations, like the Turks, but others, like high-level South Asian migrants, tend to desire lives in their new homes, raising anew the problem of reproduction in a deterritorialized context.

Deterritorialization, in general, is one of the central forces of the modern world because it brings laboring populations into the lower-class sectors and spaces of relatively wealthy societies, while sometimes creating exaggerated and intensified senses of criticism or attachment to politics in the home state. Deterritorialization, whether of Hindus, Sikhs, Palestinians, or Ukrainians, is now at the core of a variety of global fundamentalisms, including Islamic and Hindu fundamentalism. In the Hindu case, for example, it is clear that the overseas movement of Indians has been exploited by a variety of interests both within and outside India to create a complicated network of finances and religious identifications, by which the problem of cultural reproduction for Hindus abroad has become tied to the politics of Hindu fundamentalism at home.

At the same time, deterritorialization creates new markets for film companies, art impresarios, and travel agencies, which thrive on the need of the deterritorialized population for contact with its homeland. Naturally, these invented homelands, which constitute the mediascapes of deterritorialized groups, can often become sufficiently fantastic and one-sided that they provide the material for new ideoscapes in which ethnic conflicts can begin to erupt. The creation of Khalistan, an invented homeland of the deterritorialized Sikh population of England, Canada, and the United States, is one example of the bloody potential in such mediascapes as they interact with the internal colonialisms of the nation-state (e.g., Hechter 1975). The West Bank, Namibia, and Eritrea are other theaters for the enactment of the bloody negotiation between existing nation-states and various deterritorialized groupings.

It is in the fertile ground of detemtorialization, in which money, commodities, and persons are involved in ceaselessly chasing each other around the world, that the mediascapes and ideoscapes of the modem world find their fractured and fragmented counterpart. For the ideas and images produced by mass media often are only partial guides to the goods and experiences that detemtorialized populations transfer to one another. In Mira Nair's brilliant film *India Cabaret*, we see the multiple loops of this fractured deterritorialization as young women, barely competent in Bombay's metropolitan glitz, come to seek their fortunes as cabaret dancers and prostitutes in Bombay, entertaining men in clubs with dance formats derived wholly from the prurient dance sequences of Hindi films. These scenes in turn cater to ideas about Western and foreign women and their looseness, while they provide tawdry career alibis for these women. Some of these women come from Kerala, where cabaret clubs and the pornographic film industry have blossomed, partly in response to the purses and tastes of Keralites returned from the Middle East, where their diasporic lives away from women distort their very sense of what the relations between men and women might be. These tragedies of displacement could certainly be replayed in a more detailed analysis of the relations between the Japanese and German sex tours to Thailand and the tragedies of the sex trade in Bangkok, and in other similar loops that tie together fantasies about the Other, the conveniences and seductions of travel, the economics of global trade, and the brutal mobility fantasies that dominate gender politics in many parts of Asia and the world at large.

While far more could be said about the cultural politics of deterritorialization and the larger sociology of displacement that it expresses, it is appropriate at this juncture to bring in the role of the nation-state in the disjunctive global economy of culture today. The relationship between states and nations is everywhere an embattled one. It is possible to say that in many societies the nation and the state have become one another's projects. That is, while nations (or more properly groups with ideas about nationhood) seek to capture or co-opt states and state power, states simultaneously seek to capture and monopolize ideas about nationhood (Baruah 1986; Chatterjee 1986; Nandy 1989a). In general, separatist transnational movements, including those that have included terror in their methods, exemplify nations in search of states. Sikhs, Tamil Sri Lankans, Basques, Moros, Quebecois—each of these represents imagined communities that seek to create states of their own or carve pieces out of existing states. States, on the other hand, are everywhere seeking to monopolize the moral resources of community, either by flatly claiming perfect coevality between nation and state, or by systematically museumizing and representing all the groups within them in a variety of heritage politics that seems remarkably uniform throughout the world (Handler 1988; Herzfeld 1982; McQueen 1988).

Here, national and international mediascapes are exploited by nation-states to pacify separatists or even the potential fissiparousness of all ideas of difference. Typically, contemporary nation-states do this by exercising taxonomic control over difference, by creating various kinds of international spectacle to domesticate difference, and by seducing small groups with the fantasy of self-display on some sort of global or cosmopolitan stage. One important new feature of global cultural politics, tied to the disjunctive relationships among the various landscapes discussed earlier, is that state and nation are at each other's throats, and the hyphen that links them is now less an icon of conjuncture than an index of disjuncture. This disjunctive relationship between nation and state has two levels: at the level of any given nation-state, it means that there is a battle of the imagination, with state and nation seeking to cannibalize one another. Here is the seedbed of brutal separatisms—majoritarianisms that seem to have appeared from nowhere and microidentities that have become political projects within the nation-state. At another level, this disjunctive relationship is deeply entangled with the global disjunctures discussed throughout this chapter ideas of nationhood appear to be steadily increasing in scale and regularly crossing existing state boundaries, sometimes, as with the Kurds, because previous identities stretched across vast national spaces or, as with the Tamils in Sri Lanka, the dormant threads of a transnational diaspora have been activated to ignite the micropolitics of a nation-state.

In discussing the cultural politics that have subverted the hyphen that links the nation to the state, it is especially important not to forget the mooring of such politics in the irregularities that now characterize disorganized capital (Kothari 1989c; Lash and Urry 1987). Because labor, finance, and technology are now so widely separated, the volatilities that underlie movements for nationhood (as large as transnational Islam on the one hand, or as small as the movement of the Gurkhas for a separate state in Northeast India) grind against the vulnerabilities that characterize the relationships between states. States find themselves pressed to stay open by the forces of media, technology, and travel that have fueled consumerism throughout the world and have increased the craving, even in the non-Western world, for new commodities and spectacles. On the other hand, these very cravings can become caught up in new ethnoscapes, mediascapes, and, eventually, ideoscapes, such as democracy in China, that the state cannot tolerate as threats to its own control over ideas of nationhood and peoplehood. States throughout the world are under siege, especially where contests over the ideoscapes of democracy are fierce and fundamental, and where there are radical disjunctures between ideoscapes and technoscapes (as in the case of very small countries that lack contemporary technologies of production and information); or between ideoscapes and financescapes (as in countries such as Mexico or Brazil, where international lending influences national politics to a very large degree); or between ideoscapes and ethnoscapes (as in Beirut, where diasporic, local, and translocal filiations are suicidally at battle), or between ideoscapes and mediascapes (as in many countries in the Middle East and Asia) where the lifestyles represented on both national and international TV and cinema completely overwhelm and undermine the rhetoric of national politics. In the Indian case, the myth of the law-breaking hero has emerged to mediate this naked struggle between the pieties and realities of Indian politics, which has grown increasingly brutalized and corrupt (Vachani 1989).

The transnational movement of the martial arts, particularly through Asia, as mediated by the Hollywood and Hong Kong film industries (Zarilli 1995) is a rich illustration of the ways in which long-standing martial arts traditions, reformulated to meet the fantasies of contemporary (sometimes lumpen) youth populations, create new cultures of masculinity and violence, which are in turn the fuel for increased violence in national and international politics. Such violence is in turn the spur to an increasingly rapid and amoral arms trade that penetrates the entire world. The worldwide spread of the AK-47 and the Uzi, in films, in corporate and state security, in terror, and in police and military activity, is a reminder that apparently simple technical uniformities often conceal an increasingly complex set of loops, linking images of violence to aspirations for community in some imagined world.

Returning then to the ethnoscapes with which I began, the central paradox of ethnic politics in today's world is that primordia (whether of language or skin color or neighborhood or kinship) have become globalized. That is, sentiments, whose greatest force is in their ability to ignite intimacy into a political state and turn locality into a staging ground for identity, have become spread over vast and irregular spaces as groups move yet stay linked to one another through sophisticated media capabilities. This is not to deny that such primordia are often the product of invented traditions (Hobsbawm and Ranger 1983) or retrospective affiliations, but to emphasize that because of the disjunctive and unstable interplay of commerce, media, national policies, and consumer fantasies, ethnicity, once a genie contained in the bottle of some sort of locality (however large), has now become a global force, forever slipping in and through the cracks between states and borders.

But the relationship between the cultural and economic levels of this new set of global disjunctures is not a simple one-way street in which the terms of global cultural politics are set wholly by, or confined wholly within, the vicissitudes of international flows of technology, labor, and finance, demanding only a modest modification of existing neo-Marxist models of uneven development and state formation. There is a deeper change, itself driven by the disjunctures among all the landscapes I have discussed and constituted by their continuously fluid and uncertain interplay, that concerns the relationship between production and consumption in today's global economy. Here, I begin with Marx's famous (and often mined) view of the fetishism of the commodity and suggest that this fetishism has been replaced in the world at large (now seeing the world as one large, interactive system, composed of many complex subsystems) by two mutually supportive descendants, the first of which I call production fetishism and the second, the fetishism of the consumer.

By *production fetishism* I mean an illusion created by contemporary transnational production loci that masks translocal capital, transnational earning flows, global management, and often faraway workers (engaged in various kinds of high-tech putting-out operations) in the idiom and spectacle of local (sometimes even worker) control, national productivity, and territorial sovereignty. To the extent that various kinds of free-trade zones have become the models for production at large, especially of high-tech commodities, production has itself become a fetish, obscuring not social relations as such but the relations of production, which are increasingly transnational. The locality (both in the sense of the local factory or site of production and in the extended sense of the nation-state) becomes a fetish that disguises the globally dispersed forces that actually drive the production process. This generates alienation (in Marx's sense) twice intensified, for its social sense is now compounded by a complicated spatial dynamic that is increasingly global.

As for the *fetishism of the consumer*, I mean to indicate here that the consumer has been transformed through commodity flows (and the mediascapes, especially of advertising, that accompany them) into a sign, both in Baudrillard's sense of a simulacrum that only asymptotically approaches the form of a real social agent, and in the sense of a mask for the real seat of agency, which is not the consumer but the producer and the many forces that constitute production. Global advertising is the key technology for the worldwide dissemination of a plethora of creative and culturally well-chosen ideas of consumer agency. These images of agency are increasingly distortions of a world of merchandising so subtle that the consumer is consistently helped to believe that he or she is an actor, where in fact he or she is at best a chooser.

The globalization of culture is not the same as its homogenization, but globalization involves the use of a variety of instruments of homogenization (armaments, advertising techniques, language hegemonies, and clothing styles) that are absorbed into local political and cultural economies, only to be repatriated as heterogeneous dialogues of national sovereignty, free enterprise, and fundamentalism in which the state plays an increasingly delicate role: too much openness to global flows, and the nation-state is threatened by revolt, as in the China syndrome, too little, and the state exits the international stage, as Burma, Albania, and North Korea in various ways have done. In general, the state has become the arbitrageur of this *repatriation of difference* (in the form of goods, signs, slogans, and styles). But this repatriation or export of the designs and commodities of difference continuously exacerbates the internal politics of majoritarianism and homogenization, which is most frequently played out in debates over heritage.

Thus the central feature of global culture today is the politics of the mutual effort of sameness and difference to cannibalize one another and thereby proclaim their successful hijacking of the twin Enlightenment ideas of the triumphantly universal and the resiliently particular. This mutual cannibalization shows its ugly face in riots, refugee flows, statesponsored torture, and ethnocide (with or without state support). Its brighter side is in the expansion of many individual horizons of hope and fantasy, in the global spread of oral rehydration therapy and other lowtech instruments of well-being, in the susceptibility even of South Africa to the force of global opinion, in the inability of the Polish state to repress its own working classes, and in the growth of a wide range of progressive, transnational alliances. Examples of both sorts could be multiplied. The critical point is that both sides of the coin of global cultural process today are products of the infinitely varied mutual contest of sameness and difference on a stage characterized by radical disjunctures between different sorts of global flows and the uncertain landscapes created in and through these disjunctures.

The Work of Reproduction in an Age of Mechanical Art

I have inverted the key terms of the title of Walter Benjamin's famous essay (1969) to return this rather high-flying discussion to a more manageable level. There is a classic human problem that will not disappear however much global cultural processes might change their dynamics, and this is the problem today typically discussed under the rubric of reproduction (and traditionally referred to in terms of the transmission of culture). In either case, the question is, how do small groups, especially families, the classical loci of socialization, deal with these new global realities as they seek to reproduce themselves and, in so doing, by accident reproduce cultural forms themselves? In traditional anthropological terms, this could be phrased as the problem of enculturation in a period of rapid culture change. So the problem is hardly novel. But it does take on some novel dimensions under the global conditions discussed so far in this chapter.

First, the sort of transgenerational stability of knowledge that was presupposed in most theories of enculturation (or, in slightly broader terms, of socialization) can no longer be assumed. As families move to new locations, or as children move before older generations, or as grown sons and daughters return from time spent in strange parts of the world, family relationships can become volatile, new commodity patterns are negotiated, debts and obligations are recalibrated, and rumors and fantasies about the new setting are maneuvered into existing repertoires of knowledge and practice. Often, global labor diasporas involve immense strains on marriages in general and on women in particular, as marriages become the meeting points of historical patterns of socialization and new ideas of proper behavior. Generations easily divide, as ideas about property, propriety, and collective obligation wither under the siege of distance and time. Most important, the work of cultural reproduction in new settings is profoundly complicated by the politics of representing a family as normal (particularly for the young) to neighbors and peers in the new locale. All this is, of course, not new to the cultural study of immigration.

What is new is that this is a world in which both points of departure and points of arrival are in cultural flux, and thus the search for steady points of reference, as critical life choices are made, can be very difficult. It is in this atmosphere that the invention of tradition (and of ethnicity, kinship, and other identity markers) can become slippery, as the search for certainties is regularly frustrated by the fluidities of transnational communication. As group pasts become increasingly parts of museums, exhibits, and collections, both in national and transnational spectacles, culture becomes less what Pierre Bourdieu would have called a habitus (a tacit realm of reproducible practices and dispositions) and more an arena for conscious choice, justification, and representation, the latter often to multiple and spatially dislocated audiences.

The task of cultural reproduction, even in its most intimate arenas, such as husband–wife and parent–child relations, becomes both politicized and exposed to the traumas of deterritorialization as family members pool and negotiate their mutual understandings and aspirations in sometimes fractured spatial arrangements. At larger levels, such as community, neighborhood, and territory, this politicization is often the emotional fuel for more explicitly violent politics of identity, just as these larger politics sometimes penetrate and ignite domestic politics. When, for example, two offspring in a household split with their father on a key matter of political identification in a transnational setting, preexisting localized norms carry little force. Thus a son who has joined the Hezbollah group in Lebanon may no longer get along with parents or siblings who are affiliated with Amal or some other branch of Shi'i ethnic political identity in Lebanon. Women in particular bear the brunt of this sort of friction, for they become pawns in the heritage politics of the household and are often subject to the abuse and violence of men who are themselves torn about the relation between heritage and opportunity in shifting spatial and political formations.

The pains of cultural reproduction in a disjunctive global world are, of course, not eased by the effects of mechanical art (or mass media), for these media afford powerful resources for counternodes of identity that youth can project against parental wishes or desires. At larger levels of organization, there can be many forms of cultural politics within displaced populations (whether of refugees or of voluntary immigrants), all of which are inflected in important ways by media (and the mediascapes and ideoscapes they offer). A central link between the fragilities of cultural reproduction and the role of the mass media in today's world is the politics of gender and violence. As fantasies of gendered violence dominate the B-grade film industries that blanket the world, they both reflect and refine gendered violence at home and in the streets, as young men (in particular) are swayed by the macho politics of self-assertion in contexts where they are frequently denied real agency, and women are forced to enter the labor force in new ways on the one hand, and continue the maintenance of familial heritage on the other. Thus the honor of women becomes not just an armature of stable (if inhuman) systems of cultural reproduction but a new arena for the formation of sexual identity and family politics, as men and women face new pressures at work and new fantasies of leisure.

Because both work and leisure have lost none of their gendered qualities in this new global order but have acquired ever subtler fetishized representations, the honor of women becomes increasingly a surrogate for the identity of embattled communities of males, while their women in reality have to negotiate increasingly harsh conditions of work at home and in the nondomestic workplace. In short, detemtorialized communities and displaced populations, however much they may enjoy the hits of new kinds of earning and new dispositions of capital and technology, have to play out the desires and fantasies of these new ethnoscapes, while striving to reproduce the family-as-microcosm of culture. As the shapes of cultures grow less bounded and tacit, more fluid and politicized, the work of cultural reproduction becomes a daily hazard. Far more could, and should, be said about the work of reproduction in an age of mechanical art: the preceding discussion is meant to indicate the contours of the problems that a new, globally informed theory of cultural reproduction will have to face.

Shape and Process in Global Cultural Formations

The deliberations of the arguments that I have made so far constitute the bare bones of an approach to a general theory of global cultural processes. Focusing on disjunctures, I have employed a set of terms (*etbnoscape, financescape, technoscape, mediascape,* and *ideoscape*) to stress different streams or flows along which cultural material may be seen to be moving across national boundaries. I have also sought to exemplify the ways in which these various flows (or landscapes, from the stabilizing perspectives of any given imagined world) are in fundamental disjuncture with respect to one another. What further steps can we take toward a general theory of global cultural processes based on these proposals?

The first is to note that our very models of cultural shape will have to alter, as configurations of people, place, and heritage lose all semblance of isomorphism. Recent work in anthropology has done much to free us of the shackles of highly localized, boundary-oriented, holistic, primordialist images of cultural form and substance (Hannerz 1989; Marcus and Fischer 1986; Thornton 1988). But not very much has been put in their place, except somewhat larger if less mechanical versions of these images, as in Eric Wolf's work on the relationship of Europe to the rest of the world (1982). What I would like to propose is that we begin to think of the configuration of cultural forms in today's world as fundamentally fractal, that is, as possessing no Euclidean boundaries, structures, or regularities. Second, I would suggest that these cultural forms, which we should strive to represent as fully fractal, are also overlapping in ways that have been discussed only in pure mathematics (in set theory, for example) and in biology (in the language of polythetic classifications). Thus we need to combine a fractal metaphor for the shape of cultures (in the plural) with a polythetic account of their overlaps and resemblances. Without this latter step, we shall remain mired in comparative work that relies on the clear separation of the entities to be compared before serious comparison can begin. How are we to compare fractally shaped cultural forms that are also polythetically overlapping in their coverage of terrestrial space?

Finally, in order for the theory of global cultural interactions predicated on disjunctive flows to have any force greater than that of a mechanical metaphor, it will have to move into something like a human version of the theory that some scientists are calling chaos theory. That is, we will need to ask not how these complex, overlapping, fractal shapes constitute a simple, stable (even if large-scale) system, but to ask what its dynamics are: Why do ethnic riots occur when and where they do? Why do states wither at greater rates in some places and times than in others? Why do some countries flout conventions of international debt repayment with so much less apparent worry than others? How are international arms flows driving ethnic battles and genocides? Why are some states exiting the global stage while others are clamoring to get in? Why do key events occur at a certain point in a certain place rather than in others? These are, of course, the great traditional questions of causality, contingency, and prediction in the human sciences, but in a world of disjunctive global flows, it is perhaps important to start asking them in a way that relies on images of flow and uncertainty, hence *chaos*, rather than on older images of order, stability, and systematicness. Otherwise, we will have gone far toward a theory of global cultural systems but thrown out process in the bargain. And that would make these notes part of a journey toward the kind of illusion of order that we can no longer afford to impose on a world that is so transparently volatile.

Whatever the directions in which we can push these macrometaphors (fractals, polythetic classifications, and chaos), we need to ask one other old-fashioned question out of the Marxist paradigm: is there some pregiven order to the relative determining force of these global flows? Because I have postulated the dynamics of global cultural systems as driven by the relationships among flows of persons, technologies, finance, information, and ideology, can we speak of some structural-causal order linking these flows by analogy to the role of the economic order in one version of the Marxist paradigm? Can we speak of some of these flows as being, for a priori structural or historical reasons, always prior to and formative of other flows? My own hypothesis, which can only be tentative at this point, is that the relationship of these various flows to one another as they constellate into particular events and social forms will be radically contextdependent. Thus, while labor flows and their loops with financial flows between Kerala and the Middle East may account for the shape of media flows and ideoscapes in Kerala, the reverse may be true of Silicon Valley in California, where intense specialization in a single technological sector (computers) and particular flows of capital may well profoundly determine the shape that ethnoscapes, ideoscapes, and mediascapes may take.

This does not mean that the causal-historical relationship among these various flows is random or meaninglessly contingent but that our current theories of cultural chaos are insufficiently developed to be even parsimonious models at this point, much less to be predictive theories, the golden fleeces of one kind of social science. What I have sought to provide in this chapter is a reasonably economical technical vocabulary and a rudimentary model of disjunctive flows, from which something like a decent global analysis might emerge. Without some such analysis, it will be difficult to construct what John Hinkson calls a "social theory of postmodernity" that is adequately global (1990, 84).

Part II

GLOBALIZATION AND COMMUNICATION

The two selections in this section offer perspectives on historically relevant as well as contemporary issues in media communication as it traverses across borders and cultures. Oliver Boyd-Barrett analyzes the origin and demise of NWICO debate that was a call for more equal relationship and exchange between affluent, industrially advanced nations and the culturally rich, developing world, and asserts the continuing relevance of NWICO as well as the center-periphery model.

The 1956 book *Four Theories of the Press,* by Siebert, Peterson and Schramm, initiated much interest in media theory. The book proposed that in a nation, the press reflects the socio-political configuration. They proposed a taxonomy: liberal, soviet, authoritarian and social responsibility. Downing's essay draws from *Four Theories* to interpret patterns of media systems around the world, and also points to critical gaps that afflict current global media theory.

DRAWING A BEAD ON GLOBAL COMMUNICATION THEORIES

By John D. H. Downing

John D. H. Downing (PhD, London School of Economics and Political Science) is John T. Jones, Jr., Centennial Professor of Communication at the University of Texas at Austin. He writes on international communication, radical alternative media and social movements, and ethnicity, racism, and media. He teaches African and Latin American cinemas, media in Russia, and media theory.

A "bead," as the word is used in the title of this chapter, is the small piece of raised metal at the far tip of a rifle barrel that enables accurate targeting. Theorizing has the same function, or it should. It is not an end in itself but a way of getting a phenomenon clearly in our sights—though hopefully not of killing it, which is where the analogy collapses.

This is why it makes sense to argue about different theories. It's one thing to have a "fact" staring you in the face. For instance, there are many times more telephones and TV sets per head in Japan than in the 50 nations of the African continent—but how did that happen, and what does it mean? We need to attempt an explanation, a theory. What did it mean at the turn of the last century and into this one to have a single corporation—News Corporation—own one of the four major TV networks in

John D. H. Downing, "Drawing a Bead on Global Communication Theories," *Global Communication*, ed. Yahya Kamalipou, pp. 21-34. Copyright © 2001 by Wadsworth, a part of Cengage Learning, Inc. Reprinted with permission.

the United States; Star TV satellite television, which beamed programs to China and India (accounting for more than 40% of the world's population); a bunch of major newspapers in Britain and Australia; and a whole lot more media besides? Again, we need to attempt an explanation, a theory.

To answer such questions, someone has to produce a theory or at least spin some guesswork. Most of us would rather deal seriously with an idea that someone has thought out carefully than with guesswork. Careful, focused thinking is what "theorizing," properly speaking, means. Thinking carefully and with focus doesn't mean that a theory is automatically right or even mostly correct. That's one reason we argue about theories. But theorizing is a serious attempt to think connectedly and deeply about something.

There are better theories and worse theories, just as there are smarter guesses and stupider ones. If we are to understand international media, we have to train ourselves to think through these theories and evaluate them. What follows is a start on doing just that. We will begin by reviewing critically the first systematic attempt to analyze media across the planet. In the second section, we will examine a different approach to the same task.

"NORMATIVE" THEORIES

One of the earliest attempts to think about media internationally was a book published in the 1950s entitled *Four Theories of the Press* (Siebert, Peterson & Schramm, 1956). Its authors set out to create what is sometimes called a taxonomy, which means dividing up all the various versions and aspects of a topic into systematic categories and sometimes subcategories as well. The taxonomy the authors proposed was that the world's various media systems could be grouped into four categories or models: authoritarian, Soviet, liberal, and social responsibility. It compared the systems with each other, which in principle makes it easier to see the differences and then to see each system's particular characteristics—all too often, familiar only with the media system with which we grew up, we assume it is the only imaginable way of organizing media communication. Comparisons are not just interesting for what they tell us about the rest of the world. They help us sharpen our understanding of our own nation's media system (see Sidebar, which cites a leading media scholar's summary of normative theories).

Authoritarian effectively meant dictatorial, and the authors had especially in mind the nightmare fascist regimes of Hitler in Germany and Mussolini in Italy. *Soviet* referred to the communist dictatorships at that time in Russia and its surrounding ring of client regimes in Eastern Europe, the Transcaucasus, and Central Asia. The prime difference between the Soviet bloc dictatorships and "authoritarian" regimes lay, the authors proposed, in the particular political ideology that undergirded the Soviet regimes, namely Communism, which claimed to show the way to construct a just and equal society.

By *liberal*, the authors meant not "left-wing," as in current American parlance, but free market–based, which is the sense of the term in current continental European parlance. The contrast with both of the first two categories was, clearly, between media systems ruled by state regulation and censorship, and media systems ruled by capitalist money-making priorities. By *social responsibility*, the authors effectively meant a different order of reality again, namely, media operating within a capitalist dynamic but simultaneously committed to serving the public's needs. These needs were for a watchdog on government and business malpractice and for a steady flow of reliable information to help the citizens of a democracy make up their minds on matters of public concern.

A strong underlying assumption in all four models was that news and information were the primary roles of media, a view that rather heavily downplayed their entertainment function, ignoring the significant informative and thought-provoking dimensions that entertainment also carries. Indeed, despite the title *Four Theories of the Press*, the book effectively even sidelined many types of print media (comics, trade magazines, fashion magazines, sports publications, and so on). Effectively, its obsession was with the democratic functions of serious, "quality" newspapers and weekly newsmagazines, with their contribution to rational public debate and policy making. The model the authors endorsed as the best was the social responsibility model.

These theories—of which we shall review two later ones in a moment—were what is called deontic, or normative. That is to say, they did not seek simply to explain or contrast comparative media systems but to define how those systems ought to operate according to certain guiding principles. In particular, by touting the social responsibility model as superior, the authors effectively directed attention to what they saw as the highest duties of media in a democracy. They did not, however, explain why media should follow that model other than as a result of the high ethical principles of their owners and executives. Whether media owners actually worked by such codes, and what might stimulate them to do so, were left unexplained. The social responsibility model was simply a series of ethically inspired decisions by owners and editors for the public good.

The two later categories/models (cf. McQuail, 1994, pp. 131–132) added still further variety. One was the development model; the other, the participatory/democratic model. The *development* model meant media that addressed issues of poverty, health care, literacy, and education, particularly in Third World settings. Media were defined as being vitally responsible for informing the public—for example, about more efficient agricultural methods or about health hazards and how to combat them. Radio campaigns against the spread of HIV and AIDS would be a typical example. Development media were also held to have an important role in fostering a sense of nationhood in countries with highly disparate groups in the population, territories often artificially created by European colonialists as recently as the late 19th century.

Participatory media, the sixth category/model, typically designated local, small scale, and more democratically organized media, such as community radio stations or public access video, with their staff and producers having considerable input into editorial decisions. This alone sharply distinguished them from mainstream media of all kinds. But in addition, participatory media were defined as closely involved with the ongoing life of the communities they served, so that their readers or listeners could also have considerable influence over editorial policies. Sometimes these media shared the same development goals as the previous model cited, but not on any kind of authoritative top-down basis or as agents of government development policies. Public participation and a democratic process were central to their operation.

These six models did indeed cover a great variety of media structures internationally. Whether they did so satisfactorily is another matter. Let us look briefly at some of their shortcomings. Aside from their typical failure to engage with entertainment, already mentioned, their distinction among Soviet, authoritarian, and development models was very blurred in practice.

For instance, the mechanisms of Soviet and authoritarian media control were often very similar, and many Third World regimes hid behind "development priorities" and "national unity" to justify their iron control over any media critique of their behavior. The liberal model of free capitalist competition spoke to a bygone age, already vanishing by the time the original *Four Theories* book was published, an age when many small newspapers and radio stations competed with each other. In the current era of global media transnational corporations—giants valued in tens, twenties, or even approaching hundreds of billions of U.S. dollars—it is quaintly archaic to be imagining still a free media market where all media are on a level playing field.

But perhaps the chief problem with the four (or six) theories approach goes back to the deontic, or normative, dimension of the theories. The two terms used above—*categories* and *models*—illustrate this problem, for though they can be synonyms, *model* implies something that ought to be followed. While media, like any cultural organization, clearly do follow certain guiding principles and do not reinvent their priorities day by day, what media executives claim those principles are and how the same media executives behave in actuality may often be light-years apart. Let us look at some examples.

Communist media in the former Soviet bloc claimed their purpose was to serve the general public, the industrial workers, and the farmers who made up the vast majority of the population. Yet when the opportunity arose in those countries in the late 1980s, public criticism of the cover-ups and distortions of Communist media became a tidal wave.

In the social responsibility model, objectivity is trumpeted as the journalists' core principle, the driving force of their daily investigation and writing. Yet as media researchers in a number of countries have demonstrated, journalists readily place patriotism above objectivity and define objectivity in practice as the middle point between two opposing views, often those of rival political parties, not troubling to question whether truth may lie somewhere else. In the 1990s and into the next decade, the pathetic U.S. news media coverage of battles over how to reconstruct the ever more problematic U.S. health care system offered a sadly accurate confirmation of the failure of objectivity once it was defined as the midpoint between the Republican and Democratic parties (Blendon, 1995; Fallows, 1996, pp. 204–234).

Development media, as noted, were often steered away from sensitive topics by arrogant, autocratic regimes in the name of national unity and the need to focus on bettering economic production. Even media activists working for peanuts in participatory media sometimes claimed a dedication to "the cause" that masked their own obsession with wielding petty power in their community.

In other words, media researchers need to penetrate well below the surface of media professionals' assertions that they are driven by distinguished values, such as development or social responsibility or the public good, and to examine the full range of forces actually at work in media. Not to do so is hopelessly naive and blots out the prime force in media at the beginning of this century all across the planet: the ferocious elimination, as a result of the worship of market forces, of any ethical values in media save naked profitability.

COMPARING MEDIA GLOBALLY: A DIFFERENT APPROACH

In this section, we will examine some lessons that can be drawn from the now extinct Soviet Russian media system in order to understand media internationally, rather than basing our examination on a single nation. The system lasted, in different forms, from the revolution late in 1917 to December 25, 1991, when the last Soviet president, Mikhail Gorbachev, formally signed a document dissolving the Soviet Union. Many people would agree that some of the USSR's principal features persisted well after that date, with new private banks supplanting the old Communist Party as media bosses. However, although the Soviet media system is extinct in its original form, its history has a lot to contribute to our understanding of media elsewhere in the world.

First, as noted, Soviet media had a strong overlap with media under other dictatorships and with so-called development media. As an illustration, in the first 40 years of Taiwan's existence as an entity separate from mainland China, following the end of Japanese colonial rule in 1945, the media system of Taiwan was that of a dictatorial one-party state (whose leader, Chiang Kai-shek, had been schooled in Soviet Russia). Chiang Kai-shek was fiercely opposed to Communism, but that certainly did not mean he gave his own media any freedom. Another example is India, which was not a dictatorship like Taiwan but a country where, until the beginning of the 1990s, broadcast media were government-owned in the name of national development and unity, and where the Soviet model of the state as the basic agency of economic development had held sway ever since independence from British rule in 1947. Thus the study of Soviet Russian media throws light on a variety of the world's media systems.

Second, those of us who live in economically advanced and politically stable countries are in a poor position to understand how media work on much of the rest of the planet. Most if not all of what we read about research based on the United States or Britain, two nations with a considerable shared culture and the same majority language. We have little information even about media in Canada, France, Germany, Italy, or Japan—the other members of the elite Group of Eight (G8) countries—and least of all about Russia, the odd-man-out number 8 that is, as I will argue below, much more like the world at large.

In the world at large, issues of extreme poverty, economic crisis, political instability even to the point of civil war, turbulent insurgent movements, military or other authoritarian regimes, and violent repression of political dissent are the central context of media. To pretend that we can generalize about what all media are by just studying U.S. or British media, or even just media in the G8 countries minus Russia, is wildly silly. Statements such as "broadcasting is … " or "the Internet is … " or "newspapers are … " are inaccurate, however authoritative they may look at first glance—not because "every country is a bit different," but because of the major factors named at the beginning of this paragraph.

To be sure, some countries not in G8 are politically stable and economically affluent (Denmark and New Zealand, for example), even some crisis-torn nations have many positive dimensions that offset their acute problems (the Congo and Indonesia, for example). The media of affluent countries spend so little time on the constructive dimensions of other nations that the average media user in those countries can be forgiven up to a point for being unaware that there are any. But to return to the basic point here: Russia, the outsider in the G8 group, is a valuable entry point for understanding media in the world at large and thus for avoiding being imprisoned in superficial assumptions about what media are. I have argued this case elsewhere in much more detail than can be offered here (Downing, 1996), but let us see why, at least in outline.

At least the four following important issues must be considered—namely, how we understand the relation of mainstream media to (1) political power, (2) economic crisis, (3) dramatic social transitions, and (4) small-scale alternative media (such as samizdat, a term explained below). Each of the Russian examples below offers a contrast case to the usual U.S./U.K. profile of media and provokes a basic question about media in capitalist democracies.

Political Power

The relation between political power and Communist media always seemed a no-brainer. Communist media were seen as simple mirror-opposites of media in the West. Communism equaled repression and censorship, in the name of a forlorn ideal of justice, but capitalist democracy (the West) won out in the end, and over the years 1989–1991 the whole Communist system foundered, never to return. Soviet media were the favorite counterexample for proving what was right with Western media.

Now, it is indeed true that state control over media was extremely detailed in Soviet Russia, even more so than in some other dictatorships. The Communist Party's Propaganda Committee established ideological priorities. Its cell-groups in every newspaper, magazine, publishing house, and broadcast channel kept a close watch over any subversive tendencies. Media executives were chosen from a list of party members who had proven their loyalty. And the KGB (the political police) would quickly intervene if any trouble seemed evident or imminent. With all this, the official censorship body, known as Glavlit, had relatively little to do. Typewriters were licensed by the state, and a copy of the characters produced on paper by their keys—which were always slightly out of sync and therefore could be used to identify where a subversive document had originated—was on file with the local KGB. When photocopy machines came into use, access to them was governed in microscopic detail. Bugging technology was one of the most advanced aspects of Soviet industry.

This outrageous and unnerving machinery of control over communication did not, in the end, win. Many factors served to subvert it, including samizdat media (see below). But one factor perhaps was the least controllable of all—namely, the extreme difficulty of producing media that were credible or interesting inside this straitjacket. Communist Party members read *Pravda* (The Truth) daily because they knew they were expected to, not because they were convinced it was factually informative. People in general expected authentic news to arrive by conversational rumor, and honest opinion by samizdat. Only if that rumor confirmed what Soviet media announced did many people take the latter as reliable (and then only on the given topic).

Thus in the later decades of the Soviet system in Russia a dual-level public realm developed: official truths that the media blared out, that everyone mouthed, and that few believed; and an unofficial realism that was the stuff of everyday private conversation or samizdat. When Gorbachev came to power in 1985, intent on reform, he gradually introduced a new degree of frankness and directness in media (the famous glasnost policy), intended to reduce the gap between these two levels.

This media credibility dilemma is a significant one in any dictatorship. And perhaps the longer the dictatorship lasts, the worse the dilemma.

Question for Stable, Affluent Nations. The fascinating contrast is with the relatively ready trust in mainstream media, the bulk of which are owned by very large and unaccountable capitalist firms. Were Soviet media so bluntly and clumsily controlled that skepticism was a self-evident response? Are Western media sufficiently subtle, flexible, and savvy so that their message is much more attractive and their plausibility much tougher to question?

Economic Crisis

Economic crisis was a daily experience for the majority of Russians, especially from the time of the Soviet bloc's collapse up to the time of writing this essay, but it had been gathering momentum from the early 1980s onward. It continues to be a daily experience of citizens in many of the world's nations, including the impoverished sectors within the other G8 countries. The "Structural Adjustment Policies" of the International Monetary Fund, as the IMF so abstractly termed them over the 1980s and 1990s, blighted the lives of untold hundreds of millions in the countries to which the fund applied its ruthless capitalist logic. The health and housing and education prospects of children, women, the aged, peasant farmers, and slum dwellers have been sacrificed to the dictates of debt repayment to international banks, to the point that great chunks of national income go back to the banks in interest payments instead of to the public (cf. Nielsen 1995; Peabody 1996; Stein 1995; Weisbrot 1997).

"It's their governments' fault," cry the public relations specialists of the banks and the IMF, holding up their holy hands in pious denial. Their denial blots out the banks' full knowledge of what kind of governments they were dealing with at the time they contracted the loans in question: kleptocracies, or thief regimes, that spend a good chunk of the loan on themselves, and another chunk on buying weapons from the West's arms factories to put down civil unrest directed against their rule—or to manufacture wars with their neighbors in order to divert attention from their own abuses.

The Soviet and post-Soviet Russian experience of economic crisis has been profound, except during the 1970s and early 1980s, when oil revenues shot up on the world market. But during the 1990s, Russian life expectancy actually fell, which in turn meant that infant mortality increased, for the death rate among children under one year old is the prime factor in average life expectancy. Once again, among the G8 countries, Russia is the exception that stands in for much of the rest of the planet. Russian media, until the last few years of the old Soviet Union, were silent about this decline in living standards and stagnation in productivity and asserted that the capitalist countries were suffering from acute and irremediable economic problems. In the post-Soviet period, Russian media have often found it easier to point the finger at the IMF—not, it must be said, without reason—than to take aim at the Russian kleptocracy as well.

How do media in general deal with these economic crises? Do they explore them or avoid them? Do they blame them on distant scapegoats? On the IMF if theirs is the country affected? Or on Third World governments if they are in an affluent nation? Or on domestic scapegoats—immigrants, Gypsies, Chinese, Jews, refugees, Muslims?

Question for Stable, Affluent Nations. How thoroughly do media really explain economic crisis? How well do they explain strategies to deal with it that do not hit the poor and poorest much harder than the wealthy? Although global indices indicated that living standards in the United States in the 1990s were remarkably high and crisis was remote, wages had fallen way below what they were in real terms during the 1960s. Typically both parents had to work full-time to retain a stable income level, and single-parent households, a sizable proportion of the total number of households, mostly struggled to get by. The U.S. media at the turn of the millennium suggested universal prosperity, but the facts suggested a slow-burning invisible crisis, one in which the public, despite working many hours, was mostly one or two paychecks away from "welfare," a racially defined form of public humiliation that few embraced if they could avoid it. When did you last see a TV program or watch an ad or read a newspaper that got into these realities in a way that struck you?

Dramatic Social Transitions

The third issue is the relation of media to dramatic social transitions. Russia went through many transitions in the 20th century, beginning with the disastrous World War I, which opened the way to the 1917 revolution and the three-year civil war that followed the revolution. Next came the tyrannical and savage uprooting of Russian and Ukrainian farmers in 1928–1933 and Stalin's ongoing terror and vast prison camp population. Then came the loss of 20 to 25 million lives in the war against Hitler in 1941–1945, the severe economic disruptions of Gorbachev's attempt to reform the system in the late 1980s, and the economic chaos of the 1990s. This is a dimension that, with the exception of the two world wars, has not characterized the affluent nations' experience, but once again Russian experience in this regard has been much more characteristic of the world's. Colonial rule, invasion, war, vast social movements, civil war, entrenched ethnic conflicts, wrenching changes of government, and dictatorships were common experiences across the planet. Media in Russia also went through many transitions during the 20th century. Let us briefly note them.

Before the revolution, there was an active newspaper, magazine, and book industry, but it was restricted to people who could read, perhaps a quarter of the population at most, and they were nearly all concentrated in towns. Furthermore, the imperial censorship made it very risky indeed for anyone to print anything directly critical of the czars. Jail or exile in frozen Siberia were standard penalties for challenging the status quo, which included, during the war against Germany in 1914–1917, any criticism of the slaughter into which many Russian generals forced their troops. Came the revolution, the Bolshevik leadership sought peace with Germany, and criticism of the old status quo was everywhere. Literacy campaigns began, in part to enable the new revolutionary regime to get its message across. This was the first media transition.

At the time of the revolution, the arts in Russia were in ferment and had been for more than a decade. Some of the most inventive and spectacular artistic work in Europe was being done by a new generation of Russian artists. For the first 10 years or so of the revolutionary era, these artists were actively encouraged by the new regime to express their talents in theater, advertising, public campaigns, cinema, photography, and music, along with painting and sculpture. Russian media were on the cutting edge, especially in the then newer technologies of cinema and photography. However, with the rise of Stalin to power as Soviet dictator, this innovative work was shoved aside in the name of "Soviet progress." Those who did not bend to the new orthodoxy suffered at least disgrace and, at worst, prison camps or even death. This was the second media transition.

Next, for a period of about 25 years until Stalin's death in 1953, Russian media marched to the dictator's tread, looking neither right nor left. Not only did they follow the official line unwaveringly, but their language was also wooden, saturated with political jargon, endlessly grinding out the messages given them from above. Whenever the official line changed—when Stalin suddenly signed a pact in 1939 with the Nazi regime; when the Nazis invaded in 1941; when the United States supported the USSR in the Lend-Lease program; when, in the aftermath of the Nazis' defeat, Stalin annexed three Baltic and five east-central European countries, along with a chunk of eastern Germany; when Stalin began a comprehensive anti-Semitic campaign in the years just before he died—each time the media instantly changed their tune to support the switch. George Orwell's famous novel *1984* conveys some of the flavor of the way that media during the Cold War massaged such 180-degree reversals, including the World War II portrayal of Stalin in U.S. media as "friendly Uncle Joe" and the redefinition of him as a monster after the war.

In the decade that followed Stalin's death, some Russian media professionals made cautious attempts to open up the media, with intermittent encouragement from Khrushchev, Stalin's successor. A famous short novel, Aleksandr Solzhenitsyn's *One Day in the Life of Ivan Denisovich*, was the first publication of anything about the vast prison camp system Stalin had brought into being. It was in some ways the high point of the attempt to open up the media system, even just a little, but in 1964 Khrushchev was thrown out of office and the lid was jammed back on Russian media. Some other brave dissidents who tried to publish works critical of the regime were sentenced to long terms of hard labor in highly publicized trials meant to scare off any would-be imitators. Another media transition.

Only in the mid-1980s, as the Russian economic system began to grind to a halt, was there a push in favor of media reform, the glasnost era, led by the USSR's last leader, Mikhail Gorbachev. This ultimately led to an avalanche of media, which challenged the long-established status quo, even to the point, eventually, of attacking the original revolution in 1917 and thus the very foundations of the Soviet system. A further media transition.

Finally, after the collapse of the USSR in 1991, yet another media transition emerged: a print media sector that was mostly allowed to follow its own path and commercial dictates; a TV sector that was under heavy government surveillance and control; and a radio sector somewhere between. Independent media existed to a greater extent than under the Soviet regime, but Russians were still largely deprived of anything approaching a genuinely democratic media system.

This postage-stamp account of Russian media in the 20th century has shown the significant transitions through which they passed. Again, in much of the world, such wrenching changes in media have been an everyday experience. Many specifics might vary, but the Russian type of experience is not unique. In the stable nations of the West, with the exception of the Nazi era in Europe, this kind of experience of media was foreign. But we cannot take that minority experience as typical. If we are to think intelligently about media, the Russian experience is much more the norm. To assume that a particular media system is permanent or normal, that transition is not inherent in media, flies in the face of the media experience of most of humankind in the 20th century.

Question for Stable, Affluent Nations. Media seem so familiar, so much part of the landscape, so central in the way we entertain ourselves, that even rapidly changing delivery technologies—fiber optic cables, compression technologies, digitization, satellites—seem to promise only sexy new options. Yet what does the bewilderingly rapid concentration of media ownership into the hands of giant transnational corporations mean for our media future (Bagdikian, 2000; McChesney, 1999)? Is citizen influence over media, despite being an obvious necessity for a true democracy, due to dwindle slowly and imperceptibly away to nothing? We are in the midst of our own media transition, and we had better find out. And watch out.

Small-Scale Alternative Media

I have made several references to the term *samizdat media*. The term refers to the hand-circulated pamphlets, poems, essays, plays, short stories, novels, and, at a later stage, audio- and videocassettes *(magnitizdat)* that began to emerge in Soviet Russia and later in other Soviet bloc countries from the 1960s onward. They contained material that was banned by the Soviet regimes. Writing, distributing, or possessing these materials carried sentences in hard-labor camps. Samizdat contained widely varied messages—some religious, some nationalist, some ecological, some reformist, some revising the myths of official Soviet history, some attacking Soviet policies, some defending citizens victimized by arbitrary arrest and imprisonment. The term *samizdat* literally means "self-published," in contradistinction to state-published, that is, approved by the Soviet regime as "safe."

These micromedia took a long time to make a dent in the Soviet system—more than a generation. But their impact was extraordinary, for up until the last year of the USSR, even when the east-central European regimes had already shaken off Soviet rule, the Soviet Union appeared to be one of those facts of life institutions that few observers imagined could collapse. Those Russians, Ukrainians, Poles, and others who labored over those decades to create samizdat, and often paid a heavy price in jail for their pains, showed amazing spirit, determination, and foresight. They were aided by the foreign shortwave radio stations that broadcast in the region's languages into Soviet bloc territory: the BBC World Service, Radio Liberty, Radio Free Europe, Deutsche Welle, and Voice of America. These stations would read samizdat texts over the air as part of their programming and thus amplified their message outside the major urban centers, which were normally the only places where samizdat was circulated. Sometimes the Soviet bloc governments jammed their broadcasts but not always.

Historically and comparatively, small-scale radical media of this kind have been common (Downing, 2001). They have been used in the United States from the time of the War of Independence through the abolitionist and suffragist movements to the civil rights and the anti-Vietnam War movements. Yet their significant role in slowly rotting away at Soviet power flags their importance in developing our own definition *media*. All too often, we mistake size and speed for significance, as if they were the only way that media can wield power. In relation to the dizzying speed with which transnational corporations are merging media ownership, it is all too easy to slip into a fatalistic acceptance that these colossuses are too much for us to take on. Yet the samizdat story and its parallels in many other parts of the world suggest a diametrically different conclusion.

Question for Stable, Affluent Nations. The Internet greatly expanded citizens' communication options in economically advanced nations during the 1990s. Can it (a) be extended to lots of ordinary citizens outside those nations and (b) be preserved from virtually total corporate control? Corporate control can take various forms—for example, charging long-distance phone tariffs to Internet users, putting ever higher prices on access to informational Web sites, and reserving high bandwidth access to corporate users or wealthy clients. Can this trend be fought off successfully?

CONCLUSIONS

I set out in this essay to challenge the easy assumption that by studying media in just the United States or Britain, the currently dominant nations in media research publication, we can manage to "draw a bead" on media. In a deliberate paradox, I selected what seems to be a closed chapter in recent history—namely, the story of Soviet media—to illustrate some heavy-duty media issues that conventional theories fail to get in their sights. But, as I argued, those media issues are common in most of the contemporary world. I also argued that, in certain ways, they direct our attention back to pivotal media issues even in stable, affluent nations. Global comparisons need to be central to media research.

For more information on the topics that appear in this chapter, use the password that came free with this book to access InfoTrac College Edition. Use the following words as key-terms and subject searches: mass communication theories, normative theories, participatory media, Communist media, social transitions, alternative media.

QUESTIONS FOR DISCUSSION

1. What are the chief problems with deontic, or normative, theories of media?
2. Why does a study of Russian media, whether during or since the 1917–1991 Soviet era, help us understand our own media system more clearly?
3. How do our own news media present economic crises, either at home or in other parts of the planet?
4. What roles do media play in the sometimes wrenching process of transition from one type of government to another (for example, from a military government to a civilian one)?
5. What roles may alternative or underground media play in energizing active democracy and social movements?

REFERENCES

Bagdikian, B. (2000) *The media monopoly* (6th ed.). Boston: Beacon Press.

Blendon, R. J. (1995). Health care reform: The press failed to inform the public of alternative strategies. *Nieman Reports, 49*(3), 17–19.

Downing, J. (1996). *Internationalizing media theory: Transition, power, culture: Reflections on media in Russia, Poland, and Hungary, 1980–95.* London: Sage.

Downing, J. (2001). *Radical media: Rebellious communication and social movements.* Thousand Oaks, CA: Sage.

Fallows, J. (1996). *Breaking the news: How the media undermine American democracy.* New York: Pantheon.

McChesney, R. (1999). *Rich media, poor democracy.* Urbana: University of Illinois Press.

McQuail, D. (1994). *Mass communication theory: An introduction* (3rd ed.). London: Sage.

Nielsen, K. (1995). Industrial policy and structural adjustment: A case of planned versus creeping institutional change. *American Behavioral Scientist, 38*(5), 716–740.

Peabody, J. W. (1996). Economic reform and health sector policy: Lessons from structural adjustment programs. *Social Science and Medicine, 43*(5), 823–835.

Siebert, F., Peterson, T., & Schramm, W. (1956). *Four theories of the press.* Urbana: University of Illinois Press.

Stein, H. (Ed.). (1995). *Asian industrialization and Africa: Studies in policy alternatives to structural adjustment.* New York: St. Martin's Press.

Weisbrot, M. (1997). Structural adjustment in Haiti. *Monthly Review, 48*(8), 25–39.

GLOBAL COMMUNICATION ORDERS

By Oliver Boyd-Barrett

DEFINING THE CONCEPT

The concept of the New World Information and Communication Order (NWICO) is 25 years old at the time of writing. As a political tool, it had little influence on the world's communication media. What then did it signify, and why am I writing about it now?

In this chapter, I review the definition and origins of NWICO and its political and intellectual contexts. I look at the various phases of its history, at differences of viewpoint about its significance, and at evaluations of communication experts. I examine the paradox of its political demise and continuing relevance.

NWICO was a position statement, molded principally by the countries of the developing world in alliance with the communist nations of the Soviet Union and Eastern Europe. Their voices were represented through the United Nations, and through the movement of the Non-Aligned Nations, whose purpose was to resist incorporation within the sphere of influence of either of the then two superpowers. NWICO was a protest, whose proponents argued that the structure and operation of global communication had grossly inequitable consequences. They said that this

---

Oliver Boyd-Barrett, "Global Communication Orders," from *International and Development Communication: A 21st-Century Perspective*, edited by Bela Mody, pp. 35–52. Copyright © 2003 Sage. Permission to reprint granted by the publisher.

structure advantaged established media proprietors and their sponsors in the developed world, allowing them to dominate global communication with the perspectives of the developed world. Developing countries, on the other hand, lacked equivalent means to originate expression, were overly dependent on information transmitted from the developed world, and were largely dependent on Western-based media to articulate and disseminate information even about the developing world itself. NWICO signified a strategy to end such inequalities.

The NWICO debate is of historical interest for anyone wanting to monitor relations between developed and developing, rich and poor nations. It is significant for its contribution to the articulation of human rights within the United Nations. Many structural inequalities addressed by NWICO still remain in evidence; some have intensified. NWICO constituted a timely recognition that communications—then largely regarded as a national policy matters, except for esoteric regulatory issues concerning allocation of access to the electromagnetic spectrum—had acquired a significant global dimension. The operation of international communication had implications for national sovereignty, and therefore they had to be regulated for reasons of national security.

NWICO signifies a transition between world orders. Governance of the earlier order was articulated by nation states, whose dialogue was given form by national media. The new order is governed by a neoliberal economic presumption of an open and global marketplace regulated by rules of competition. This order is adjudicated and adjusted by "global" institutions such as the World Trade Organization, the World Bank, and the International Monetary Fund, in which the wealthy nations exercise most influence. The new order is associated with the ascendancy of transnational corporations in the global economy. It is identified with communication media that are increasingly owned by international capital. Communications facilitate the operations of the transnational corporations, of which there were approximately 60,000 in 2000, with 600,000 affiliates. In number and importance, most are based in the United States, Britain, and Japan, countries that constitute the most important transnational corporation markets and in which most of their direct employees are based.

NWICO emerged when the United States as a global superpower was threatened by its failure in Vietnam, a war that had been fought to contain the spread of communism, at the cost of many hundreds of thousands of lives. Coincidentally, it was a war whose U.S. objective was attained two decades later by the tentative entry of Vietnam into the world economy. A further defeat, indirectly linked to Vietnam, was the exposure of U.S. government duplicity at the highest levels during Watergate. Such public exposure, leading to the successful ouster of President Richard Nixon, provoked a crisis of confidence both between press and government and between government and society. Vietnam and Watergate fueled a new radicalism in American society among those disillusioned by the economic, social, and foreign policies of their country's power elite. Adding to the general malaise of war defeat was the newfound strength of the Organization of Petroleum Exporting Countries (OPEC), which exerted its collective control over the volume of oil production and raised prices.

Non-oil countries feared the economic impact of higher gasoline prices, and the possibility that the OPEC example might be adopted by other alliances of primary goods exporters in the developing world.

The economic miracle of Japan and its developing supremacy in the manufacture and global sale of audiovisual equipment and cars underlined U.S. vulnerability to labor at home, lower wages abroad, and global competition. The persistence of Soviet and Chinese communism and the nuclear arms race between the United States and the Soviet Union, and their global rivalry for political influence, constituted an all-absorbing investment of attention and resources. This atmosphere of fear and rivalry provided the pretext, in the name of "freedom," for U.S. support of outrageously brutal and corrupt dictatorships. In Chile, for example, the United States helped to overthrow a democratically elected socialist government and to install and sustain the murderous regime of a military dictator, Augusto Pinochet.

Computer innovation—benefiting from considerable military and defense investment—was beginning to demonstrate its technical revolutionary potential, aided in part by the relaxation of antitrust legislation to permit collaboration between otherwise competing corporations in research and development.

There is important work to be done in tracing linkages between the threatened supremacy of the United States in the 1970s and the new world order initiated by Republican Ronald Reagan in the United States and Conservative Margaret Thatcher in the United Kingdom from the early 1980s. This new world order rejected strategies of compromise with the developing world in the forums of the United Nations and its agency, UNESCO (United Nations Educational, Scientific and Cultural Organization). The number of members of the United Nations had grown significantly with the success of independent movements and the subsequent creation of new nations. The United States and its allies no longer enjoyed uncontested control over the United Nations. Debates about the new world economic order and its sister concept, NWICO, were nurtured precisely through such forums. In place of the old world order of sovereign national states operating autonomously in international trade, communications, and other flows, the United States and its allies, working through the General Agreement on Tariffs and Trade (GATT), the International Monetary Fund, and the World Bank, proposed an order of increasingly open markets. The prospect of opening up their domestic markets to greater external competition was a small price to pay for the immeasurably greater advantage, to already powerful economies, of gaining unfettered access to overseas markets. Whether this transition of world orders is an overall positive or negative thing is a matter of considerable contention. Advocates of the new world order may say that it has brought relief to the peoples of the erstwhile stagnant economies of the communist world and that free flows of capital distribute job opportunities and wealth globally. The large, continuous U.S. trade deficit demonstrates just how much the U.S. domestic market is open to foreign producers, and the fluid movement of capital undermines older oligarchies and supports democracy, where practicable, as providing a relatively stable business environment. Critics of the new world order are particularly concerned that the increasing volume and penetration of international capital weaken state control and undermine the health of the "public sphere." They fear that state-sanctioned, unfettered pursuit of corporate profit is dangerous to the environment, creates economic disparities within and between nations, and destroys cultural identity.

Communication industries are important to the neoliberal new world order. They are sizable industries in their own right, generate international trade, and grow more important as digitization enhances communication capacity and speed. Older regulatory structures were based on presumptions of the scarcity of communication space (airwaves), and on egalitarian ideologies of universal service, but have collapsed before the prospect of a seeming infinity of bandwidth. The conquest of space and time has been of great benefit to transnational corporations. These advances accelerate the distribution of global capital and financial markets. They consolidate alliances between financial elites around the world. They promote the emergence of a global class of the super-rich and yet they also promote alliances of movements of resistance. Applied to communication industries, neo-liberalism intensifies the global process of communication commercialization—even of the "public service media." It subverts the authority and wealth of state-sponsored communication monopolies in broadcasting and telecommunications. Many of these have been privatized, or forced to compete with new, commercial competitors, domestic and foreign. The new order favors media products that maximize profit by attracting either large or wealthy audiences and delivering these audiences to advertisers. It favors a media environment that respects the needs of capital, at the expense of the state and civil society. But the decline of state involvement in media, where this has occurred, is not everywhere mourned. The "public service" models of Western Europe, best exemplified by the British Broadcasting Corporation, did not translate easily to other parts of the world. They had and still have much to commend them. But they have also been accused of cultural elitism, of being insufficiently vigorous in their resistance to contentious political controls and interference. The potential contribution of communication media to the wider civil society remains an inspiration for those who engage critically with current global trends and is reason in itself for pondering the fate of NWICO.

ORIGINS AND CONTEXTS

History of NWICO

Nordenstreng (1995) summarized the cornerstones of NWICO as the "four Ds": decolonization development, democratization, and demonopolization. He traced its roots to the League of Nations. Many "international instruments"—resolutions or commitments agreed on between nations—have touched directly on communications and, less directly, on human rights as these might pertain to communications. The Universal Declaration of Human Rights was passed in 1948. U.N. consideration of freedom of information and an international code of ethics for journalists date back to the 1940s. A 1952 U.N. General

Assembly resolution called for resources for independent, domestic, information enterprises, as contributors to the development of public opinion. The U.N. Economic and Social Council, (ECOSOC) addressed the issue of global imbalance of information structures as early as 1961. The U.N. General Assembly in 1962 noted that 70% of the world's population lacked adequate information facilities and were denied the effective enjoyment of the right to information. The U.N. General Assembly, in 1966 and 1972, addressed issues of satellite broadcasting and resolved in favor of national sovereignty, upholding "the principle of prior consent" by the receiving country.

In 1974, the United Nations presented the Declaration on the New International Economic Order (NIEO). This advocated an equitable economic relationship between nations of the First and Third Worlds. It proposed improved terms of trade for the Third World, greater Third World control over productive assets, more interaction between Third World countries, more Third World presence in First World markets, and more Third World influence in global economic institutions. NWICO, sister to NWEO, was created to foster more equitable communications between First and Third Worlds. It proposed news-exchange agreements, greater Third World countries' control over their own communications assets, improvements in the quantity and quality of news about Third World countries in Third World media, a stronger Third World media presence in the First World, and enhancement of Third World influence in UNESCO/International Telecommunication Union or other forums.

Specifically, Nordenstreng (1995) traces NWICO back to Tunis at the end of March 1976. Its emergence postdated the Helsinki agreements between 33 European nations, the United States, and Canada. These enhanced international cooperation in practically all fields—from commerce and industry to culture and communication. The Helsinki accords, says Schiller (1976), represented a U.S. relaxation of its doctrine of "free flow," a doctrine that employed the concept of freedom as an excuse for imperialistic domination. Another significant contribution to the birth of NWICO was the Intergovernmental Meeting of Experts at UNESCO in Paris, December 1975. Its purpose was to prepare the Declaration on Fundamental Principles Governing the Use of the Mass Media in Strengthening Peace and International Understanding and in Combating War Propaganda, Racism and Apartheid. This was a Soviet and East European initiative, backed by militant developing countries. It had been discussed at the UNESCO General Assembly in 1974. Progress was complicated by Arab countries' calls for the inclusion of references to Zionism as a form of racism and racial discrimination.

The 1976 Tunis Non-Aligned Symposium on Information was organized by the Non-Aligned Movement (NAM), based on a mandate by the previous NAM summit and bringing together nearly 200 representatives from 38 NAM member states, some international organizations (including the United Nations and UNESCO), and some countries as invited guests. In opening the symposium, Tunisia's prime minister made reference to NAM's "global majority" and its entitlement to readjustment of international relations leading to the establishment of a new economic order based on a more equitable distribution of resources. During the meeting, a Peruvian delegate, German Carnero Roque, noting that the fight for national emancipation was often distorted by international communication media, made reference to the "new international information order."

NAM had already helped to establish an alternative news agency, the Non-Aligned News Agencies Pool (NANAP). From the Conference of the Press Agencies Pool of the Non-Aligned Pool in New Delhi, in July 1976, there emerged the New Delhi Declaration. This referred to the inadequacy and imbalance of global information flows and noted that the right to freedom of information could be secured only by material means and that a new international order for information was as necessary as the new international economic order.

A resolution adopted at the fourth meeting of the Inter-Governmental Coordinating Council for Information of Non-Aligned Countries in Baghdad, in June 1980, was an outspoken articulation of NWICO principles within the context of international law. Its preamble invoked relevant decisions of NAM summits in Algiers (1973), Colombo (1976), and Havana (1979); the U.N. decisions concerning NIEO, disarmament, and information; and the Mass Media Declaration of UNESCO. The 1980 Baghdad document talks of

- the right of every nation to develop its own independent information system and to protect its national sovereignty and cultural identity, in particular by regulating the activities of the transnational corporations;
- the right of people and individuals to acquire an objective picture of reality by means of accurate and comprehensive information as well as to express themselves freely through various media of culture and communication;
- the right of every nation to use its means of information to make known worldwide its interests, its aspirations, and its political, moral, and cultural values;
- the right of every nation to participate, on the governmental and nongovernmental level, in the international exchange of information under conditions of equality, justice, and mutual advantage; and
- the responsibility of the producers of information for its truthfulness and objectivity as well as for the particular social objectives to which the information activities are dedicated.

Following publication of the MacBride report, Many Voices, One World (International Commission for the Study of Communication Problems, 1980), the UNESCO General Conference in Belgrade that same year passed a milder version of the NAM document. This noted that NWICO could be based on

- elimination of imbalances and inequalities;
- elimination of the negative effects of certain monopolies and excessive concentrations;
- removal of internal and external obstacles to a fee flow and wider and better balanced dissemination of information and ideas;
- plurality of sources and channels of information;

- freedom of the press and information;
- freedom and responsibility of journalists and all professionals in the communication media;
- respect for each people's cultural identity and the right of each nation to inform the world public about its interests, its aspirations, and its social and cultural values;
- respect for the right of all peoples to participate in international exchanges of information on the basis of equality, justice, and mutual benefit; and
- respect for the right of the public, of ethnic and social groups, and of individuals to have access to information sources and to participate actively in the communication process.

Postcolonialism

A full explanation of developing countries' interest in NWICO must extend beyond the internal dynamics of international organizations. Hamelink (1997) locates NWICO within the context of postcolonialism. He cites the challenges that recently liberated states faced when trying to achieve national integration in territories whose boundaries were artificial constructs, many of whose peoples were multiethnic and multilingual and whose economies had been developed to suit Western business interests. Western technologies were transferred to cultural contexts for which they were not always suitable, at a high price in precious foreign exchange, often within programs of tied aid, and they created a dependent relationship on provider companies for spare parts and repairs. NAM forums offered an opportunity for dialogue both between the ex-colonial powers and countries of the South and among the countries of the South. Growing disillusion with postcolonialism contributed to suspicion of multinational corporations and cynicism about the Western political interests.

Intellectual Radicalism: New Waves

The arguments of developing countries drew in part on a new generation of communications thinking. Up to the mid-1960s, the United Nations and UNESCO promoted a two-dimensional approach: free flow of information and development communication. Development communication was conservatively defined as the transfer of technology, skills, and culture from prosperous Western countries to developing countries. Some experts tolerated government control of media: They believed media had a responsibility to facilitate modernization, defined in a way that prioritized state efforts to achieve national integration and industrialization. But they gave insufficient attention to which interests defined modernization and which interests were served by the media, or to media working practices that shaped their content.

NWICO debates corresponded with important shifts in scholarly thinking. A new radicalism was reflected in Third World voices such as those of Fritz Fanon (1967) and Paulo Freire (1970); in protests against American intervention in Vietnam; in European student movements that rocked campuses in hostile reaction to Vietnam, cultural conservatism, and the "massification" of higher education. Social scientists such as Baran and Sweezy (1968), Noam

Chomsky (1990), Herbert Marcuse (1964), C. Wright Mills (1956), and Herbert Schiller (1969) rediscovered and reinterpreted Marx. They subverted fundamental mainstream ideas about economics, history, language, psychology, social structure, and communications, mainly by tracing the links between micro and macro levels of analysis, and analyzed phenomena in their full historical, political, cultural, and economic contexts. With their help, communication research wrenched itself free of quantitative scientism and psychology that had numbed scholarly ability to ask socially relevant questions, think critically, and identify methodologies appropriate to the questions that were asked. Communication scholarship notably in the works of Curran and Seaton (1980), Murdock and Golding (1977), Halloran, Elliot, and Murdock (1970), Mattelart (1979), Nordenstreng (1984), Schiller (1969), Tunstall (1977), and Varis (1973) showed how media worldwide were subject to forces that filtered their representations of the world in the interests of hegemonic power. They fingered corporate and political interests of the United States, and of a small handful of other countries, among them Britain, France, and Japan. Some of the best work from this tradition became available only after NWICO had lost steam under counterattack.

These influences conceptualized significant issues, among them (a) the *imbalance* of communication flows between First and Third Worlds, (b) the *content* of that flow (which in news, for example, prioritized the First World and further undermined the Third World), and (c) *control* of that flow (principally by Western countries, in their own interests).

The NWICO movement's response to these issues, as reflected in the 1980 MacBride report, was to urge the development of national communication policies in developing countries, elaborate guiding principles for mass media in the international sphere, restructure the international information system to achieve greater national autonomy and equity between nations, and stimulate indigenous cultural expression and local communication industry.

PHASES

Nordenstreng (1995) identifies three different phases of the debate. The first was the "decolonization offensive," in which the Third World articulated a collective protest to the First World. Then the West counterattacked, with the help, among others, of the International Press Institute and the Inter-American Press Association. The U.S. Senate Committee on Foreign Relations prepared reports and hearings. Western governments prepared deals, offering material help to build mass media infrastructures. This led to the compromise Mass Media Declaration of 1978, and later to the International Programme for the Development of Communication (IPDC), whose purpose, said critics, was to deflect attention from ideology toward technical aid issues. Radical statements were still to be heard, as at the Intergovernmental Conference on Communication Policies in Asia and Oceania, in Kuala Lumpur in 1979, and at the Intergovernmental Conference on Communication Policies in Africa, in Yaoundé in July 1980. The latter noted that communication problems cannot be reduced to issues of technology transfer or resource distribution. These are essential, certainly, but there are more important issues of ideology and journalistic practice. These were expressed at a conference of 300,000 organized journalists in Mexico City in 1980, which proposed 10 principles for an international code of journalistic ethics.

But the United States was disengaging from the debate. Maintaining a semblance of accommodation, the United States walked away well satisfied from the 1979 World Administrative Radio Conference of the International Telecommunication Union in Geneva, which had met to allocate the international airwaves. Conservatives grew more vocal in opposition to NWICO, which *Time* (October 6, 1980) deemed to directly undermine press freedom. The managing director of Reuters opposed a policy that he claimed would support government control of expression. The United States and Western Europe supported the setting up of IPDC, a policy one U.S. diplomat described as the outcome of "our practical, nonideological approach" in place of "Soviet-inspired ideological approaches." Within six months of the UNESCO General Conference in Belgrade that had endorsed the MacBride report and established IPDC, came the Talloires meeting of 63 delegates from 21 countries to take a united stand against NWICO. Its main resolution urged UNESCO to abandon attempts to regulate global information and strive instead for practical solutions to Third World media advancement. The "Talloires approach" urged developing country media to cooperate with the private sector in the West in setting up, training, and maintaining media infrastructure and personnel.

NWICO references continued until the late 1980s. A compromise formulation by UNESCO's 1983 General Conference referred to "a new world information and communication order, seen as an evolving and continuous process, conducive to a free flow and better balanced dissemination of information." This was one year before U.S. withdrawal from UNESCO, followed by Britain and Singapore, actions that crippled UNESCO economically. Reference to NWICO appeared in a resolution from the 1985 General Conference. With the ascent of Federico Mayor as director general in 1987, UNESCO ceased to promote NWICO altogether, resorting instead to free flow. NWICO discussion continued in NAM, but NAM influence collapsed with the disintegration of Yugoslavia and the end of European communism. Annual meetings continue of the MacBride Round Table on Communication, a coalition of nongovernmental organizations and professional and academic supporters of NWICO.

KEY POSITIONS

NWICO was a dialogue between three distinct power blocs (Wells, 1987). The Soviets wanted resolutions to secure the conditions necessary for peace, including the responsible use of communications and information. They argued that information must serve the interests of the state as representative of the people. Journalists had to educate their reading publics in socialist principles and serve the cause of international peace. Their work was subject to state control, to prevent dissemination of undesirable material. The Soviets distrusted the Western presumption of "freedom of information" as an ultimate good. Individuals could not exercise their right to freedom unless they had access to the means of communication, and such access was denied when the means of communication were controlled mainly by the wealthy. "Freedom of communication" if applied internationally, contravened national sovereignty. Governments also had to guarantee that citizens had access to "correct" information.

The Soviet position was alien to the West. Of course, Soviet principles clashed with actual Soviet practice. Their media were no less concentrated in state hands than Western media were concentrated in the hands of commercial interests. But Soviet philosophy of the 1970s is still a challenge to the West, particularly with respect to the protection of national sovereignty. Global neoliberal hegemony rarely exhibits a defense of national ideology that does not prioritize openness to the global market. This perspective has attained the state of "naturalness" that in the West is a hallmark of the most successful, all-pervasive, and all-invasive of ideologies. Yet the self-definition of many states is emphatically ideological, unsympathetic to invasion of communication space from programming content that violates cherished social, political, and cultural beliefs and values. Why should communications not be directed by the state? The West argues that state control is dangerous to international peace and to human rights. Human rights, at least in theory, were respected both by Soviet insistence on the "responsibility" of journalists and the rights of citizens to "correct" information. The state had considerable power even in many countries of the West, for example, over national broadcasting institutions. The essential difference between the two positions was the higher value the Soviets placed on collective interest (even if in practice it was the party and state that were served) and to the higher value the West placed on the individual (even if in practice it was business that was served). For the West it was incredulous that anyone should seriously trust the state to police "correct" information; Westerners imputed the mere suggestion to nefarious motives.

The Western bloc held fast to the "free flow of information" and the principle of freedom from state interference with its presumption that actual state influences in the West are mostly benign. Not accepting the Soviet notion that the state ensures media responsibility, the West saw a relationship between international conflict and state manipulation of information flows. The West suspected that many of the collective "rights" referred to by NWICO were a cloak for reinforcement of state control. Advertising, far from being a pernicious barrier to the supply of public-serving information, was seen as the guarantor of freedom from the state and of media credibility. This argument underestimated public capacity to pay for media content without the intermediary filter of advertising. The West was concerned (sensibly) about loosely drafted legal and extra-legal propositions, and about measures that might justify the distribution of subsidies only to media that did the bidding of governments. Issues of responsibility and ethics, in the Western bloc, were considered best achieved voluntarily, through codes of ethics and journalist training. The West treated things that alarmed the non-Western countries as of only marginal concern: for example, the might of private capital through media ownership, advertising, and secret or informal alliances with political parties, and the power of even Western states to corrupt the validity, relevance, and accessibility of public information and to curtail the scope for public participation in social communication.

The developing world, represented principally by NAM, was closer to the Soviet than to the Western position, but distinct. It was hostile to Western laissez-faire principles of free flow, freedom that was of benefit mainly to countries and institutions that were already strong, freedom for Western media whose wealth derived from affluent domestic markets. Having covered their costs on domestic markets, they had an unbeatable advantage in foreign markets. They enjoyed links with big industry (through advertising) and with the state (through informal alliance and shared ideology). The main beneficiaries were media proprietors and their allies in government, defense, and other industries with which the media were associated through ownership and partnership. They had the freedom to push information, advertising, ideology, and propaganda anywhere in the world. Developing countries lacked the wealth to arrest this one-way flow, and they lacked the credibility and sophistication to penetrate Western markets. Their protests were more than an expression of hurt national pride. It was a question of investment. In "coups and earthquakes," Western coverage of the developing world (Rosenblum, 1979), Western media were "free" to construct whatever negative images they wanted, without fear of reprisal or serious challenge and with little concern for the damage that such coverage inflicted on investment flows.

Developing countries in the 1970s seemed unable to protect infant media industries. The "dumping" of Western television products at cheap rates made it difficult to nurture local production and talent at a competitive price. Simultaneously, they were targeted by developed country corporations, tying them into expensive media technologies that were not necessarily cost-effective in developing country conditions. Television in itself required an infrastructure of electricity supply that was not widely available. Content came mainly from developed countries, and much of it clashed with traditional values. Developing countries were strong defenders of cultural pluralism in international media flow (in strong contrast to their domestic policies). They were concerned about structured information imbalance and distortions in content, for example, Western news focus on elite countries, elite people, the exceptional, the trivial, failures rather than successes, entertainment rather than information, events rather than processes. These features did not serve long-term political and cultural interests. The developing world supported UNESCO attempts to secure rights to inform, to be heard, to full sovereignty over information, to a free and *balanced* flow, and the right to preserve a way of life. In this perspective, unfortunately, too little was heard of domestic tyrannies, of the absence of political and media representation of many ethnic and other groups, of the use of cultural industries to establish ethnic and political hegemony, of political corruption, and of local alliances with multinational corporations.

ISSUES

The debate revolved around five critical contradictions:

1. Contradiction between ideas of freedom and of sovereignty, for example, between the freedom of publishers to disseminate their media products around the world and the sovereign rights of states to control information flows into and out of national territories.
2. Contradiction between ideas about media responsibility for the nation and about their responsibility to the people. The media, some say, have a responsibility for the achievement of national development, international peace, and other publicly desirable objectives, whether by actively promoting such objectives or passively declining to cover issues or ideas that might impede them. But the media may also have a responsibility to protect the people against the state as concrete representative of the "nation." The role of the press as a watchdog or a fourth estate pits it as ever vigilant against abuse of communications by the state, which typically appeals to national development, security, or integration as excuses for abuse or covers for factional interest. This contradiction can be thought of as a three-way tension between ideas of information as social development, information as political control, and information as social criticism.
3. Contradiction between freedom of the press (referring mainly to the rights of owners) and freedom of information (referring to the rights of individuals and groups to express ideas through media, exercise control over media, and to access media).
4. Contradiction between a communications ideology of professional service that positions audiences as clients or consumers, as against a communications ideology of social participation that engages audiences as equal partners with the media in debate about public issues for the public good.
5. Contradiction between principles of communications equity, requiring some form of state or other form of intervention to achieve equality of access to expression, representation, and reception, and principles of communications choice, which guarantee freedom for audiences to make market choices between technologies, content, and consumption behaviors.

EVALUATION AND CONTEMPORARY RELEVANCE

Outcomes of NWICO have been modest, NWICO was a victim of the very imbalances it critiqued, and it was the target of counter-reaction from threatened interests. Antagonists included Freedom House, Heritage, the Inter American Press Council, the International Press Institute, and the World Press Freedom Committee. Their views were influential in the Western press. Among common misrepresentations was the charge that UNESCO (as opposed to particular UNESCO delegates) favored government control of information, and wanted governments to license journalists.

One significant outcome, IPDC, represented a victory for the United States. It restricted UNESCO to facilitation of communications infrastructure by technical assistance, It evaded issues of media ownership and content, and it preserved the principle of free flow. IPDC funds could be made available to capitalist interests in developing countries.

News-exchange agreements and alternative news agencies are often regarded as a positive outcome of NWICO. Some initiatives, such as NANAP and the Pan-African News Agency (PANA), date from early in the debate, or even preceded it. Subsequent evaluations (see Boyd-Barrett & Rantanen, 1998; Boyd-Barrett & Thussu, 1992) are not encouraging. The popularity of NANAP, never great, was undermined by the collapse of Yugoslavia, whose national agency, TANJUG, was the pool's main coordinator. PANA, once owned by the Organization of African Unity, became a semi-commercial agency in 1998, owned by national news agencies of African countries and African private or commercial interests. This change highlights a record of feckless government or intergovernmental intervention in efforts to transform information flow. Some news agencies that had been established in line with NWICO principles, such as Shihata of Tanzania, have disappeared. Others, such as the News Agency of Nigeria (cf. Musa, 1997), developed in ways that are not identifiably different in news philosophy from conventional agencies; others still are in political and/or economic difficulty. News-exchange arrangements in themselves are incapable of challenging dominant Western news agencies. Mainstream Western agencies have achieved vertical integration in their home markets, have gained privileged access to news clients and news sources in wealthy domestic markets, have the benefits of established worldwide first-copy costs, and have the safeguards of diversification (Somarajiwa, 1984). Effective operation of news-exchange mechanisms is undermined by the lack of credibility that results from dependence on governments for patronage and/or revenue, inability of many members to pay, excessive "protocol" news, lack of facilities and training, inappropriate editing for international markets, invisibility in developing world media, and little play in developed world media.

By 1980, NWICO had secured a place on the global political agenda. There were international mechanisms for the development of communications in the developing world, and basic principles had been articulated for mass media conduct in international relations. There were no legally binding obligations on nations to act on any of these principles. Little finance was committed. Some kind of U.N. intervention was necessary in support of NWICO, but the United Nations is made up of governments, and people who attend U.N. conferences are diplomats and bureaucrats. For NWICO supporters, these considerations presented no problem because of their belief that states must take responsibility for their respective media. But Western media philosophy is hostile to government intervention in media practice, even though this position sometimes may seem hypocritical.

Perhaps NWICO proponents focused too narrowly on news. Hamelink (1994) argued that there should have been more attention to media technology and communication policy, more demand for fundamental political changes within developing countries, more vigorous control by Western governments over transnational corporations, and more significant concessions to the role of market forces in socialist countries.

Nordenstreng (1995) argues that what emerged after NWICO was almost the opposite of what was intended, namely, a media world that was every day more concentrated in fewer hands. Yet NWICO did not disappear; many of its issues remain. The main lessons that Nordenstreng draws are that power rather than reason sets the rules of the debate and that in the final analysis it is the political that determines the global (political) agenda. The withdrawal of the United States and the United Kingdom from UNESCO was not due to any single issue but reflected increasing opposition to multilateralism. The anti-NWICO campaign, he argues, was a "big lie" that presented NWICO as an enemy to media freedom—quite the reverse of what it actually represented—and it claimed, wrongly as it happens, that Third World dictators would use NWICO as a pretext for information suppression. Nordenstreng recognizes that the concept lacked sufficient precision to survive politically. Self-critically, he notes that the NWICO concept remained relatively shallow and its relation to the big narratives of modernization, dependency, imperialism, and so on was left without sufficient articulation. He concludes that NWICO's significance lies in the debate and its lessons rather than in the actual operations of communication industries.

Is NWICO relevant to the contemporary world? Mainly, yes. The significance of geographical boundary has changed. The international media influence of a few countries (most notably the United States) in areas such as cinema, computing, and telecommunications is immense. The fundamental issue is control over communications space, which in almost every domain appears to be monopolized by the twin forces of either private capital or the state, or both, at the expense of the public sphere (cf. Boyd-Barrett, 1999). This battlefield is less about struggle between national interests than it is between corporate giants for global markets. Issues of equity, participation, corporate control, and responsibility are no less pressing now than they were in the 1970s. The role of the nation in communications analysis has been underrated in globalization discourse (Curran & Park, 2000). A worldwide process continues that redirects regulatory systems away from principles of public good toward principles of competition, and whose purpose is to articulate the rules of engagement for surviving oligopolies.

Writing in 1997, Hamelink looks at the MacBride report's five key areas: communication policies, technology, culture, human rights, and international cooperation. The proposal for national, comprehensive communication policies, he concludes, had little impact because communication issues reach the public agenda relatively rarely. The notion of integrated policy making usually runs against the preferences of powerful local lobbies for existing institutional and regulatory arrangements. The proposal did not chime with the mood for deregulation in the 1980s. In technology, the commission had proposed responsible technology decision making with extended public involvement and regulatory measures that favored developing countries. Again, this had little impact. The pace of technology change and anxiety not to be "left behind" militated against prudent, comparative assessment of different technologies from a public good perspective. In the meantime, business has become increasingly influential in regulatory forums. The commission recommended policies that fostered cultural identity and cultural dialogue. But national culture policies have not emerged. The commission simplified the notion of culture, underestimated the extent of cultural heterogeneity, and exaggerated the mutual interest that people have in each other's culture. In human rights, the commission recommended that the media expose human rights violations and support human rights. But in practice, media coverage of human rights is distorted and uneven, and the media themselves are part of the problem that NWICO addressed. The proposed right to communicate has not been codified. Finally, MacBride recommended the establishment of a New World Information and Communication Order and the improvement of multilateral assistance for communication development. In practice, both NIIO and NWICO have disappeared as formative concepts. IPDC never became a genuine multilateral fund, and it continues to be short of finance. Governments have given low priority to communication development, leaving this to "market forces." As a set of policies, the formulation of NWICO lacked precision and strategy: "Fundamental principles were taken for granted; wrong choices about major addressees were made; existing communication policies were ignored; and the commission's work itself revealed an inadequate understanding of social reality" (Hamelink, 1997, p. 91).

Hancock and Hamelink (1999) reviewed the conclusions of the MacBride report's recommendations. MacBride's commitment to communication as a basic human right linked it to the concept of a free and balanced flow of information, and to the view that communication policies were necessary to realize communication rights. But the recommendations did not, nor could not, fuse together to form a coherent philosophy. The report had two somewhat incompatible audiences: the UNESCO and U.N. system, on the one hand, and the general audience, on the other.

The call for cohesive national communication policies, including language and literacy policies, had little response. IPDC has had some successes, but the emphasis on the national now seems insensitive to intra- and cross-national interests and has been subverted by the continuing internationalization of media and culture. Attempts to politicize communication and elevate investment in public communications infrastructure and capacity have been undermined by deregulation and commercialization. Some tariff reductions have been achieved, but spectrum division is still unequal. Communications is a more central component of both communication and development policies within international organizations such as UNESCO, the Food and Agriculture Organization of the United Nations (FAO), and UNICEF (United Nations Children's Fund), but public participation in communications has grown weaker, whereas media monopolization and commercialization is greater and more complex.

Recommendations to preserve national and cultural identity confused communication and culture and overemphasized national culture to the detriment of local culture(s). Development of informatics has been facilitated, mainly by the Internet. MacBride wanted to improve journalism through such means as educational training; strengthening values of truthfulness, accuracy, and respect for human rights, with mechanisms to hold journalists accountable (mainly voluntary measures); and codes of professional ethics. UNESCO has continued to be active in these areas, and the status of journalists has been enhanced in some countries (though there is a lamentable continuation of aggression against journalists worldwide).

The report wanted to widen the sources of information available to citizens in their everyday life, abolish censorship or arbitrary control of information, reduce concentration of media ownership and commercial influence, establish effective legal measures to circumscribe the actions of transnationals, and reduce the editorial influence of advertising. Progress toward these ends has been helped in part by the collapse of authoritarian regimes, yet political controls still range from severe to overwhelming in many parts of the world, and issues of concentration and monopoly are strong almost everywhere. Independence and autonomy are normally championed in relation to freedom from government, but much less is said in mainstream public discourse about the relationship between economic factors and editorial independence.

Positive endorsement of diversity and choice was to be achieved by strengthening infrastructure, increasing resources, securing a plurality of information sources, and safeguarding the needs of women and minorities. Hancock and Hamelink (1999) note that principles of individual and community participation are largely incompatible with the modus operandi of the mass media. There is now more abundant information and more sources, and more favorable attention is directed toward the interests of women and minorities, although there is considerable scope for improvement. Media management is hardly more democratic.

How has communication scholarship in general handled the NWICO debate? Broadly, it has been sympathetic to the original developing world perspective. Closer to the time of the debate, sympathetic analyses incorporated NWICO within a broader critique of cultural and media imperialism or dominance-dependency relationships, drawing on specific case studies of flows of television and news products (cf. Harris, 1977). This critique has been transformed subsequently into a broader critique of globalization, the neoliberal global order, relations between local and global, and the multimedia mega-corporations (cf. Golding & Harris, 1997). A related but distinct literature, also sympathetic to the original developing world perspective, has focused its attention on practical solutions, for example, the role of radio in health and agricultural campaigns. There has also been an important counter-critique to NWICO, which has used empirical study to challenge some of its presumptions (cf. Weaver, Wilhoit, Stevenson, Shaw, & Cole, 1980).

CHALLENGES FOR SCHOLARSHIP

Analysis of communications in national and international context has continued to improve since NWICO. Scannell and Cardiff (1990) and Martín Barbero (1993), among others, illuminated the relationship between the development of mass communication and the formation of national and cultural identities. Habermas (1988) contributed the concept of "public sphere" as an ideal type by which to judge the extent to which media nurture public dialogue. His main criteria were equality of access, relevance of content to the public good, freedom from the intervention of state or capital, and the role of rationality as the final arbiter of value. Curran (1996), Gaining (1999), and Winseck (1995) offered helpful models for depicting relationships between state, capital, civil society, and media. Notable North American scholars Edward Herman and Noam Chomsky (1988), Robert McChesney (1999; Herman & McChesney, 1997), Herbert Schiller (1976), and Dan Schiller (1999) charted continuing processes of concentration and convergence, and the capture of media by industrial, political, and military interests. Sreberny (2000) explored the complexity of relationships between the global and the local, and the many different influences that act upon culture. Hamelink (1994) identified the principal forces of change in international communication as digitization, deregulation, convergence, concentration, commercialization, and globalization. To these, Boyd-Barrett (2000, 2001) added *competitivization* and democratization. Competitivization happens when new markets are created or old markets are considerably expanded as the result of technological innovation or deregulation, in a way that temporarily reduces the costs of market entry. The result is a dramatic increase of new players, and a scramble for market influence among old and new. What starts as enhanced competition then leads to industrial consolidation through aggression and fear. Democratization also initially stimulates media abundance and diversity. In the 1980s and 1990s, democratization typically involved an opening up of national markets to the global market. This encourages the formation of alliances between national and international enterprises, and a gradual delocalization and consolidation of media interests. It reflects the ascendancy of neoliberal ideology, implemented through international financial institutions, which, as Braman (1990) observed, foster principles of economic exchange that do not distinguish cultural commodities from any others. This ideology therefore is hostile to forms of state subsidy for cultural industries, or to state intervention to protect national media markets from foreign competition. It would seek to penalize states that persist in such subsidies and interventions.

The rate at which states subscribe to this regulatory order is uneven. At the end of the Uruguay Round of GATS (General Agreement on Trade and Services), only 13 countries made commitments (rising to 19 by 1998 as a result of accessions) in the audiovisual services sector. A substantially larger number sought exemptions. Only 2 countries, the Central African Republic and the United States, made commitments in all six subsectors. Most commitments are subject to limitations. The most common include limits on foreign shareholdings and on the share of screening time allotted to foreign productions, and exclusion from national treatment in respect to domestic subsidies. Several audiovisual industry representatives of member countries during the Uruguay Round suggested that the cinema and broadcasting sectors should be excluded from the agreement in order to protect national industries and cultures from being overwhelmed by foreign products. An alternative approach was to suggest exemptions from certain disciplines in recognition of the cultural specificity of these industries. No agreement was reached. Even where exemptions are sought, however, they are hard to police. The European Union's "Television Without Frontiers" directive to preserve a proportion of television time for local consumption has not been well enforced, and such standards are easy to evade (e.g., through coproductions) and are sometimes ignored with impunity (as in the case of many cable and satellite channels). Countries continue to be under pressure to reduce state protections, as a condition of full entry to global nontariff markets, and as a form of leverage for the securing of international financial loans. In summary, neoliberal ideology commits states to the principle of free flow and in relation to all commodities, cultural and other.

Assessing the actual balance between local, national, regional, and global factors in the functioning and role of communication media is a contentious exercise. Warning against errors of determination (e.g., attribution of deterministic power to concepts such as globalization rather than to actions of responsible human agents), I have called for a sharper focus on issues of access, fairness, and representation (Boyd-Barrett, 1999).

There are important lessons here for communication research. Research should be embedded within a thorough understanding of the social, cultural, political, and economic context of the subject that it addresses. It should consciously articulate and balance a range of theoretical perspectives available for making sense of its subjects. It should take equal account of each phase of the communication process, namely, production, content, and reception, and should build on and contribute to a solid framework of empirical data systematically collected, quantitative and qualitative. In international communication research, a strong ethnographic and empirical base of information concerning peripheral countries is as important as in the case of core countries. Special care should be taken when the subject under investigation is also high on political agendas. Advocacy is best left to politicians. Yes, scholars ought sometimes to identify themes and issues of public concern that have a sociological reality but have not penetrated political discourse. Otherwise, scholarship should examine the underlying premises and ideologies that inform political discourses, what is said and not said, holding them up against alternative perspectives and evidence. In the 1970s, NWICO was a sufficiently daunting challenge with respect to postcolonial theories of cultural imperialism and dominance-dependency. The challenge to scholars at the turn of the 21st century with respect to communications and globalization is even greater, even more interdisciplinary, macro, elusive, and enjoys much higher political visibility because it is more plainly relevant, in both positive and negative implications, to peoples of both developed and developing worlds. It is not different from NWICO: NWICO was an early manifestation of concern about processes that were later to be identified as component forces of globalization. Communication processes, as we have seen, are central to globalization. We have not been examining a concept that was alive and whose significance has now lapsed, but a concept that helps give us a purchase, albeit imperfectly, on the state of the world as it is today.

REFERENCES

Baran, P., & Sweezy, P. (1968). *Monopoly capital* Harmondsworth, UK: Pelican.

Boyd-Barrett, O. (1999). Media imperialism reformulated. In D. K. Thussu (Ed.), *Electronic empires: Global media and local resistance* (pp. 157–176). London: Edward Arnold.

Boyd-Barrett, O. (2000). Cyberspace and the public sphere. In *DIAC-2000 symposium*. Proceedings of the Shaping the Network Society: The Future of the Public Space in Cyberspace. Seattle, WA: Computer Professionals for Social Responsibility.

Boyd-Barrett, O. (in press). Globalization and cyberspace. In D. Schules & P. Day (Eds.), *Shaping the network press*. Cambridge: MIT Press.

Boyd-Barrett, O., & Rantanen, T. (1998). *The globalization of news*. London: Sage.

Boyd-Barrett, O., & Thussu, D. (1992). *Contra-flow in global news*. London: John Libbey.

Braman, S. (1990). Trade and information policy. *Media, Culture & Society, 12,* 361–385.

Chomsky, N. (1990). *Deterring democracy*. London: Verso.

Curran, J. (1996). Mass media and democracy revisited. In J. Curran & M. Gurevitch (Eds.), *Mass media and society* (2nd ed., pp. 81–119). London: Edward Arnold.

Curran, J., & Park, M.-J. (2000). *De-Westernizing media studies*. London: Routledge.

Curran, J., & Seaton, J. (1980). *Power without responsibility*. London: Fontana.

Fanon, F. (1967). *The wretched of the earth*. Middlesex, UK: Penguin.

Freire, P. (1970). *Pedagogy of the oppressed*. New York: Continuum.

Galtung, J. (1999). State, capital and the civil society: A problem of communication. In R. Vincent, K. Nordenstreng, & M. Traber (Eds.), *Towards equity in global communication: MacBride update*. Cresskill, NJ: Hampton.

Golding, P., & Harris, P. (Eds.). (1997). *Beyond cultural imperialism: Globalization, communication and the new international order*. London: Sage.

Habermas, J. (1988). *The structural transformation of the public sphere* (T. Burger, Trans.). Cambridge: MIT Press.

Halloran, J., Elliot, P., & Murdock, G. (1970). *Communications and demonstrations*. Harmondsworth, UK: Penguin.

Hamelink, C. J. (1994). *The politics of world communication*. London: Sage.

Hamelink, C. J. (1997). MacBride with hindsight. In P. Golding & P. Harris (Eds.), *Beyond cultural imperialism: Globalization, communication and the new international order* (pp. 69–93). London: Sage.

Hancock, A., & Hamelink, C. (1999). Many more voices, another world: Looking back at the MacBride recommendations. In R. Vincent, K. Nordenstreng, & M. Traber (Eds.), *Towards equity in global communication: MacBride update*. Cresskill, NJ: Hampton.

Harris, P. (1977). *News dependence: The case for a new world information order*. Final report to UNESCO of a study of the international news media. Paris: UNESCO.

Herman, E., & Chomsky, N. (1988). *Manufacturing public consent*. New York: Pantheon.

Herman, E., & McChesney, R. (1997). *The global media*. London: Cassell.

International Commission for the Study of Communication Problems. (1980). *Many voices, one world: Towards a new, more just and more efficient world information and communication order.* Paris: UNESCO.

Marcuse, H. (1964). *One-dimensional man.* Boston: Beacon.

Martín Barbero, J. (1993). *Communication, culture and hegemony: From media to mediations.* London: Sage.

Mattelart, A. (1979). *Multinational corporations and the control of culture: The ideological apparatuses of imperialism.* Brighton, UK: Harvester.

McChesney, R. (1999). *Rich media, poor democracy: Communication politics in dubious times.* Urbana and Chicago: University of Illinois Press.

Mills, C. W. (1956). *The power elite.* New York: Oxford University Press.

Murdock, G., & Golding, P. (1977). Capitalism, communication and class relations. In J. Curran, M. Gurevitch, & J. Woollacott (Eds.), *Mass communication and society* (pp. 12–43). London: Edward Arnold.

Musa, M. (1997). From optimism to reality: An overview of Third World news agencies. In P. Golding & P. Harris (Eds.), *Beyond cultural imperialism: Globalization, communication and the new international order.* London: Sage.

Nordenstreng, K. (1984). *The mass media declaration of UNESCO.* Norwood, NJ: Ablex.

Nordenstreng, K. (1995). *The NWICO debate.* Unit 20 of the M.A. in mass communications. Leicester, UK: University of Leicester, Centre for Mass Communications Research.

Rosenblum, M. (1979). *Coups and earthquakes: Reporting the Third World for America.* New York: Harper and Row.

Somarajiwa, R. (1984). Third World entry to the world market in news: Problems and possible solutions. *Media, Culture & Society, 6,* 119–136.

Scannell, P., & Cardiff, D. (1990). *A social history of British broadcasting.* Oxford, UK: Basil Blackwell.

Schiller, D. (1999). *Digital capitalism: Networking the global market system.* Cambridge: MIT Press.

Schiller, H. I. (1969). *Mass communications and American empire.* New York: A. M. Kelley.

Schiller, H. I. (1976). *Communication and cultural domination.* White Plains, NY: International Arts and Sciences Press.

Sreberny, A. (2000). Television, gender, and democratization in the Middle East. In J. Curran & M.-J. Park (Eds.), *De-Westernizing media studies* (pp. 63–78). London: Routledge.

Tunstall, J. (1977). *The media are American.* London: Constable.

Varis, T. (1973). *International inventory of television programme structure and the flow of TV programmes between nations.* Tampere, Finland: University of Tampere.

Wells, C. (1987). *The UN, UNESCO, and the politics of knowledge.* London: Macmillan.

Weaver, D. H., Wilhoit, G. C, Stevenson, R. L, Shaw, D. L., & Cole, R. (1980). *The news of the world in four major wire services.* Prepared for inclusion in the final report of the "foreign images" project undertaken by members of the International Association for Mass Communication Research for UNESCO.

Winseck, D. (1995). *The shifting context of international communication: Possibilities for a New World Information and Communication Order.* Unit 21 of the M.A. in mass communications. Leicester, UK: University of Leicester, Centre for Mass Communications Research.

Part III

STATE POWER AND COMMUNICATION

The impact of state interests and strategies is a significant concern for International Communication scholars. Essays in this selection examine how state deploys power across the international arena. The first selection in this section, Nye's essay describes state power deployed as hard power (coercion, punishment) as well as soft power (gaining consensus through persuasion). Nye underlines the significance of global deployment of soft power in terms of foreign policy and public diplomacy and describes how national governments employ media technologies to communicate with the publics of other nations.

Price's essay describes state-interest as competing with commercial and political interests to control media space or simply for access to media. New media technologies are a challenge to states that have exercised monopoly control over national media. New media are in Itheil de Sola Pools' words, "technologies of freedom," as much as they are variously used by disparate groups—often pursuing violence, inside and outside the state. Price's essay offers useful analysis of media and state sovereignty.

PUBLIC DIPLOMACY AND SOFT POWER

By Joseph S. Nye, Jr.

Power is the ability to affect others to obtain the outcomes you want. One can affect others' behavior in three main ways: threats of coercion ("sticks"), inducements and payments ("carrots"), and attraction that makes others want what you want. A country may obtain the outcomes it wants in world politics because other countries want to follow it, admiring its values, emulating its example, and/or aspiring to its level of prosperity and openness. In this sense, it is important to set the agenda and attract others in world politics, and not only to force them to change through the threat or use of military or economic weapons. This soft power—getting others to want the outcomes that you want—co-opts people rather than coerces them.[1]

Soft power rests on the ability to shape the preferences of others. At the personal level, we all know the power of attraction and seduction. Political leaders have long understood the power that comes from setting the agenda and determining the framework of a debate. Soft power is a staple of daily democratic politics. The ability to establish preferences tends to be associated with intangible assets such as an attractive personality, culture, political values and institutions, and policies that are seen as legitimate or having moral authority. If I can get you to want to do what I want, then I do not have to force you to do what you do *not* want.

Joseph S. Nye Jr., "Public Diplomacy and Soft Power," *The Annals of the American Academy of Political and Social Science*, vol. 616, no. 1, pp. 94-109. Copyright © 2008 by SAGE Publications. Reprinted with permission.

Soft power is not merely influence, though it is one source of influence. Influence can also rest on the hard power of threats or payments. And soft power is more than just persuasion or the ability to move people by argument, though that is an important part of it. It is also the ability to entice and attract. In behavioral terms, soft power is attractive power. In terms of resources, soft power resources are the assets that produce such attraction. Whether a particular asset is an attractive soft power resource can be measured through polls or focus groups. Whether that attraction in turn produces desired policy outcomes has to be judged in each particular case. But the gap between power measured as resources and power judged by the outcomes of behavior is not unique to soft power. It occurs with all forms of power. Before the fall of France in 1940, for example, Britain and France had more tanks than Germany, but that advantage in military power resources did not accurately predict the outcome of the battle.

This distinction between power measured in behavioral outcomes and power measured in terms of resources is important for understanding the relationship between soft power and public diplomacy. In international politics, the resources that produce soft power arise in large part from the values an organization or country expresses in its culture, in the examples it sets by its internal practices and policies, and in the way it handles its relations with others. Public diplomacy is an instrument that governments use to mobilize these resources to communicate with and attract the publics of other countries, rather then merely their governments. Public diplomacy tries to attract by drawing attention to these potential resources through broadcasting, subsidizing cultural exports, arranging exchanges, and so forth. But if the content of a country's culture, values, and policies are not attractive, public diplomacy that "broadcasts" them cannot produce soft power. It may produce just the opposite. Exporting Hollywood films full of nudity and violence to conservative Muslim countries may produce repulsion rather than soft power. And Voice of America (VOA) broadcasts that extol the virtues of government policies that are seen by others as arrogant will be dismissed as mere propaganda and not produce the soft power of attraction.

Governments sometimes find it difficult to control and employ soft power, but that does not diminish its importance. It was a former French foreign minister who observed that Americans are powerful because they can "inspire the dreams and desires of others, thanks to the mastery of global images through film and television and because, for these same reasons, large numbers of students from other countries come to the United States to finish their studies" (Vedrine and Moisi 2001, 3).

Soft power is an important reality. Those self-styled realists who deny the importance of soft power are like people who do not understand the power of seduction. They succumb to the "concrete fallacy" that espouses that something is not a power resource unless you can drop it on a city or on your foot.[2] During a meeting with President John F. Kennedy, senior statesman John J. McCloy exploded in anger about paying attention to popularity and attraction in world politics: " 'world opinion?' I don't believe in world opinion. The only thing that matters is power." But as Arthur Schlesinger noted, "like Woodrow Wilson and Franklin Roosevelt, Kennedy understood that the ability to attract others and move opinion was an element of power" (McCloy and Schlesinger, as quoted in Haefele 2001, 66). The German editor Josef Joffe once argued that America's soft power was even larger than its economic and military assets. "U.S. culture, low-brow or high, radiates outward with an intensity last seen in the days of the Roman Empire—but with a novel twist. Rome's and Soviet Russia's cultural sway stopped exactly at their military borders. America's soft power, though, rules over an empire on which the sun never sets" (Joffe 2001, 43). But cultural soft power can be undercut by policies that are seen as illegitimate. In recent years, particularly after the invasion of Iraq, America's soft power has declined. For example, a 2007 BBC opinion poll reported that across twenty-five countries, half of those polled said the United States played a mainly negative role in the world *(New York Times* 2007).

THE DEVELOPMENT OF PUBLIC DIPLOMACY

The soft power of a country rests primarily on three resources: its culture (in places where it is attractive to others), its political values (when it lives up to them at home and abroad), and its foreign policies (when they are seen as legitimate and having moral authority). Culture is the set of practices that create meaning for a society, and it has many manifestations. It is common to distinguish between high culture such as literature, art, and education, which appeals to elites; and popular culture, which focuses on mass entertainment. After its defeat in the Franco–Prussian War, the French government sought to repair the nation's shattered prestige by promoting its language and literature through the Alliance Francaise created in 1883. "The projection of French culture abroad thus became a significant component of French diplomacy" (Pells 1997, 31). Italy, Germany, and others soon followed suit. World War I saw a rapid acceleration of efforts to deploy soft power, as most of those governments established offices to propagandize their cause. The United States not only established its own office but was a central target of other countries. During the early years before American entry into the war, Britain and Germany competed to create favorable images in American public opinion.

The United States was a relative latecomer to the idea of using information and culture for the purposes of diplomacy. In 1917, President Woodrow Wilson established a Committee on Public Information directed by his friend, the newspaperman George Creel. In Creel's words, his task was "a vast enterprise in salesmanship, the world's greatest adventure in advertising" (Rosenberg 1982, 79). Creel insisted that his office's activities did not constitute propaganda and were merely educational and informative. But the facts belied his denials. Among other things, Creel organized tours, churned out pamphlets on "the Gospel of Americanism," established a government-run news service, made sure that motion picture producers received wartime allotments of scarce materials, and saw to it that the films portrayed America in a positive light. The office aroused suspicions sufficient enough that it was abolished shortly after the return of peace.

The advent of radio in the 1920s led many governments into the arena of foreign-language broadcasting, and in the 1930s, communists and fascists competed to promote favorable images to foreign publics. In addition to its foreign-language radio broadcasts. Nazi Germany perfected the propaganda film. As Britain's Foreign Secretary Anthony Eden realized about the new communications in 1937, "It is perfectly true, of course, that good cultural propaganda cannot remedy the damage done by a bad foreign policy, but it is no exaggeration to say that even the best of diplomatic policies may fail if it neglects the task of interpretation and persuasion which modern conditions impose" (as quoted in Wagnleitner 1994, 50).

By the late 1930s, the Roosevelt administration was convinced that "America's security depended on its ability to speak to and to win the support of people in other countries" (Pells 1997, 33). President Roosevelt was particularly concerned about German propaganda in Latin America. In 1938, the State Department established a Division of Cultural Relations, and supplemented it two years later with an Office of Inter-American Affairs that, under Nelson Rockefeller, actively promoted information about America and its culture to Latin America. In 1939, Germany beamed seven hours of programming a week to Latin America, and the United States about twelve. By 1941, the United States broadcast around the clock.

After America's entry into the war, the government's cultural offensive became global in scope. In 1942, Roosevelt created an Office of Wartime Information (OWI) to deal in presumably accurate information, while an intelligence organization, the Office of Strategic Service, included among its functions the dissemination of disinformation. The OWI even worked to shape Hollywood into an effective propaganda tool, suggesting additions and deletions to many films and denying licenses to others. And Hollywood executives were happy to cooperate out of a mixture of patriotism and self-interest. Well before the cold war, "American corporate and advertising executives, as well as the heads of Hollywood studios, were selling not only their products but also America's culture and values, the secrets of its success, to the rest of the world" (Pells 1997, xiii). Wartime soft power resources were created partly by the government and in part independently. What became known as the Voice of America grew rapidly during World War II. Modeled after the BBC, by 1943 it had twenty-three transmitters delivering news in twenty-seven languages.

With the growth of the Soviet threat in the cold war, public diplomacy continued to expand, but so did a debate about the extent to which it should be a captive purveyor of government information or an independent representative of American culture. Special radios were added such as Radio Liberty and Radio Free Europe, which used exiles to broadcast to the Eastern bloc. More generally, as the cold war developed, there was a division between those who favored the slow media of cultural diplomacy—art, books, exchanges—which had a "trickle down effect," and those who favored the fast information media of radio, movies, and newsreels, which promised more immediate and visible "bang for the buck." Although the tension has never fully been resolved to this day, public diplomacy of both sorts helped to erode faith in communism behind the Iron Curtain.[3] When the Berlin Wall finally went down in 1989, it collapsed under the assault of hammers and bulldozers, not an artillery barrage.

With the end of the cold war, Americans were more interested in budget savings than in investments in soft power. From 1963 to 1993, the federal budget grew fifteen-fold, but the United States Information Agency (USIA) budget grew only six and a half times larger. The USIA had more than 12,000 employees at its peak in the mid-1960s but only 9,000 in 1994 and 6,715 on the eve of its takeover by the U.S. State Department (U.S. Department of State n.d.). Soft power seemed expendable. Between 1989 and 1999, the budget of the USIA, adjusted for inflation, decreased 10 percent. While government-funded radio broadcasts reached half the Soviet population every week and between 70 and 80 percent of the populace of Eastern Europe during the cold war, at the beginning of the new century, a mere 2 percent of Arabs heard the VOA (Blinken 2003, 287). Resources for the USIA mission in Indonesia, the world's largest Muslim nation, were cut in half. From 1995 to 2001, academic and cultural exchanges dropped from forty-five thousand to twenty-nine thousand annually, while many accessible downtown cultural centers and libraries were closed (Johnson and Dale 2003, 4). In comparison, the BBC World Service had half again as many weekly listeners around the globe as did the VOA. Public diplomacy had become so identified with fighting the cold war that few Americans noticed that with an information revolution occurring, soft power was becoming more rather than less important. Government policies reflected popular attitudes. For example, the percentage of foreign affairs articles on the front page of U.S. newspapers dropped by nearly half (Hiatt 2007). Only after September 2001 did Americans begin to rediscover the importance of investing in the instruments of soft power.

PUBLIC DIPLOMACY IN AN INFORMATION AGE

Promoting positive images of one's country is not new, but the conditions for projecting soft power have transformed dramatically in recent years. For one thing, nearly half the countries in the world are now democracies. The competitive cold war model has become less relevant as a guide for public diplomacy. While there is still a need to provide accurate information to populations in countries like Burma or Syria, where the government controls information, there is a new need to garner favorable public opinion in countries like Mexico and Turkey, where parliaments can now affect decision making. For example, when the United States sought support for the Iraq war, such as Mexico's vote in the UN or Turkey's permission for American troops to cross its territory, the decline of American soft power created a disabling rather than an enabling environment for its policies. Shaping public opinion becomes even more important where authoritarian governments have been replaced. Public support was not so important when the United States successfully sought the use of bases in authoritarian countries, but it turned out to be crucial under the new democratic conditions in Mexico and Turkey. Even when foreign leaders are friendly, their leeway may be limited if their publics and parliaments have a negative image of the United States. In such circumstances, diplomacy aimed at public opinion can become as important to outcomes as the traditional classified diplomatic communications among leaders.

Information is power, and today a much larger part of the world's population has access to that power. Long gone are the days when "small teams of American foreign service officers drove jeeps to the hinterlands of Latin America and other remote regions of the world to show reel-to-reel movies to isolated audiences" (Ross 2003, 252). Technological advances have led to a dramatic reduction in the cost of processing and transmitting information. The result is an explosion of information, and that has produced a "paradox of plenty" (Simon 1998, 30–33). Plenty of information leads to scarcity of attention. When people are overwhelmed with the volume of information confronting them, it is hard to know what to focus on. Attention rather than information becomes the scarce resource, and those who can distinguish valuable information from background clutter gain power. Editors and cue-givers become more in demand, and this is a source of power for those who can tell us where to focus our attention.

Among editors and cue-givers, credibility is the crucial resource and an important source of soft power. Reputation becomes even more important than in the past, and political struggles occur over the creation and destruction of credibility. Governments compete for credibility not only with other governments but with a broad range of alternatives including news media, corporations, nongovernmental organizations (NGOs), intergovernmental organizations, and networks of scientific communities.

Politics has become a contest of competitive credibility. The world of traditional power politics is typically about whose military or economy wins. Politics in an information age "may ultimately be about whose story wins" (Arquila and Ronfeldt 1999). Governments compete with each other and with other organizations to enhance their own credibility and weaken that of their opponents. Witness the struggle between Serbia and NATO to frame the interpretation of events in Kosovo in 1999 and the events in Serbia a year later. Prior to the demonstrations that led to the overthrow of Slobodan Milosevic in October 2000, 45 percent of Serb adults were tuned to Radio Free Europe and VOA. In contrast, only 31 percent listened to the state-controlled radio station, Radio Belgrade (Kaufman 2003). Moreover, the domestic alternative radio station, B92, provided access to Western news, and when the government tried to shut it down, it continued to provide such news on the Internet.

Reputation has always mattered in world politics, but the role of credibility becomes an even more important power resource because of the "paradox of plenty." Information that appears to be propaganda may not only be scorned, but it may also turn out to be counterproductive if it undermines a country's reputation for credibility. Exaggerated claims about Saddam Hussein's weapons of mass destruction and ties to Al Qaeda may have helped mobilize domestic support for the Iraq war, but the subsequent disclosure of the exaggeration dealt a costly blow to American credibility. Similarly, the treatment of prisoners at Abu Ghraib and Guantanamo in a manner inconsistent with American values led to perceptions of hypocrisy that could not be reversed by broadcasting pictures of Muslims living well in America. In fact, the slick production values of the new American satellite television station Alhurra did not make it competitive in the Middle East, where it was widely regarded as an instrument of government propaganda. Under the new conditions of the information age, more than ever, the soft sell may prove more effective than the hard sell. Without underlying national credibility, the instruments of public diplomacy cannot translate cultural resources into the soft power of attraction. The effectiveness of public diplomacy is measured by minds changed (as shown in interviews or polls), not dollars spent or slick production packages.

THE DIMENSIONS OF CURRENT PUBLIC DIPLOMACY

In 1963, Edward R. Murrow, the noted broadcaster who was director of the USIA in the Kennedy administration, defined public diplomacy as interactions not only with foreign governments but primarily with nongovernmental individuals and organizations, and often presenting a variety of private views in addition to government views (as cited in Leonard 2002). Skeptics who treat the term *public diplomacy* as a mere euphemism for propaganda miss the point. Simple propaganda often lacks credibility and thus is counterproductive as public diplomacy. Good public diplomacy has to go beyond propaganda. Nor is public diplomacy merely public relations campaigns. Conveying information and selling a positive image is part of it, but public diplomacy also involves building long-term relationships that create an enabling environment for government policies.

The mix of direct government information with long-term cultural relationships varies with three dimensions of public diplomacy, and all three are important (Leonard 2002). The first and most immediate dimension is daily communications, which involves explaining the context of domestic and foreign policy decisions. After making decisions, government officials in modern democracies usually devote a good deal of attention to what and how to tell the press. But they generally focus on the domestic press. The foreign press has to be an important target for the first stage of public diplomacy. The first stage must also involve preparation for dealing with crises. A rapid response capability means that false charges or misleading information can be answered immediately. For example, when Al Jazeera broadcast Osama bin Laden's first videotape on October 7, 2001, U.S. officials initially sought to prevent both Al Jazeera and American networks from broadcasting further messages from bin Laden. But in the modern information age, such action is not only as frustrating as stopping the tide, but it runs counter to the value of openness that America wants to symbolize. A better response would be to prepare to flood Al Jazeera and other networks with American voices to counter bin Laden's hate speech. While Al Jazeera and other foreign networks are hardly free of bias, they also need content. As their Washington bureau chief invited, "Please come talk to us, exploit us" (as quoted in Blinken 2003).

The second dimension is strategic communication, which develops a set of simple themes much as a political or advertising campaign does. The campaign plans symbolic events and communications over the course of the next year to reinforce central themes or to advance a particular government policy. Special themes focus on particular policy initiatives. For example, when the Reagan administration decided to implement NATO's two-track decision of deploying missiles while negotiating to remove existing Soviet intermediate-range missiles, the Soviet Union responded with a concerted campaign to influence European opinion and make the deployment impossible. The United States's themes stressed the multilateral nature of the NATO decision, encouraged European governments to take the lead when possible, and used nongovernmental American participants effectively to counter Soviet arguments. Even though polls in Germany showed residual concerns about the policy, they also showed that the German public was pro-American by a two-thirds majority. As former secretary of state George Schultz later concluded, "I don't think we could have pulled it off if it hadn't been for a very active program of public diplomacy. Because the Soviets were very active all through 1983 ... with peace movements and all kinds of efforts to dissuade our friends in Europe from deploying" (as quoted in Tuch 1990).

The third dimension of public diplomacy is the development of lasting relationships with key individuals over many years through scholarships, exchanges, training, seminars, conferences, and access to media channels. Over time, about seven hundred thousand people, including two hundred heads of governments, have participated in American cultural and academic exchanges, and these exchanges helped to educate world leaders like Anwar Sadat, Helmut Schmidt, and Margaret Thatcher. Other countries have similar programs. For example, Japan has developed an interesting exchange program bringing six thousand young foreigners from forty countries each year to teach their languages in Japanese schools, with an alumni association to maintain the bonds of friendship that develop.[4]

Each of these three dimensions of public diplomacy plays an important role in helping to create an attractive image of a country that can improve its prospects for obtaining its desired outcomes. But even the best advertising cannot sell an unpopular product. Policies that appear as narrowly self-serving or arrogantly presented are likely to prohibit rather than produce soft power. At best, longstanding friendly relationships may lead others to be slightly more tolerant in their responses. Sometimes friends will give you the benefit of the doubt or forgive more willingly. This is what is meant by an enabling or a disabling environment for policy.

A communications strategy cannot work if it cuts against the grain of policy. Actions speak louder than words, and public diplomacy that appears to be mere window dressing for hard power projection is unlikely to succeed. In 2003, former speaker of the House of Representatives Newt Gingrich attacked the State Department for failing to sell America's policy (Gingrich 2003). But selling requires paying attention to your markets, and on that dimension, the fault did not rest with the State Department. For example, Gingrich complained about America's removal from the UN Human Rights Commission in 2001. But that was in retaliation for America's failure to pay its UN dues (a policy that originated in the U.S. Congress) and the unilateral policies of the new Bush administration (that often originated in other executive departments despite the warnings of the State Department). As Republican Senator Charles

Hagel noted, after 9/11 many people in Washington were suddenly talking about the need for renewed public diplomacy to "get our message out." But, he pointed out, "Madison Avenue–style packaging cannot market a contradictory or confusing message. We need to reassess the fundamentals of our diplomatic approach. ... Policy and diplomacy must match, or marketing becomes a confusing and transparent barrage of mixed messages" (Hagel 2003).

Effective public diplomacy is a two-way street that involves listening as well as talking. We need to understand better what is going on in the minds of others and what values we share. That is why exchanges are often more effective than mere broadcasting. By definition, soft power means getting others to want the same outcomes you want, and that requires an understanding of how they are hearing your messages and adapting them accordingly. It is crucial to understand the target audience. Yet research on foreign public opinion is woefully underfunded.

Preaching at foreigners is not the best way to convert them. Too often, political leaders think that the problem is simply that others lack information, and that if they simply knew what we know, they would see things our way. But all information goes through cultural filters, and declamatory statements are rarely heard as intended. Telling is far less influential than actions and symbols that show as well as tell. That is why the Bush administration initiatives on increasing development assistance or combating HIV/AIDS were potentially important before they vanished under the burdens of Iraq. It is interesting that provision of Tsunami relief to Indonesia in 2004 helped to reverse in part the precipitous slide in America's standing in Indonesian polls that began after the Iraq war.

Broadcasting is important but needs to be supplemented by effective "narrowcasting" via the Internet. While the Internet reaches only the elites in many parts of the world where most people are too poor to own a telephone (much less a computer), its flexibility and low cost allows for the targeting of messages to particular groups. It also provides a way to transfer information to countries where the government blocks traditional media. And the Internet can be used interactively and in combination with exchanges. Face-to-face communications remain the most effective, but they can be supplemented and reinforced by the Internet. For example, a combination of personal visits and internet resources can create both virtual and real networks of young people who want to learn about each other's cultures. Or the United States might learn a lesson from Japan and pay young foreigners to spend a year teaching their language and culture in American schools. The alumni of these programs could then form associations that would remain connected over the Internet.

Some countries accomplish almost all of their public diplomacy through actions rather than broadcasting. Norway is a good example. It has only 5 million people, lacks an international language or transnational culture, is not a central location or hub of organizations or multinational corporate brands, and is not a member of the European Union. Nonetheless, it has developed a voice and presence out of proportion to its modest size and resources "through a ruthless prioritization of its target audiences and its concentration on a single message—Norway as a force for peace in the world" (Leonard 2002, 53). The relevant activities include conflict mediation in the Middle East, Sri Lanka, and Colombia, as well as its large aid budget and its frequent participation in peace-keeping missions. Of course, not all Norwegian actions are consistent in their message. The domestic politics of whaling sometimes strikes a discordant note among environmentalists, but overall, Norway shows how a small country can exploit a diplomatic niche that enhances its image and role.

Not only do actions need to reinforce words, it is important to remember that the same words and images that are most successful in communicating to a domestic audience may have negative effects on a foreign audience. When President Bush used the term *axis of evil* to refer to Iraq, Iran, and North Korea in his 2002 State of the Union address, it was well received domestically. However, foreigners reacted against lumping together disparate diplomatic situations under a moralistic label. Similarly, while declaring a "war on terrorism" helped mobilize public and congressional support after 9/11, many foreign publics believed that the United States was making cooperative efforts against terrorism more difficult, particularly when the idea of a war of indefinite duration could be used to incarcerate prisoners at Guantanamo without full legal rights. In 2006, the British Foreign Office prohibited its diplomats from using the phrase because they believed that it played into Al Qaeda's narrative of global jihad (Nye 2007).

Even when policy and communications are "in sync," wielding soft power resources in an information age is difficult. For one thing, as mentioned earlier, government communications are only a small fraction of the total communications among societies in an age that is awash in information. Hollywood movies that offend religious fundamentalists in other countries or activities by American missionaries that appear to devalue Islam will always be outside the control of government. Some skeptics have concluded that Americans should accept the inevitable and let market forces take care of the presentation of the country's culture and image to foreigners. Why pour money into VOA when CNN, MSNBC, or Fox can do the work for free? But such a conclusion is too facile. Market forces portray only the profitable mass dimensions of American culture, thus reinforcing foreign images of a one-dimensional country.

Developing long-term relationships is not always profitable in the short term, and thus leaving it simply to the market may lead to underinvestment. While higher education may pay for itself, and nonprofit organizations can help, many exchange programs would shrink without government support. Private companies must respond to market forces to stay in business. If there is no market for broadcasting in Serbo-Croatian or Pashtu, companies will not broadcast in those languages. And sometimes private companies will cave in to political pressures from foreign governments if that is better for profits—witness the way Rupert Murdoch dropped the BBC and its critical messages from his satellite television broadcasts to China in the 1990s.

At the same time, postmodern publics are generally skeptical of authority, and governments are often mistrusted. Thus, it often behooves governments to keep in the background and to work with private actors. Some NGOs enjoy more trust than governments do, and though they are difficult to control, they can be useful channels of communication. American foundations and NGOs played important roles in the consolidation of democracy in Eastern Europe after the end of the cold war. Similarly, for countries like Britain and the United States, which enjoy significant immigrant populations, such diasporas can provide culturally sensitive and linguistically skilled connections. Building relationships between political parties in different countries was pioneered by Germany, where the major parties have foundations for foreign contacts that are partly supported by government funds. During the Reagan administration, the United States followed suit when it established the National Endowment for Democracy, which provided funds for the National Democratic Institute and the International Republican Institute, as well as trade unions and chambers of commerce, to promote democracy and civil society overseas.

American companies can also play an important role. Their representatives and brands directly touch the lives of far more people than government representatives do. Some public-spirited businesspeople have suggested that companies develop and share sensitivity and communications training for corporate representatives before they are sent abroad. Companies can also take the lead in sponsoring specific public diplomacy projects such as "a technology company working with Sesame Workshop and a Lebanese broadcaster to coproduce an English language children's program centered on technology, an area of American achievement that is universally admired" (Reinhard 2003, 30).

Another benefit to indirect public diplomacy is that it is often able to take more risks in presenting a range of views. It is sometimes domestically difficult for the government to support presentation of views that are critical of its own policies. Yet such criticism is often the most effective way of establishing credibility. Part of America's soft power grows out of the openness of its society and polity and the fact that a free press, Congress, and courts can criticize and correct policies. When the government instruments avoid such criticism, they not only diminish their own credibility but also fail to capitalize on an important source of attraction for foreign elites (even when they are fiercely critical of government policies). In fact, some observers have suggested that the United States would get a better return on its investment if it turned Alhurra into an international C-SPAN that broadcasts seminars, town meetings, and congressional debates.

The military can sometimes play an important role in the generation of soft power. In addition to the aura of power that is generated by its hard power capabilities, the military has a broad range of officer exchanges, joint training, and assistance programs with other countries in peacetime. The Pentagon's international military and educational training programs include sessions on democracy and human rights along with military training. In wartime, military psychological operations ("psyops") are an important way to influence foreign behavior. An enemy outpost, for example, can be destroyed by a cruise missile or captured by ground forces, or enemy soldiers can be convinced to desert and leave the post undefended. Such psyops often involve deception and disinformation that is effective in war but counterproductive in peace. The dangers of a military role in public diplomacy arise when it tries to apply wartime tactics in ambiguous situations. This is particularly tempting in the current ill-defined war on terrorism that blurs the distinction between normal civilian activities and traditional war. The net result of such efforts is to undercut rather than create soft power [see Table 20.1].

Table 20.1. Soft Power Sources, Referees, and Receivers

SOURCES OF SOFT POWER	REFEREES FOR CREDIBILITY OR LEGITIMACY	RECEIVERS OF SOFT POWER
Foreign policies	Governments, media, nongovernmental organizations (NGOs), intergovernmental organizations (IGOs)	Foreign governments and publics
Domestic values and policies	Media, NGOs, IGOs	Foreign governments and publics
High culture	Governments, NGOs, IGOs	Foreign governments and publics
Pop culture	Media, markets	Foreign publics

Finally, it is a mistake to see public diplomacy simply in adversarial terms. Sometimes there is a competition of "my information versus your information," but often there can be gains for both sides. German public diplomacy during the cold war is a good example. In contrast to French public diplomacy, which sought to demonstrate independence from the United States, a key theme of German public diplomacy was to portray itself as a reliable ally in American eyes. Thus, German and American policy information goals were mutually reinforcing. Political leaders may share mutual and similar objectives—for example, the promotion of democracy and human rights. In such circumstances, there can be joint gains from coordination of public diplomacy programs. Cooperative public diplomacy can also help take the edge off suspicions of narrow national motives.

In addition, there are times when cooperation, including enhancement of the public image of multilateral institutions like NATO or the UN, can make it easier for governments to use such instruments to handle difficult tasks like peacekeeping, promoting democracy, or countering terrorism. For example, during the cold war, American public diplomacy in Czechoslovakia was reinforced by the association of the United States with international conventions that fostered human rights. In 1975, the multilateral Helsinki Conference on Security and Cooperation in Europe (CSCE) legitimized discussion of human rights behind the Iron Curtain and had consequences that were unforeseen by those who signed its Final Act. As former CIA director Robert Gates concluded, despite initial American resistance, "the Soviets desperately wanted the CSCE, they got it, and it laid the foundations for the end of their empire" (as quoted in Thomas 2003, 257).

CONCLUSIONS

Power in a global information age, more than ever, will include a soft dimension of attraction as well as the hard dimensions of coercion and inducement. The ability to combine hard and soft power effectively is "smart power." The United States managed to deploy smart power throughout much of the cold war. It has been less successful in melding soft and hard power in the period since 9/11. The current struggle against transnational terrorism is a struggle over winning hearts and minds, and the current overreliance on hard power alone is not the path to success. Public diplomacy is an important tool in the arsenal of smart power, but smart public diplomacy requires an understanding of the role of credibility, self-criticism, and the role of civil society in generating soft power. Public diplomacy that degenerates into propaganda not only fails to convince, but can undercut soft power.

NOTES

1. I first introduced this concept in *Bound to Lead: The Changing Nature of American Power* (Nye 1990). It builds on what Peter Bachrach and Morton Baratz (1963) called the "second face of power." I developed the concept more fully in *Soft Power: The Means to Success in World Politics* (Nye 2004).
2. The term is from Steven Lukes (2005).
3. See Yale Richmond (2003). Also, see Nye (2004, chap. 2).
4. See David McConnell (forthcoming).

REFERENCES

Arquila, John, and D. Ronfeldt. 1999. *The emergence of neopolitik: Toward an American information strategy.* Santa Monica, CA: RAND.

Bachrach, Peter, and Morton Baratz. 1963. Decisions and nondedsions: An analytical framework.

American Political Science Review 57 (September): 632–42.

Blinken, Anthony J. 2003. Winning the war of ideas. In *The battle for hearts and minds: Using soft power to undermine terrorist networks,* ed. Alexander T. J. Lennon, Cambridge, MA: MIT Press.

Gingrich, Newt. 2003. Rogue State Department. *Foreign Policy,* July, p. 42.

Haefele, Mark, 2001. John F. Kennedy, USIA, and world public opinion. *Diplomatic History* 25 (1): 66.

Hagel, Senator Chuck. 2003. Challenges of world leadership. Speech to the National Press Club, June 19, Washington, DC.

Hiatt, Fred. 2007. The vanishing foreign correspondent. *Washington Post,* January 29.

Joffe, Josef. 2001. Who's afraid of Mr. Big? *The National Interest* 64 (Summer): 43.

Johnson, Stephen, and Helle Dale. 2003. How to reinvigorate U.S. public diplomacy. *The Heritage Foundation Backgrounder,* No. 1645, April 23, p. 4.

Kaufman, Edward. 2003. A broadcasting strategy to win media wars. In *The battle for hearts and minds.* Washington, DC: Center for Strategic and International Studies.

Leonard, Mark. 2002. *Public diplomacy.* London: Foreign Policy Centre.

Lukes, Steven. 2005. *Power: A radical view.* 2nd ed. London: Palgrave.

McConnell, David. Forthcoming. Japan's image problem and the soft power solution: The JET Program as cultural diplomacy. In *Soft power influx: National assets in Japan and the United States,* ed. Yasushi Watanabe and David McConnell. Armonk, NY: M. E. Sharpe.

New York Times. 2007. Global view of U.S. worsens, poll shows. January 23.

Nye, Joseph. 1990. *Bound to lead: The changing nature of American power.* New York: Basic Books.

—. 2004. *Soft power: The means to success in world politics.* New York: Public Affairs.

—. 2007. Just don't mention the war on terrorism. *International Herald Tribune.* February 8.

Pells, Richard. 1997. *Not like us.* New York: Basic Books.

Reinhard, Keith. 2003. Restoring Brand America. *Advertising Age,* June 23, p. 30.

Richmond, Yale. 2003. *Cultural exchange and the cold war.* University Park: Pennsylvania State University Press.

Rosenberg, Emily, 1982. *Spreading the American dream.* New York: Hill & Wang.

Ross, Christopher. 2003. Public diplomacy comes of age. In *The battle for hearts and minds.* Washington, DC: Center for Strategic and international Studies.

Simon, Herbert A. 1998. Information 101: It's not what you know, it's how you know it. *Journal for Quality and Participation.* July–August, pp. 30–33.

Thomas, Daniel C. 2001. *The Helsinki Effect: International Norms, Human Rights, and the Demise of Communism.* Princeton, NJ: Princeton University Press.

Tuch, Hans N. 1990. *Communicating with the world: U.S. public diplomacy overseas,* chap. 12. New York: St. Martin's.

U.S. Department of State. n.d., History of the Department of State during the Clinton presidency (1993–2001). Washington, DC: Office of the Historian, Bureau of Public Affairs.

Vedrine, Hubert, and Dominique Moisi. 2001. *France in an age of globalization.* Washington, DC: Brookings Institutions Press.

Wagnleitner, Reinhold. 1994. *Coca colonization and the cold war.* Chapel Hill: University of North Carolina Press.

MEDIA AND SOVEREIGNTY

The Global Information Revolution and Its Challenge to State Power

By Monroe E. Price

Every new medium, every new technology for transmitting information, causes responses by those who feel threatened. A half-millennium ago, revolutions in print caused fears over dominion and sovereignty, and those in control responded. Even before print, when graven images held great sway, iconoclasts imposed a law of their own. The bonding of religion and state meant prohibitions too on symbols of those whose faiths were found discordant. Homing pigeons were an early technology for flying over boundaries with messages. Biblical stories of spies entering the Promised Land predate the present revolutionary technologies of boundary penetration and surveillance.

Each mode of gathering or transmitting information caused its own reaction. The introduction of radio broadcasting was no different. Almost from the beginning, radio was seen to be a threat to national sovereignty, much as the Internet is now. The very first broadcasts were ship to shore, a harbinger of pirate broadcasting. Radio, intrinsically, knew no political boundaries until it was tamed and domesticated. The 1920s and 1930s were chapters in regulatory history that confirmed state interests in maintaining control of information flows within their boundaries, though even then the growth of propaganda underscored other potentials for the radio medium. By the 1970s, satellite

Monroe E. Price, "Media and Sovereignty: The Global Information Revolution and its Challenge to State Power," *Media and Sovereignty: The Global Information Revolution and its Challenge to State Power*, pp. 27-29, 31-36. Copyright © 2002 by MIT Press. Reprinted with permission.

distribution of signals presented what seemed a decisive moment in the sundering of political lines. Now the Internet, with its silent, abundant ubiquity, seems to be the capstone of this tendency to obliterate borders.

Central to much of modern scholarship is the idea that modern technologies can be, in Ithiel de Sola Pool's memorable phrase, "technologies of freedom" precisely because of the capacity to overwhelm boundaries—whether physical or legislative—and as a result they become key to the spread of democracy. Political transitions now taking place seem clear manifestations of this view. Technologies of freedom are the stuff of every morning's news: new generations of satellites, the promise of far more abundant telephony, and signals reverberating around the globe. It is a small jump from the profusion of these new technologies to the evanescence of national boundaries as gates or walls against the free flow of information. It is asserted almost everywhere that national borders are increasingly irrelevant, and that technology traverses boundaries so effectively that it continues to confound current modes of media and political organization.

Most of what is written and celebrated emphasizes this overwhelming and determined nature of technology to weaken national controls over information and cultural images within their borders. Seamlessness is tied to the promotion of human rights and democratic values. Information and its growth expand national economies and international trade. Enlarging the marketplace of ideas helps to reduce intense and troublesome separatist identities as well as the possibilities of genocide and war. The general benefits of the free flow of information are apparent. Still it is important to check enthusiasm, track popular resistance, and observe the efforts by states to continue control.

It is certainly inevitable, and often desirable, that states concern themselves with the sustenance of their language, enrichment of their history, and strengthening of their internal political and creative processes. Yet each of these has implications for the weight and impact of information across national borders. States have national security needs and these too, as we have seen in the wake of September 11, have radically transformative consequences for media policies. It is vital to examine the complexities and contradictions in Western attitudes toward unmediated distribution of information, the historic problem of oscillating between demands for freedom and concern over content. We do not yet know what constitutes an ideal global Republic of Information.

Given the active strategies of states responding to challenges to their authority in a post-global age, those who ring the death knell of the state may ring too soon. There is a curious and present contradiction between the exaltations of theory and the less sublime practices of the everyday world. At the same time that the function of the state and its capacity to describe and enforce law is brought into doubt, law-making and invocation of the need and power to control imagery increase. It is not without precedent that these two phenomena, a disparagement of the capacity of law on the one hand, and a widespread turn to invoking law on the other, should coexist (perhaps one is a sign of the other), but there is something remarkable about it. The market is so powerful, technology so ubiquitous, that we are often reminded that the process of law making, especially in the field of media regulation, is like building castles in the sand where complex structures will be forcefully erased by an overwhelming cascade of waves. Yet simultaneously, there is a passion for moral controls, for regulation of indecency, and for restoring some sense of an order and security.

The relationship between media and borders is always in transition. However, that transition is not only what it is widely considered to be: technologies of freedom sweeping past traditional media monopolies designed to keep out new and dissenting cultural and political voices. That transition includes the efforts, not only in Malaysia, China, and India but also throughout the world to design new boundary technologies that will allow some continuing control over internal information space. The transition includes the use of new technologies to create diasporic boundaries: intense opportunities for the unification of physically dispersed populations. Political boundaries affect media boundaries, and the opposite is true as well: the radical changes in the media map will alter the physical map in ways yet unknown. [...]

In an earlier book, *Television, the Public Sphere, and National Identity* I identified a "market for loyalties," in which large-scale competitors for power, in a shuffle for allegiances, use the regulation of communications to organize a cartel of imagery and identity among themselves. Government is usually the mechanism that allows the cartel to operate and is often part of the cartel itself. This market produces "national identity" or "community," to use the less discriminating Americanism. Management of the market yields the collection of ideas and narratives employed by a dominant group or coalition to maintain power. For that reason alone, control over participation in the market has been, for many countries, a condition of political stability. This market, I contended, has existed everywhere and at all times. What differs in today's market is the range of participants, the scope of its boundaries, and the nature of the regulatory bodies capable, of establishing and enforcing rules for participation and exclusion.

> The "sellers" in this market are all those for whom myths and dreams and history can somehow be converted into power and wealth—classically states, governments, interest groups, businesses, and others. The "buyers" are the citizens, subjects, nationals, consumers—recipients of the packages of information, propaganda, advertisements, drama, and news propounded by the media. The consumer "pays" for one set of identities or another in several ways that, together, we call "loyalty" or "citizenship." Payment, however, is not expressed in the ordinary coin of the realm: It includes not only compliance with tax obligations, but also obedience to laws, readiness to fight in the armed services, or even continued residence within the country. The buyer also pays with his or her own sense of identity.

It is easiest to understand the functioning of such a market for loyalties in the traditional context of a single state. One can make the general and expansive claim that much domestic broadcast regulation is an effort, within a society, to maintain or adjust the distribution of power among those who are dominant, with due recognition for subsidiary groups. While such legislation is often justified as a means of preserving or strengthening national identity, national identity can be reframed as essentially the set of political views and cultural attitudes that help maintain the existing power structure. Certainly that is often the operational goal (though hardly ever explicit) of those in control. I have suggested that while there were several ways to define "national identity," including a discovery of the "true" or "historic" national identity of a state, this slightly cynical definition (the construction of identity by the power structure so as to maintain its power) enhances our understanding of media legislation by providing an underlying analytic explanation. If familiar regulation of domestic media can be seen, at least in part, as the use of law to reinforce or adjust a political status quo, then much of contemporary national response to media globalization may have a similar explanation. Reregulation or the incentive to change media law and policy occurs, within a state, when the cartel of political allegiances can no longer maintain its position of civil dominance. In that sense the pressures of globalization lead to changes in domestic media laws and structures if either (1) existing domestic broadcasting laws are inadequate at protecting the cartel, or (2) national identity is changing or has changed and legislation is necessary to be more inclusive, to legitimate new players, and to protect them, in turn, against unregulated challenge.

Media globalization and new information technologies yield a crisis of domestic law and policy if barriers to entry are lowered for those excluded from the old political cartel, especially if the new entrants could be threats to the control of the *ancien régime*. In response, a government can either redefine the cartel and accommodate new entrants or take effective steps, through law or force, to try to raise the barriers to entry again. "Failed states" or states made to fail by force (Taliban-led Afghanistan, for example) lose control over their media space as force is exerted against them. External entities (corporations, states, and diasporic groups) also participate in the market for loyalties when they advocate the use of technology or international norms to force a state to enlarge the membership of a local cartel.

Media globalization also fosters the reinforcement of power across national lines and the development of international agreements to render new organizations of identity effective. A competition emerges among those who supply different ideologies for command of large-scale sectors. For example, an international cartel could, as a means of shaping a transnational market for loyalties, establish a set of rules on a global level or encourage or impose a set of rules favoring its "products" in the bosom of a significant group of states. Tacit or explicit arrangements among states, or between states and multinational corporations or nongovernment organizations, may be designed to affect the nature of a global market in cultural and political attitudes and facilitate the predominance of one ideology over another. Thus, while the apparent determinant of the relationship between regulation and control remains the nation-state, communication avenues in any given state would increasingly be a matter of international action, justified under the aegis of stability, trade, and human rights.

International norms like Article 19 of the Universal Declaration of Human Rights, domestic constitutional rules like the First Amendment in the United States, and regional constraints, like the European Convention on Human Rights and the Television without

Frontiers Directive in the European Union have a special role in limiting the cartelization of the market for loyalties. These provisions are usually considered curbs on the power of local political cartels to use law and regulation to screen out voices that seek to alter the current power structure, and especially those who seek to use broadcasting despite its power to force such change. Increasingly these norms are used swordlike by those external to the state, often NGOs and media corporations with existing global power, to encourage a more favorable legal regime within a state. To be sure, such expansion often serves the honorable principle of the right to receive and impart information, but it is about the extension of power and influence as well. [...]

Let me turn to the example of India, about which there is a verdant media literature. The effort to control media space domestically has, over the half-century since Independence, been maintained through the state's monopoly on terrestrial broadcasting, more expansive a monopoly than in many other states that assert democratic traditions. The rise of foreign satellite channels, distributed by and large through relatively unregulated cable television systems, specifically threatened this enduring practice and possibly the political arrangements that depended on it. In 1997 a report of the Ministry of Information and Broadcasting summarized official views and decried the "adverse impact ... on Indian values and culture" of the "large number of foreign satellite TV channels beaming their programmes over Indian sky." Describing the early moments of the satellite invasion when he was minister of information, P. Unendra said, "A file was put up in the Ministry as to how to counter the satellite invasion. What steps should be taken to stop it? I wrote back saying you cannot stop the sun shining by holding an umbrella. The more you try, the more you encourage people to watch."

Long preoccupied by concerns over the consequences of what might be called an "unbridled" press or a press controlled by entities not, in the historic view, sensitive to the complexities of local conditions, successive governments opposed Western broadcasting influences. India has seen itself as frequently subject to significant security threats from Pakistan (and vice versa). During the 1999 conflict with Pakistan over incursions in Kashmir, the minister of information issued a ban on broadcasting the signal of Pakistan-TV by cable television services on the grounds that India's opponent was spreading misinformation that might lead to disunity within the state. During the same period, Videsh Sanchar Nigam Limited (VSNL), then virtually a monopoly Internet service provider, removed *Dawn*, the Islamabad-based daily, from distribution probably at the behest of the government. Even after the ban on Pakistan-TV was lifted, the government's right to impose such a ban was generally accepted.

Section 10 of India's draft Broadcast Bill of 1997 embraced a list of concerns that reflected India's history and security consciousness. In a relatively standard list of prohibitions, the statute provided that any licensee, terrestrial or satellite, would be obliged to ensure that programming would not "offend against good taste or decency." There would be a prohibition on programs "likely to encourage or incite to crime or to lead to disorder or to be offensive to public feeling." Similarly the draft statute included standards requiring that programs reflect India's history and demography. Religious programs were to avoid "improper exploitation of religious susceptibilities" or offending "the religious views and beliefs of those belonging to a particular religion or religious denomination." Statutory standards would require that "due emphasis [be] given ... to promote values of national integration, religious harmony, scientific temper and Indian culture." Officials were still smarting from fears that internal dissension and communal violence might become a significant problem if uncontrolled signals such as news coverage by the BBC not subject to national censorship, are allowed.

These are a few fragments from a rich history in India. Restraint and restriction are based on the idea of maintaining a democratic state at a time of centripetal forces: national security needs, fears of internal violence because of religious strife, the need to protect morals from forces that endanger cultural traditions, and the need to use media for the balance between the notion of India as a whole and its several parts. The range of justifications for excluding certain entrants into the market is almost as broad as exists anywhere. [...]

Part IV

DIASPORA AND COMMUNICATION

The selections in this section examine the proliferation and nature of transnational media outside of the mainstream international media. Georgiou and Silverstone argue that diasporic media used by transnational cultural communities are sites of transnational political ideologies and spaces where cultural expressions of identity are played out. Indeed since the mainstream global and national media often tend to exclude voices from the periphery, diasporic media tend to be the alternative sites for the development of ideologies and representations intersecting routes of the diasporic journeys.

Pednekar-Magal and Oppenheim describe how diasporic communities use media-communication technologies for a plethora of everyday activities and create networked spaces connecting nations and cultures. These everyday practices, they argue, constitute the microprocesses of globalization.

Rego and Pastina describe the trajectory of Brazilian Telenovas as a significant component of the increasing global proliferation of Latin American media products. They argue that upsurge in the flow of media products from Latin America that claim wider markets in North Africa, Eastern Europe, France, Russia and Japan present a counter-hegemonic challenge to Hollywood.

The last chapter in this section, Issues in World Cinema underscores national cinema as a powerful cultural practice that 'reflects and inflects' the discourse of nationhood. Wimal Dissanayake argues that non-Western cinema are often sites in which changing cultural meanings are generated and fought over. The increase in global audiences for national cinema deepens the linkages between the local and the global.

DIASPORAS AND CONTRA-FLOWS BEYOND NATION-CENTRISM

By Myria Georgiou and Roger Silverstone

The debates on the direction of communication flows have long moved away from the original cultural imperialism thesis, which implies linearity and one-way relationships of causality between producer (West) and receiver (and the rest). More recent debates on multiple flows, asymmetrical interdependence and transnational corporate networks have studied the global and regional complexities, shaking off the stigma of linearity and causality.

Studies of national and regional adaptation of production forms and the emergence of hybrid media genres, as well as analyses of the role of national elites and audiences have brought forward the importance of consumption, cultural proximity and regional dynamics. What has not been shaken off (and there has not been a real desire to do so) is the central role of *the national* in inter-national communications. For all the debates on the local and the global, the transnational corporations and the regional players, the study of communication flows and contra-flows is still preoccupied with national corporations (which turn transnational or regional players), governments and national audiences. It is obvious that we cannot, and should not, erase the nation as a site of both political and cultural activity and regulation

Roger Silverstone and Myria Georgiou, "Diasporas and ContraFlows: Beyond National Centricism," *Media on the Move: Global Flow and Contra Flow*, pp. 30-43. Copyright © 2007 by Taylor & Francis Group LLC. Reprinted with permission.

completely. There remain the recalcitrance of the transnational and the instabilities and movements of communication and cultural forms, whose understanding is not reducible to the singularity of the national.

In this chapter we address the diaspora as a locus of the transnational, and use the dispersal of populations as the basis for an enquiry into the dispersal of communications. Our argument is that the mediated communications generated around and by such groups provide a key route into the understanding of the contra-flows of global media. Just as migration itself disturbs the boundaries of the state and the culture of a nation, so too do the communications that migration generates. Statehood remains, but its boundaries are ignored and the dominance of the existing media players, themselves of course equally unconstrained by such boundaries, is challenged by the presence of alternative threads of global communication that observe different rules and move in different directions.

The case of diaspora is, therefore, the most visible challenge to ideologies of the boundedness of people, cultures, identities and the media. Diasporas are transnational cultural communities.[1] They are communities of people originating in a geographical location (often a nation-state) and settling in another. Their travels and (re-)settlement are usually plural and include multiple mobilities of people and diverse cultural practices. Diasporas are ultimately transnational as they are forced in some way or another to flee an original homeland and to seek (a better) life somewhere else. Diasporic identity is about the roots as much as it is about the routes of the diasporic journey (Clifford, 1994; Gilroy, 1995). As diasporas find themselves spread across at least two—and usually many more—nation-states, their political and cultural identity and practices are far from reproductions or extensions of the nation. Questions of multiple or parallel loyalties, connections to more than one public sphere, and association with political causes that surpass boundaries are some of the key ways in which the *nation-ness* of political identities is cancelled.

The diasporic everyday has to do as much with the family and the life left behind (or imagined to have been left behind), as it is about the neighbour in the country of settlement and the relatives and friends in a number of countries where diasporic networks expand. As a reflection of this complexity, communication flows in diasporic space—which is a transnational space—go in all different directions. They include primary forms of communication, such as telephone, travel, interpersonal encounters, and advanced communication technologies, such as radio, television and the Internet.

Diasporic communication flows are variously flows against the dominant (what this volume is identifying as contra-flows), but they complement others and co-exist with many more. If we argue that *contra* implies some form of opposition, either intentional or not, to hegemonic ideologies, then in the case of the diaspora these oppositional contra-flows should be seen in relation to the dominant forms of the political and of the production and consumption of culture, both national and transnational. As such, the complexity and plurality of their relationship to these other, perhaps more dominant or insistent flows of communication needs to be asserted (Silverstone, 2006).

Indeed diasporic media and communication practices are sites where national and transnational political ideologies and cultural expressions, or counter-expressions, of identity are often seen and heard. Diasporic media are involved in the development of ideologies and representations outside the major global and national media and the mainstream national and international political arenas, which often exclude voices from the periphery and from non-mainstream political organisations. Very often the *raison d'être* of diasporic media is the development of such contra-flows, or at least the creation of the ideology of their development.

MEDIA AS SITES OF POLITICS, OR POLITICS AS SITES OF MEDIATION

Mediation is a political process in so far as control over mediated narratives and representations is denied or restricted to individuals, groups and regions by virtue of their status or their capacity to mobilise material and symbolic resources in their own interests. Mediation is also a political process in so far as dominant forms of imaging and storytelling can be resisted, appropriated or countered by others. This can take place both inside media space, and through the development of contra-flows of information and communication (through diasporic or other alternative and minority media), or on the edge of it, through the everyday tactics of symbolic engagement. The latter create another informal and mundane form of contra-flow (as expressed in the stubborn refusal to embrace dominant and hierarchical forms of mediated communication, in gossip and communication outside the media, in participation in multiple and conflicting mediascapes).

The media, seen through the lens of these contested processes, provide frameworks for identity and community, equally contested of course, but significantly available as components of the collective imaginary and as resources for collective agency. In this context, diasporic media can be seen as threats to the globalisation of media forms and firms, as destabilising elements in international affairs and in relation to (inter-)national politics, as often proud (even if sometimes fundamentalist) voices against global and regional hierarchies in communication and in politics. Diasporas appear, or more often do not appear, in mainstream media; and when they do appear it is often through stereotypical and alienating images. But diasporas also represent themselves (and others) in their own media, those that they produce and consume in and across the societies in which they are minorities, as well as those that they consume in such (dis)locations, but which are produced in societies where they might be, or once might have been, majorities.

Diasporic media range from the exchange of letters, videos and mobile phone texts and images, to the printed press, domestic and satellite television, and the Internet (Gillespie, 1995; Dayan, 1999). They are produced by the displaced to express and reflect their daily lives as minorities, but also by mainstream cultures elsewhere, which offer a link for the displaced to a world of home, both real and imagined (or to a world once left but not conceptualised as home). As such, diasporas and their media have a key role to play in the development of contra-flows and in the diversification of media-scapes outside the (full) control of nation-states and corporate transnationalism.

Media provide frameworks for inclusion, and by the same token, frameworks for exclusion. Those frameworks are at once transnational, national, ethnically specific, regional and local. The cultures that sustain and that are sustained by them are differentially placed with respect to each other and to their mainstreams. They are never homogeneous; and the media which are both produced and consumed reflect differences of gender and generation, as well as differences of politics and religion within cultures and communities.

As already indicated, diasporic mediascapes consist of online media and more conventional media, such as television, radio and press. All of those, especially the electronic ones, have also diversified and now include public, state-run, commercial and community broadcasts and products that integrate technologies and content, connecting people in local and transnational spaces. The presence of such media threads and flows raises a number of questions. The first is that of the integrity or the fragmentation of the emerging public sphere, its singularity or its plurality. As Arjun Appadurai notes: 'The challenge for this emergent order will be whether such heterogeneity is consistent with some minimal conventions of norm and value, which do not require a strict adherence to the liberal social contract of the modern West' (1996:23). It follows that the next question would need to address the capacity of such flows to provide genuine political and cultural alternatives, and maybe even conflicting ones, to the mainstream. The emerging situation is much more complex than simply a negative or positive reply to these questions would reflect. Nationalistic and cosmopolitan ideologies are in constant tension in the diaspora and they often take place around the media.

DIASPORA IN MEDIA CULTURE

Pluralism appears as central to any understanding of the representation of diasporic populations in media culture, and this too at a number of different levels. Media representation involves both participation and recognition. And participation is a matter of the capacity to contribute to the mainstream (that being national and/or transnational), to enable the minority voice or visibility on (trans-)national channels or the national press, but it is also a matter of the capacity to gain a presence on one's own terms on the nationally owned spectrum or on the global commons of the Internet. Participation ultimately involves the equal sharing of a common cultural space. There are different issues that can be addressed here, and different politics, but all raise the questions of whether or how to enable smaller groups (or groups with less access to media and political centres of power) to speak, but also, and this is crucial, to enable them to be heard. Who is speaking and on behalf of whom? But we must ask too, who is listening and with what consequences?

Diasporic minorities are producers; they are audiences and they are addressees. As audiences they have the distinct advantage, it might be suggested, of being able to choose, often quite radically, between different representational spaces, different programmes, different languages and different accounts of global or national conflicts. Greek Cypriots in the diaspora for example, have access to media from Cyprus, from Greece, from their country of settlement, from other countries where Greek diasporas live. Additionally, they access and use various national and global media, which are broadcast in languages they understand (Georgiou, 2006). Mixing and choosing between a huge variety of locally and globally produced media and media produced by members of the diaspora, the *homeland* media industry, but also media produced by major or minor media players in transnational cultural spaces, is a part of the banal everyday living of diaspora. Such choices are material with consequences for both their own sense of themselves and their position in national cultures, but inevitably they are also material for those national cultures themselves and the degree to which states can meaningfully include all of its residents and citizens.

The politics of the national mediascapes are often politics of struggle and conflict. Many European governments are hesitant to accept Kurdish satellite Med TV in their territory, as the station has been accused of being attached to a militant Kurdish party (Hassanpour, 2003). The American government forced the only Somali Internet service provider connecting the Somali diaspora to shut down because of suspected links with terrorists (Karim, 2003). Diasporic communications increasingly find themselves caught in national and global politics and important decisions. As satellite television and the Internet in particular are being increasingly used to bring diasporic politics into the public sphere, governments and transnational political institutions pay a closer attention to them. The case of Al-Jazeera, of course, has become the most noticeable example, attracting attention and attacks from some of the most significant players in national and global politics.

As addressees, diasporas emerge as problematic perhaps most significantly in diasporic websites, such as those designed to support asylum seekers or refugees. Here choices are made between a general mode of address, one that seeks to engage both the subjects of the site but also looks to a wider public for both financial and political support. This is a both/and rather than an either/or mode of address, which could be as self-defeating as it is productive. The refugee and migrant network of support and communication, seen in the UK in sites such as that of the Refugees, Asylum Seekers and the Mass Media Project (http://www.ramproject.org.uk/) and Refugees Online (http://www.refugeesonline.org.uk/) brings activists and refugees closer together into a community of interest and political action. These sites, at the same time, raise awareness around issues of diversity, when they address the general public and potentially advance dialogue between minorities and the mainstream. However, in attempting to reach the broader public and in their attempt to condemn racism and xenophobia, these websites often adopt an instrumental discourse (e.g. focusing on presenting directories and statistical information; selling items for support of network). The complexity of diasporic identity and diasporic transnationalism is often overlooked in the development of 'popular' and 'accessible' models of diversity (Siapera, 2005).

There is a tension expressed in all that follows, both within, and surrounding, diasporic media and the symbolic and material presence of diasporic minorities within national and transnational mainstream media, which is articulated at the interface between plurality and power. Questions of identity are central but intensely difficult to resolve both theoretically and in the experienced realities of everyday life. In this respect, the media context is no different from the wider cultural and social context in which the dilemmas of difference and visibility are endemic in diverse societies which are, once again, becoming increasingly ambivalent with regard to the manifestations of otherness within national borders.

What, however, is not at issue is the nature of the change in media culture and the challenges to national politics and to national broadcasting systems in particular. The significance and strength of these challenges vary hugely, of course, from one country to another, but taken together they promise a sea-change in the way in which global communication, both public and private, is conducted. The metaphors used to describe these changes are familiar enough: *networks*, *rhizomes* and *mediascapes* variously capture both the fluidity and freedoms now apparent in personal and collective communication. At stake is the continuing capacity of the nation to insist on its cultural specificity, with possibly significant consequences for its inhabitants' participation in, and identification with, national community. At stake too is the capacity of diasporic groups to form their own transnational or global media cultures, which, for better or worse, could offer frameworks for participation and agency no longer grounded in singular residence and no longer oriented exclusively to the project of national or singular citizenship. At the same time, the struggle for power takes place around defining the global as a space for communication and for belonging outside its corporate transnationalising interpretations.

TRANSNATIONAL PUBLIC SPHERES AGAINST TOP-DOWN INTERNATIONAL AFFAIRS?

The politics of popular culture is, arguably, gaining ground against mainstream politics (cf. Street, 1997), but the established national political sphere is still of major importance and has implications for the diasporic communities and for the nation-states of both their origin and settlement. Looking into the possibilities for liberating and participatory diasporic politics, Appadurai argues that there is a growing potential for the development of diverse and inclusive diasporic public spheres (1996) and he suggests that, as electronic media become predominant in mediated communication, the formal literacy in a common language becomes less of an obstacle to participation in transnational public spheres. The potential for decentralised, transnational diasporic spheres emerges, therefore, as the nation-state begins to lose its monopoly of social, political and cultural exchanges and as images, sounds and people are less bounded and grounded within singular political and cultural territories.

The challenges against nation-centric political ideologies which emerge with the presence of diasporic populations are the product of communication practices in all three dimensions of their living space: the transnational, the national and the local, but especially in the transnational and the local. The transnational is largely mediated by two technologies: satellite and the Internet. The local—and we will be talking about the urban local in particular here—is challenged in communication practices which are not necessarily framed within a narrow media setting. Mediation and media cultures are not all about television and the Internet. Music, interpersonal communication, mobility in and out of communication spaces, such as Internet cafés, local libraries, community centres and clubs are as much part of the diasporic media cultures as are the Internet and satellite television. The national is the site for a more assimilative move in the direction of providing spaces for minorities to appear, as individuals (for example presenters), characters (in soap operas) or in the 'colouring' of existing genres (in ethnically or culturally distinct sit-coms). But the national is also the site for the location of both the production and consumption of diasporic media, the location of the lived everyday and the focus of any longing for a displaced homeland amongst diasporic populations. It is the latter characteristic of the national that we will focus on rather than the former.

THE TRANSNATIONAL: THE CONTRA-FLOW OF THE IMAGINARY

Projects of diasporic politics, those referring to the country of origin, political participation (or refusal to participate) in the country of settlement, and to minority politics which oppose dominant ideologies within diasporic groups, have all found a space of expression on the Internet as in no other medium. As Manuel Castells has put it:

> the internet is not simply a technology: it is a communication medium (as the pubs were), and it is the material infrastructure of a given organisational form: the network (as the factory was). On both counts the internet became the indispensable component of the kind of social movements emerging in the network society. (Castells, 2002:139)

Diasporic politics, as opposing, antagonising and competing with national politics, is part of the growing culture of cyberpolitics, which in turn is largely transnational and which adopts tactics of connecting offline locations (and politics) with online transnational networking activities. Campaigners for a Kurdish or for a Palestinian state can reach sections of their diasporic groups (and seek support among them) as never before. So can fundamentalist groups. The reasons Internet users turn to such sites cannot be predicted and only in-depth research can try to answer the extent to which their visible presence translates into practical action.[2] This is not our task here. No matter what individual Internet users are looking for, the point is that diasporic political movements can reach audiences in geographical and numerical scale in unprecedented ways. The Internet has become a tangible setting where alternative, fragmented, or transnational public spheres emerge. In some of these cases at least (for example, among the Tamil where even the state, Eelam, in Sri Lanka, to which they are attached does not formally exist (Jeganathan, 1998), we see a form of imagined community emerging or finding a space of expression. It may be possible to suggest therefore that transnational political communities become realisable—to extend Anderson's original thesis (1983)—albeit in the mind of each Internet user as she seeks, finds and connects to like-minded diasporic fellows sharing the same communication space.

But beyond the Internet, there is another communication technology which is increasingly appropriated by diasporic populations; this is satellite broadcasting. Al-Jazeera has shaken the world with its stubborn success against Western global media. Chapter 7 in this book discusses the case of Al-Jazeera in more detail, but this example being widely known outside specific diasporic audiences, is no more than one of the very successful diasporic media claiming a voice and a role in the provision of political information and agenda-setting in international affairs. The powerful global media have been trying to regain influence among audiences, which would rather watch the news on a diasporic news bulletin (or watch the diasporic as well as the mainstream news and thus become more critical and demanding viewers). Research on Arabic audiences, for example, has shown how the diversity of news consumption—in mainstream Western and diasporic satellite media—becomes an everyday mechanism for audiences to critically engage with all media (El-Nawawy and Iskander, 2002; After September 11 Research Project, 2002). Satellite diasporic television is booming and it is definitely here to stay and play a role in international political information and communications.

THE LOCAL: THE CONTRA-FLOW OF THE CITY

In the city, the taken-for-granted domination of the nation-state on cultural and political ideologies is challenged. The city is the location where nationhood is questioned from within. The particular dynamics of the city and of urban life allow different populations to live together, different cultures to co-exist and intermix in new urban, multicultural and hybrid settings while not necessarily embracing the national project. Studying diasporic cultures in the urban context where they are experienced—and where many of the media develop and are consumed—involves contextualising diasporic (media) cultures in the space where they become possible. As James Donald (quoted in Robins, 2001:89) notes, the city poses 'the internal impossible question of how we strangers can live together'. As we live together, hybrid cultures, identities and alternative scenarios for inclusion and participation emerge, next to others of exclusion, discrimination and racism.

Diasporic populations are an integral part of contemporary urban economic and cultural life, even if their contribution in national and mainstream transnational ideologies is not acknowledged as such. The city—where diasporic populations usually live—is the space where the private and the public and the experience of mediation take their meanings in relation to urban cultural practices and in co-existence with other city dwellers. The *mobile foreign subjects*, who are not foreign anymore, challenge the purity of the nation and suburban privatised closure and instead participate in the construction of diverse, creative and sometimes anarchic urban cultures. Diasporic populations' participation in the formation of a working-class cosmopolitanism (Werbner, 1999) brings dialogue and new encounters between strangers, between people of different backgrounds, in the city.

In urban meetings and mixings, in the public performance of diverse cultures and in the anarchy of co-existence and competition for ownership and participation, distinct kinds of publicness and exposure emerge in public life and in cultural representation. The different kinds of music heard and imposed around town, the large satellite dishes insulting middle-class/white aesthetics, the loud, colourful and supposedly tasteless hybrid spaces hosting Internet cafés, combined with hair-salons and/or grocers, create aural and visual cultural fusions and spatial amalgams, in cacophony as much as in harmony. The city expresses the movement of the Other from the periphery of the empire to its core (the metropolis—the city) (Eade, 2001). As migrants and diasporas move to the centre, they occupy a symbolic and physical space that is powerful in its presence and in the active alteration of what it used to be through participation in economic, cultural and social life. The emergence of horizontal cultural formations challenges the vertical divisions of the nation-state and of consumerist transnationalism.

THE NATIONAL: THE CONTRA-FLOW OF THE POLITICAL

Diasporic audiences are capable of shifting their attention and their commitments from their own media (local and transnational) to the national mainstream media, and in so doing finding opportunities for comparison but also possibilities for choice. Research has shown that even those with minimum knowledge of the dominant language of the country of settlement flick between mainstream national channels for a favourite soap opera or for catching up with (fractions and/or images of) the local and national news (Aksoy and Robins, 2000; Ogan, 2001; Georgiou, 2006). As diasporic media co-exist and compete with others, the appropriation of both is filtered by the diverse experience of their audiences. Diasporic media audiences have a media literacy that surpasses particularistic consumption. This diversity of consumption is important not just in terms of diasporas' capacity to sustain their own culture and identity but also for the character of the mainstream national media culture, indeed the culture of the nation-state itself, as the latter can no longer easily control and contain the images, voices and narratives which have for so long laid exclusive claims on the attention of its citizens.

Awareness of the significance of diasporic media for the political mobilisation of the diaspora is evident in both top-down initiatives—by the governments of the original homeland

and by community leaders—and bottom-up everyday practice—as people turn to the media to keep up to date with political developments. The diasporic and national hegemonic ideologies of transporting nationalism in transnational spaces however faces some significant obstacles. Diasporisation and transnational connections imply the emergence of networks. The settlement of diasporic populations in different social and cultural contexts, as well as the increased possibility for mobility and interactivity between different nodes within diasporic networks, comes with increased cultural and political autonomy and inevitable ruptures in the umbilical cord—and the ideologies of the umbilical cord—that link the homeland and the diaspora. Hanafi (2005) describes the case of PALESTA (Palestinian Scientists and Technologists Abroad) network, which started as an initiative of the Palestinian Authority in order to strengthen links with the Palestinian diaspora. The Internet network was formed as a centralised effort where all communication was taking place around one centre—the homeland. As PALESTA grew successfully, the taken-for-granted centrality of the homeland became challenged. Its users developed their activities beyond the control of the centre and mostly in interdiasporic communication. The rupture of the umbilical cord caused tensions between the diaspora and the centre. Nonetheless, in most cases, these ruptures are conditional. The diversity of cultural references in diasporic spaces, competing nationalisms, and global, individualistic capitalism, create constant tensions between centrifugal and centripetal ideologies of (national) belonging.

On one hand, mediation and networking advance the sense of proximity to other dispersed populations and to the country of origin. On the other, they amplify the level of critical reflection and selective engagement with the imagined community as increased information and interaction remind the members of diasporic groups that the original homeland is not sacred and pure and that the dispersed populations who share a common origin are not characterised by cultural sameness. The increased exchange of images and sounds from the country of origin and other sections of the diaspora becomes a constant reminder of diversity and of the real and present face of the country of origin and the fellow members of the imagined community.

THE COMPLEXITY OF IDENTITY OR THE CONTRA-FLOWS WITHIN

The plausibility of these structural changes should not obscure the material realities of diasporic everyday life in the production and consumption of media. These realities are grounded in the struggles of connection and communication, in the conflicts around identity and identification, in the shared but fraught project of finding a voice. These empirical realities inevitably muddy the waters of grand theories and the perception of global trends. Indeed they focus, and quite properly, on the dilemmas of the everyday as individuals, families and communities seek to manage their lives on the borderland between inclusion and exclusion.

Media are sometimes crucial to this management; sometimes not. They offer security in the familiarity of sounds and images. But they also threaten that security in their many representational failures. And for those members of minorities at work within media (as well as those denied such work), the media are crucial both at an individual as well as at a collective level in constructing identities and transnational communities. Identity construction is a complex process. This complexity is often revealed in the contra-flows to hegemonic discourses within diasporic groups.

First, they are expressed in subversive everyday communication practices and the diasporic diversity of engagement with media—both in terms of which media are consumed—but also in the way diasporas engage with media in various ways, as already discussed. In terms of audiencehood (or citizenship), such contra-flows might create a distance from political projects promoting national and consumerist homogeneity, but they often lead to a distancing from equally essentialist and hierarchical projects from within. Diasporic nationalism, as well as the promotion of authoritarian and repressive discourses, is not rare in diasporic media (e.g. fundamentalist religious sites; satellite television promoting uncritical devotion to the country of origin). In such cases, in terms of production, the contra-flows to the national and commercial mainstream are more about antagonising other national and commercial interests. Such projects are usually tested and contested on the level of consumption.

These contra-flows within also refer to the relationship between minorities within minorities, i.e. the diasporic media that are peripheral, extremist, marginalised within their own diasporic mediascapes. We are thinking here in particular of fundamentalist projects. These flourish, when they do at all, especially on the Internet. With al-Qaeda developing its own website, the moral panics about the Islamic diasporic public sphere being taken over by Osama bin Laden and his comrades have reached a record high, but are not confined to the national mainstream. They are significantly the object of dismay within their own minority cultures. Less visible projects of this kind include diasporic political voices that are excluded from the mainstream diasporic politics even when they do not entice violence—e.g. the Palestinian left finds a space of expression denied in national and diasporic public domains. Cypriot gay and lesbian organisations are practically banned from the main diasporic media stages. They find their expression in local activities and transnational online fora. Often political expression and identity politics—especially when represented in the mainstream politics of communities—find an entry to the public sphere through the Internet.

In this context, questions about diverse and competing mediascapes and ideoscapes become crucial. And even if they cannot be resolved here, yet in a sense the debates that define them, above all those that centre on competing rights and (sadly less often) competing obligations, both of minorities and majorities, are central. These debates involve questions of uncompromising difference and processes of hybridisation; those that privilege the particular over the universal; those that insist on a continuing role for the nation and those that stress transnationalism; those that desire a single public sphere and those that wish for, or fear for, its rupture; those that challenge innocent, or naïve, claims for participation; and those that refuse the dominance of cultural difference over the inequities of political and economic position. All of these debates are vivid and vividly unresolved.

An examination of the production and consumption of diasporic media cultures, both in terms of the production of particularistic media and associated consumption practices critically involves a refusal of the various kinds of essentialism that bedevils many of the discussions on identity and community within and across national boundaries. In the present context, the media are seen not to be determining of (the other) *(contra)* identities, but contributing to the creation of symbolic community spaces in which identities can be constructed. Diasporic identities are not others to the mainstream. They are not *contra*. These identities are essentially plural (Silverstone, 2006; Georgiou, 2006). And this is the case at the level of the individual, where one's status as a Somali or as a Vietnamese depends on cultural context (as well as on gender, generation and class), the mode of the media's address as well as one's position in relation to it, either as consumer or producer. It is also the case at the level of the community, where media practices provide links between the group and multiple others, both within and beyond the nation. Within and across nation-states, where the discussion of contra-flows has emerged, the broadcasting culture of the twentieth century has advanced claims for national coherence and national, singular, mediated public spheres (which can extend to transnational spaces, as they are reflected in many nation-states' policies to expand their broadcasting services to *their* diasporas). Such ambitions for national and transnational coherence are increasingly vulnerable to the presence of both alternative media and alternative media voices that dig deeper into the local and, often excluding ethnically specific, spill into the multiple global discordances of satellite and Internet communication.

Participation, inclusion but also exclusion from the community is not in this case (or any more) framed within singular geographical boundaries or within inescapable dualities of dependence: diaspora/homeland or migrants/ host country. Geographical boundedness and dualities are being constantly challenged in the actual diasporic experience, which builds upon a number of complex, and even competing, links and relations. The links and flows cut across many different places and follow many different directions. Thus, members of diasporic groups sustain relations with friends in the country of origin, but also relations with friends in the local non-ethnic community. Diasporic belonging is non-exclusive and, in times of increased transnationalism, high mobility and intense mediation, it can only be conditional and parallel to other forms of belonging. People use diasporic as well as non-diasporic media; they appropriate technologies in order to renew repertoires of diasporic identity, but also in order to fulfil age group interests, professional or other political interests, hobbies and friendships in and across places.

The emphasis on the diversity of spatial contexts, of cultural content and communication flows, is a reminder of the growing significance of network structures and the transnational mechanisms of sharing images, sounds and information and their consequences for imagining a multipositioned and inevitably diverse community. In this context, boundaries have not faded away and this is not the time for romantically celebrating liberating cosmopolitanisms.

Boundaries are still there, though now they are often more symbolic than physical; they are more diverse, and they are defined as much by exclusionary mechanisms within global capitalism as they are by national and diasporic exclusionary discourses.

CONCLUSIONS

Diasporas are cosmopolitans of a different kind to the high-flying, jet-setting cosmopolitans in control of global capitalism. The discussion about diasporic communication flows is not restricted or controlled by national or corporate transnational interests. Diasporic populations are usually the invisible cosmopolitans and the unnoticed participants in the formation of transnational (media) cultures; they are initiators of urban and trans-urban networks, which are sometimes, though not necessarily, antagonistic towards the nation-state, which diversify urban spaces in creative and communication practices, and which develop parallel, competing and complementing elements of mediated consumer cultures. Diasporas build transnational networks, develop particularistic cultural formations and construct distinct identities in mediation—in the mixing denied by the ideology of boundedness and separation of the nation-state and the modernist separated spheres of economic, cultural and political life.

Diasporas are postmodern—and, in a way, pre-modern—formations, as they constitute messy, anarchic and uneven networks, emerging in equally messy flows of communication and connection. Networks of family and kin, of economic and political interests and of cultural activities, become merged, fused and confused. In their (con)fusion, they reflect a range of ideologies: from the most conservative traditionalist and nationalistic, to the cosmopolitan celebration of capitalism and the cosmopolitan resistance to nationalism and profit. The contradictions, oxymora and struggles of diaspora are expressed in public transnational dialogues and debates, which tend to be highly mediated.

The contradictory dynamics of diaspora reflect the lack of clear-cut order or singular direction for ideologies and communication within cosmopolitanism. As Ulrich Beck suggests:

> I doubt that cosmopolitan societies are any less ethical and historical than national societies. But cosmopolitanism lacks orientation, perhaps because it is so much bigger and includes so many different kinds of people with conflicting customs, assorted hopes and shames, so many sheer technological and scientific possibilities and risks, posing issues people never faced before. There is, in any case, a greater felt need for an evident ethical dimension in the decisions, both private and public, that intervene in all aspects of life and add up to the texture of cosmopolitan societies. (Beck, 2002:20)

The diasporic condition unravels some of the key characteristics of cosmopolitanism, but it does so from a distinct position which might be *beyond* nation-centrism but not *outside* the national. Diasporas do not exist outside the authority of nation-states. National media and politics can even increase their influence outside national boundaries, partly because diasporas appropriate them in transnational consumption and public spheres. Diasporas however live *beyond* nation-states, if we refer to the nation-state as defined in Western modernity to frame identity, culture and politics. The complexity of the diasporic condition is often reflected in communication practices that are diverse, contradictory and unstable.

Contemporary transnational connections and the persistence of diaspora as a relevant cultural category can only be understood in the context of transnationalism, competing cosmopolitanisms and intense mediation.

> It becomes possible to think of identities which are multiple ... An Egyptian immigrant in Britain might think of herself as a Glaswegian when she watches her local Scottish channel, a British resident when she switches over to the BBC, an Islamic Arab expatriate in Europe when she tunes into the satellite service from the Middle East, and a world citizen when she channel-surfs on to CNN. (Sinclair *et al.*, 1996:25)

The diversity characterising diasporic media consumption and appropriation illustrates some of the major existing limitations in the analyses of communication and cultural flows. The argument that the major challenges to one-way flows emerge in the production and consumption of commercial projects (either global or regional) is still rooted in the assumption of consumption within singular national frameworks. This assumption is significantly limiting. Audiences and cultural communities more often participate in co-existing media culture(s)—particularistic, diverse, mainstream—than in singular framed communities.

The direction and quality of flows and contra-flows we need to understand are not only those of mainstream media production, nor are they exclusively about privileged players within a newly emergent cosmopolitanism. They are also about the growing variety of audiences' media outlook. They are about the emergence of transnational players in media culture which are not only corporate but based within the community. And they are about the diversification of communication activities which are not constrained within the media of television, radio, press and the Internet, but which also involve various appropriations of communication technologies in localities, cities and transnational networks that stimulate new ways of communicating, informing and belonging.

NOTES

1. Diasporic communities are, of course, imagined. The use of the concept of *community* here relates to processes of imagination and identification. There is no assumption that community exists as a real structure.
2. On this issue, and with arguments based on just such empirical research albeit on transnational social movements rather than specifically diasporic groups, see Cammaerts (2005).

REFERENCES

After September 11 Research Project. Research Report (2002). Available at: http://www.afterseptember11.tv/

Aksoy, Asu and Kevin Robins (2000) 'Thinking across spaces: transnational television from Turkey', *European Journal of Cultural Studies*, 3 (3):343–65.

Anderson, Benedict [1983] (1991) *Imagined Communities: Reflections on the Origins and Spread of Nationalism*. London: Verso.

Appadurai, Arjun (1996) *Modernity at Large: Cultural Dimensions of Globalization*. Minneapolis and London: University of Minnesota Press.

Beck, Ulrich (2002) 'The cosmopolitan society and its enemies', *Theory, Culture & Society*, 19 (1– 2):17–44.

Cammaerts, Bart (2005) 'ICT-usage among transnational social movements in the networked society: to organise, to mobilise and to debate', in Roger Silverstone (ed.), *Media, Technology and Everyday Life in Europe*. Basingstoke: Ashgate, pp. 53–72.

Castells, Manuel (2002) *The Internet Galaxy: Reflections on the Internet, Business and Society*. Oxford and New York: Oxford University Press.

Clifford, James (1994) 'Diasporas', *Cultural Anthropology*, 9 (3):302–37.

Dayan, Daniel (1999) 'Media and diasporas', in J.Gripsrud (ed.), *Television and Common Knowledge*. London and New York: Routledge.

Eade, John (2001) *Placing London: From Imperial Capital to Global City*. London: Berghahn.

El-Nawawy, M. and A.Iskander (2002) *Al-Jazeera: How the Free Arab News Network Scooped the World and Changed the Middle East*. Cambridge, MA: Westview.

Georgiou, Myria (2006) *Diaspora, Identity and the Media: Diasporic Transnationalism and Mediated Spatialities*. Cresskill, NJ: Hampton Press.

Gillespie, Marie (1995) *Television, Ethnicity and Cultural Change*. London: Routledge.

Gilroy, Paul (1995) 'Roots and routes: black identity as an outernational project', in H.W.Harris, Howard C.Blue and Ezra E.H.Griffith (eds), *Racial and Ethnic Identity: Psychological Development and Creative Expression*. London and New York: Routledge.

Hanafi, Sari (2005) 'Reshaping geography: Palestinian community network in Europe and the new media', *Journal of Ethnic and Migration Studies*, 31 (3):581–9.

Hassanpour, Amir (2003) 'Diaspora, homeland and communication technologies', in Karim H.Karim (ed.), *The Media of Diaspora*. London and New York: Routledge.

Jeganathan, Pradeep (1998) 'Eelam.com: Place, nation and imagi-nation in cyberspace', *Public Culture*, 26 (3):515–29.

Karim, H.Karim (2003) *The Media of Diaspora*. London and New York: Routledge.

Ogan, Christine (2001) *Communication and Identity in the Diaspora: Turkish Migrants in Amsterdam and their Use of Media*. Lanha, MD: Lexington.

Robins, Kevin (2001) 'Becoming anybody: thinking against the nation and through the city', *City*, 5 (1):77–90.

Siapera, Eugenia (2005) 'Minority activism on the web: between deliberative democracy and multiculturalism, *Journal of Ethnic and Migration Studies,* 31 (3):499–519.

Silverstone, Roger (2006) *Media and Morality: On the Rise of the Mediapolis.* Cambridge: Polity Press.

Sinclair, John, Elizabeth Jacka and Stuart Cunningham (eds) (1996) 'Peripheral vision', in J.Sinclair, E.Jacka and S.Cunningham (eds), *New Patterns in Global Television: Peripheral Vision.* Oxford: Oxford University Press, pp. 1–32.

Street, John (1997) *Politics and Popular Culture.* Cambridge: Polity Press.

Werbner, Pnina (1999) 'Global pathways: working class cosmopolitans and the creation of transnational ethnic worlds', *Social Anthropology,* 7(1):17–35.

TRANSNATIONAL COMMUNITIES AND GLOBAL COMMUNICATION

By Vandana Pednekar-Magal and Keith Oppenheim

The particular dynamics of the city and of urban life have allowed different populations to live together, different cultures to co-exist and intermix in the urban multicultural settings. However, multiculturalism in the city, during most of the 20th century was spatially ordained. A Chinatown, Little Italy, or Little India is a familiar feature of large metropolitan cities such as New York, Philadelphia, Toronto or Singapore. These 'ethnic enclaves' are spaces in the city where diasporic populations of particular national, linguistic, cultural affinity clustered. Their shared language and cultural history enabled them to form networks and garner 'social capital' that eased their transition to the new country and facilitated economic, cultural and political life. For people dispersed from a region or a nation, these spaces of arrival in enclaves would not seem so far apart from spaces of departure.

Since the past two decades, global dispersal of populations has risen at an unprecedented degree. Movements of "new diasporas" arrived in the wake of the complex processes of what we call globalization, have altered the local urban landscape. Shifting populations: guest workers, exiles, refugees, immigrants, tourists, now constitute the metropolis. The large cross-border dispersal of populations is intensified by "flexible accumulation"—global deployment of production processes and human capital by multinational corporations (Harvey 1989, Clifford, 1994); and due to ethnic conflicts and war across many regions of the world.

Contemporary diasporic populations are prodigious in their movement and too diverse—in that they are from many varied cultural and socio-economic backgrounds, to be contained in enclaves. They now occupy spaces in the city that are symbolic in its active transformation of 'what it used to be' through participation in economic, cultural and social life (Georgiou and Silverstone, 2007). Manifestations of this trend abound in the city. Indian, Chinese, Mexican restaurants, Bosnian bakeries, nail-salons and spas run by Vietnamese women, the presence of 'foreign' information technology works in corporate offices, and foreign health workers—doctors, nurses, technical staff in hospitals, are integral to the urban scene. In this sense, the transnational social spaces (Ludger Pries, 2002) seem now woven into the fabric of the city and allow a continuous economic, cultural and social transactions between the urban local and the global.

These transnational spaces are also networked spaces of communication that are not tied immediately to territory but through electronic capabilities, are connected with multiplicity of nations and cultures across the globe. Through their everyday communicative practices from their particular nooks and corners of the city and civil society transnational communities connect the local to the global (Keane, 1995).

In this essay we focus on the contemporary diaspora and their communicative practices in the city and across borders.[i] We examine the ways in which diasporic communities are networked locally and across nations in the differently mixed milieu of the urban local. We explore how the continuous social exchange and media consumption across borders tempers the diasporic experience and also illuminates on the evolving nature of the global public sphere.

Our examination is grounded in extended interviews with diasporic families in Grand Rapids, a mid-size city, in West Michigan. The choice of this city is deliberate to bring home the point that regional urban centers too, as much as large metropolises (Chicago, New York, Los Angeles) have attracted a considerable mix of diasporic populations.

THE MANY TRAJECTORIES: A NOTE ON IMMIGRATION

The shifting 'ethnoscapes' (Appadurai, 1990) in Grand Rapids can be attributed to many recent developments in the United States as well as across borders. Among the populations we studied, the Bosnians arrived in the city as refugees of the Balkan war after the United States government granted Bosnians "Temporary Protected Status" as a result of the 1991–1995 War. According to the United Nations High Commissioner for Refugees, by 2002 there were 92,293 Bosnian refugee and asylum seekers in the USA. A substantial share of these refugees has settled in West Michigan (Ethnic Atlas of West Michigan-EAWM).

Vietnamese immigrants began arriving in the United States and subsequently to Grand Rapids during the late 1970s, following the fall of the South Vietnamese regime. A much larger wave of Vietnamese arrived in the 1990s through a political refugee program.

The Sudanese, mostly from Dinka and Nuer tribes of South Sudan reached Grand Rapids around 2001 following resettlement of orphaned young boys known as "lost boys of Sudan." The Sudanese civil war had raged from 1983 to 2005 and an estimated 17,000 lost boys had fled Sudan to refugee camps in Kenya. Several thousands were brought to the United States under the aegis of United Nations High Commissioner for Refugees, working together with the State Department, Lutheran Immigration and Refugee Services and US Catholic Conference. Over a hundred young men were settled in Grand Rapids and acquired education in local area schools and colleges. After the end of the civil war, most of the men could travel back to their villages to marry and some were able to reconnect with their extended families and subsequently begin a full-fledged life in Grand Rapids (Corbett, 2001).

The Indian (South Asian) diaspora in the city has two different trajectories. In the wake of the Civil Rights movement, President Lyndon Johnson enacted the Immigration and Nationality Act of 1965. This act radically broke with the previous immigration policy that preferred Western and Northern Europeans and allowed easy entry for people from those countries only. The new act replaced this policy based on race and exclusion (Ludden, 2006) with a preference system that focused on immigrants' skills and family relationships with citizens or US Residents. This brought a wave of skilled professionals from India- mainly doctors and engineers who then 'sponsored'—a term used for enabling entry visa—their families. A parallel wave of students seeking higher education in the United States swelled the population of Indians in America.[ii] The second wave arrived in the late 1990s, as digital revolution spread in the industrial sector, and India began to export Information Technology professionals to the Western world. A large contingent of guest workers arrived in the United States through special visa status (Faist, 2008) A steady stream of Indian technology workers began arriving in Grand Rapids as employees in the city's many corporations.

The Immigration and Nationality Act of 1965, enacted at the height of the Civil Rights movement also enabled the Chinese diaspora to flourish. Chinese immigrants first arrived in the United States in the 1920s as railway and farm workers, and were subjected to exclusionary policies that marginalized them in 'ghettos'—Chinatowns and the diaspora was unable to assimilate economically or politically in mainstream American life.(Ong Hing 2012, p. 95). The 1965 Act leveled the immigration playing field giving nearly equal shot to newcomers from around the world. In the 1970s, waves of Chinese professional and students arrived in the United States as a result of this policy. Chinese immigrant in Grand Rapids arrived as adoptees in early 2000s as Chinese government encouraged International adoptions as a corollary to its One Child Policy, and the US government issued thousands of visas to Chinese adoptees (EAWM).

The Latino immigration to the United States was fueled during WWII under the Bracero program, a labor agreement between United States and Mexico. Under this program contract workers arrived in Chicago and Detroit and were employed in manufacturing units and farms in the Midwest. Over the decades, more Spanish speaking immigrants from the Caribbean came to the Midwest via New York and Detroit. The Latino or Spanish speaking community in Grand Rapids is the largest transnational community. About 78 percent of this community is Mexican and the rest are Guatemalan, Cuban, Puerto Rican and Dominican and some from Ecuador. The Cuban and Guatemalan are the largest groups in the state of Michigan. Mexican workers from Chicago and Detroit farmed out to the Grand Rapids area for agriculture work and to take up jobs in manufacturing and the health sector in Grand Rapids (EAWM).

The visible development of transnational communities in Grand Rapids can be mapped through the sheer number of institutional infrastructures of the various communities, the spaces of economic and cultural activities: Hindu, Buddhist and Sikh temples, churches, mosques, restaurants, bakeries, specialty grocery stores, nail spas, community centers. Each group of transnational community has created spaces of gathering and cultural activities where the community comes together around cultural events: Diwali celebration, Chinese New Year, Hispanic festival. These spaces attest to the diversity of transnational peoples in the city.

ROOTS AND ROUTES[1]: DIASPORIC IMAGINATIONS AND MEDIA USE

The central concept of diasporic experience is about "belonging" and "bridging" across national borders where parts of life—family, friends, memories of lived experiences are scattered. The transnational person's life is connected to more than one country. As Hall (1993) puts it, diasporic populations inhabit the culture of their "origin…. they bear traces of particular cultures, traditions, language systems and beliefs, text and histories that have shaped them. But they are also obliged to come to terms with and make something new of the culture they have arrived into." Hall points out that the new diasporas are a product of interlocking histories and cultures … a product of a "diasporic consciousness." (Hall 1993, p. 362). Sreberny (2000) refers to this consciousness as, "cultural memory and attachment to other spaces and places." (p. 179). Diasporic communities are continuously engaged in the 'project' of being, as Ludger Pries puts it, 'both here and there.' Faist (2008) on the other hand suggests that that the new transnational approach to mobility goes beyond the traditional binary concept of emigration and immigration. By contrast, transnational mobility should be understood as manifold processes linking together countries of origin, destination, and onward migration, and as a nexus of networks for sustained and continuous cross border transactions.

---

1   The phrase by Paul Gilroy—referenced in citations

In the city, the urban locale, such cross border transactions become evident through a view of lived experience and mediated practices of diasporic populations. The diasporic accounts of transnational populations we studied are highly diverse, their trajectories differ in time and histories. This multiplicity is reflected in the narratives about notions of "homeland," displacement, migrancy, as well as more contemporary notions of connectivity and cultural reinvention.

From Somewhere Else: Accounts of transnationalism

Among the populations who arrived as forced migrants—the Bosnians, the Sudanese, the Vietnamese, the personal narratives of the transnational experience reveal a fixation to the 'homeland,' nostalgic and emotional aspects of the home country. These families make a considerable effort to maintain their separate national and cultural identity. The heritage language and traditions are of key importance in their day-to-day life in the new country.

From South Sudan

Abraham Mach Thon is one of the 500 Dinka South Sudanese men living in Grand Rapids area. He, arrived with eight other "Lost boys" in 2001 and after the first bout of civil war ceased in Sudan, he went "home" to find a wife having paid a "dowry"—as is the Dinka traditions, to the wife's family, and brought her to Grand Rapids. The couple has two children who were born in Grand Rapids. While most of Abraham's family members were killed in the war, Abraham's mother still lives in the village in Bor, and he has a brother who was settled in Canada. In Grand Rapids, the Sudanese Dinka are a close community and maintain a "deep connection" with Sudan through language and cultural ceremonies.

> "We celebrate July 9, Independence day—Dinka and Neur and all Sudanese come together. We keep doing tradition so our children catch up with it. Here in my house my kids don't speak English here. So I tell them in the house—no English—You only speak Dinka. When other friends come here, other Dinka children, I have to tell them that. I don't want to hear you speaking English here. If my kids ask for anything—if they want me to do it, they have to ask me in Dinka. If they ask me in English, I'll act like I don't know, I don't know what you are talking about. So yeah! They speak good Dinka."

> "I take them (his children) to Sudan to see my Mom. To see my village—and tell them where I was born. So if my mom and others see the kids speaking Dinka they are happy. Otherwise, I will be blamed for it (for not teaching them Dinka).

> "We still have our culture as a Dinka. My wife do cooking Sudanese food so much. My kids don't like Sudanese food. They like American fast food. I feel Dinka very much and I try to bring the two cultures together.

In the usage of media, these nostalgic aspects are of prime importance.

"Mostly I watch BBC News—that brings Sudanese news. That brings what's going on in Africa and around the world, and the "Sudanese dish network" with Sudanese programming. I teach my kids to look at Sudanese news—now they know who is President of Sudan."

From Vietnam

Hau Mai and De Tran were born in Vietnam and arrived in Grand Rapids in 1994 through a political refugee program. Since then they sponsored their seven sons and daughters and their families. They all have settled in the city with homes close to each other. Hau and De Tran's home is a gathering place for the entire family of 42 members for every celebration, religious festivals. They worship at the city's Vietnamese Buddhist Temple and have a particular connection with it as De Tran's mother's ashes are placed in the temple. It is essential to visit the ashes of the elder. In this sense, the Trans have brought their family heritage to Grand Rapids. Every member of the family including children born in the United States speaks Vietnamese. Meals made together consist of traditional Vietnamese dishes and entertainment media watched is in Vietnamese language. Films and entertainment shows are popular among the elders and the very young, as they watch these shows together. The younger children, many of them, come to the grandparent's home until their parents get off work and pick them up. Much of the shows are watched with the grand parents, in-between homework and meals.

Thanh, Hau's granddaughter is the most recent arrival from Vietnam while her parents decided to stay back—the only ones, in the Tran family. Thanh came on a student visa and is a recent graduate of a state university. She lives with her grandparents and has entered the circle of family and friends. Except, unlike her relatives who are Buddhists, Thanh attends the Catholic Church, The Lady of La Vang (the belief that Virgin Madonna appeared in La Vang at a time when Catholics were persecuted in Vietnam), led by Vietnamese priest.

Thanh straddles the "back home" and "America" through media. Unlike her relatives, Thanh is well versed in English and learned the language in Vietnam. She follows news channels such as CNN and navigates the Internet for information. Via the Internet she reads news of Vietnam, chats with friends in Vietnam.

"I have been watching American movies and listening to English music since I was young" she refers to her exposure to global media channels. Yet, prefers the ethnic language media.

"I can feel (the emotions) in a story when I read, watch in Vietnamese. It feels very relaxing to read in your own language. ... There is an emotional connection. I feel connected to Vietnam. But I use English media when I am looking for information, or scientific knowledge."

From Bosnia

Emina Aliskovic came to Grand Rapids with her sister and parents in the aftermath of the War in Bosnia. After the war her family returned to Sarajevo but Emina stayed back as she met her future husband Elmir. They married soon and now have two young children. Emina's family in this sense is straddled across borders.

> "When I moved to United States I was 18 years old. I was in school in Bosnia—I had friends I grew up with over there. My whole family lives in Bosnia. I was already ya know grown up person when I came to the United States. ... My parents are there. And (so are) my sisters. And I really love Bosnia. I loved everything about it. Even though (there was) war, and my childhood was not that happy (because of it)—I still love it. ... I am still connected with my middle school friends and high school friends as well. I speak with them as well—we use Internet all the time. Everyday we use Facebook. That's a great way to connect with everybody and see pictures and see there families and see how their their kids are growing up and what they do in their life..it's easy way and it's also free. It doesn't cost anything and I just love it."

In the city, Emina makes keen effort to reproduce the life left behind even while she must negotiate life in the United States.

> "At home, here we cook Bosnian food. We can't live without that. We have Bosnian friends here. That we hang out with and go to Bosnian events. To always stay connected with the Bosnian community or Bosnian culture. There are a few markets in town where they have a lot of Bosnian products. And lots of Bosnian people go there and buy products that are imported from Europe. Most of the time we speak Bosnian—it all depends on the situation. Sometimes because I have been living here for almost 12 years, sometimes now it's easier to express myself in English than in Bosnian. Or I am noticing that some of the words—if I want to speak with somebody—they're just not coming out. If I can't remember how to say that in Bosnian, I just say English word—and then I say—Bosnian the rest. We're starting to mix, but mainly we speak Bosnian—because of the kids as well. Because we want them to learn Bosnian language."

> "In Bosnia, I have family and friends, and I feel more comfortable down there because I feel more loved and wanted. It is different in ways. But I am getting used to this culture here and to what's there in the United States."

Among those who voluntarily crossed borders in search of opportunities, such as populations in Grand Rapids from India, or China, connectivity, settlement in the new home tend to be key notions in the narratives about their diasporic condition. There is a distinct effort to construct notions of "who they are," by looking forward, yet not necessarily giving up their heritage culture. They negotiate their transnational life through economic assimilation and cultural separation.

From China

Su Yi came in early 1990s as a student and after he found a job in the United States, went back to China to get married and brought his wife who then enrolled at a University. The couple has two children.

> "A lot of students in China wanted to come to the United States to study. I joined the cult and took the GRE test and got a scholarship. ... I was from a small town and my parents worked hard to send my siblings and me to college in Beijing. We were poor then. We all were poor in China. Now my brothers and one sister have good jobs and good businesses."

Su did not think of returning to China even as he has considerable economic opportunities in China. Yet he wants to maintain his Chinese cultural elements. The blend is of importance to him.

> "I am Americanized now," he says.

Although, his social network of friends and family in the United States is predominantly of Chinese origin. He sends his daughter to a "Saturday Chinese school," where she learns to read, speak and write in Chinese.

> "We send her back to China every summer so she stays with my family. That way, she too will learn Chinese. We (the Chinese people) have a long history and wisdom, culture. If she can't read and speak in Chinese, she will miss that. The reason I came to the United States is not just to go to school. I wanted to broaden my view and understand more."

From India

Suresh and Alka Bhargava arrived in Grand Rapids as 'sponsored' Permanent Residents in 1992. Suresh works for a utility corporation and Alka owns a retail business. They maintain a strong sense of their national, cultural identity in their everyday lives:

> "We cook Indian food every day, we speak Hindi at home, listen to Hindi music, watch Hindi films. We love the Indian attire. Alka (his wife) has an exquisite collection of *Saris* from many parts of India. We follow the Hindu religion and practices and we are actively involved in the Hindu temple. We are proud of our heritage, our (Indian) culture." (Suresh)

Their media habits reflect their effort to maintain their identity.

> "I give myself time at work to read at least two or three newspapers from India: *The Times of India, Rajathan Patrika*, we subscribe to *India Abroad*. We have dish network and I love

to watch the Indian soaps (soap operas), especially the mythological ones. The language is sankritized (based on Sanskrit), and is clean, pure language and I like to hear it and learn from it. We watch Bollywood films on weekends. The new ones are available at the Indian grocery store. There's a lot of good stuff on Indian TV, it gives us insight into what's happening in India. I want to keep in touch about politics, who is in power, about culture, about Bollywood celebrities …" (Alka).

From Latin America

Among the Spanish speaking communities a continuous practice of cross border remittances has existed for many decades. Migrants from Latin America continue to send remittances to support their family and community 'back home.' This practice has evolved into Community or Village projects of investment in infrastructure in the native communities in the 'old country.' National governments and other organizations like banks have started to build programs around commitments felt by migrants towards their home institutions. Mexico, for instance, has provided incentives to such projects. A prominent example is the *tres-por-uno* (3x1) program in which each 'migra dollar' sent by a migrant from abroad is complemented by three dollars from various governmental levels. More recently banks have joined the fray. The transnational associations provide 'local to local' relationships across national borders (Faist 2008).

In Grand Rapids, apart from the Mexicans, the Bolivian, Dominican and Colombian communities have vibrant transnational associations that invest in such projects as building schools, roads, a church, a new bridge. Some observers lament that this commitment often comes at a cost of building community in the country of arrival, and the investment abroad that is made due to emotional commitment is often under-utilized in capacity.

> "We build our lives in Grand Rapids and improve the quality of life for our families by remaining transnationally connected. The community that allows you access and our engagement are the ones left behind. It plays on your heart strings, your emotions and nostalgia … and all of this sadness that comes from being in exile has an impact, and you invest in an infrastructure project or a community service project in your native country that you or your (immediate) neighbors don't have direct access to on a day-to-day basis. Yet, I think there is a missed opportunity for deeper civic engagement, assimilation and acculturation in the country you live in. There is a missed opportunity for economic development work in the U.S. that could enhance education and economic opportunities for the immigrant communities that are here. … What you see if you travel to these destinations that are home base for immigrant communities, you see beautiful schools that have hardly any children,

paved roads no one drives on, you have beautiful mansions that are empty." (Martha Gonzalez-Cortes[2])

This connectivity to the native village, country and community reflects in media usage. Spanish speaking communities in Grand Rapids are connected to global media that provides content in Spanish, more so than local media. Local media are of no consequence due to lack of content in the heritage language.

> "Due to a very limited access we have in Grand Rapids to real time news in Spanish at the local level, everyone in the Spanish speaking community is forced to tune into International outlets, say, Univision, Telemundo, Telefutura, Tele Azteca. Every Latin American country has international cable access shows that will give you news from back home either for your state or region from where you might be from. Direct TV and Cable TV providers have made a killing on viewership and consumer dollars with the Latino community that is desperate to be connected to some degree to real time news available to us in Spanish." (Gonzalez-Cortes).

The bridging across national borders to stay connected with family, a key aspect of diasporic life is as much facilitated and enhanced by new communication technologies. Sarah Williams, a recent immigrant from Ecuador underlines the significance of communication technologies.

> "When you leave your family and friends (back home) you sort of commit social suicide. You have to find a way to connect back. While you find new relationships here (in Grand Rapids) in a way you have to reinvent yourself here. But you can do that with the support of those meaningful relationships at home. I *Skype* every day or talk to my family and friends via *Facebook*. I talk to my parents who are now in Venezuela on the phone daily, I *Skype* with my brother who is in Quito in Ecuador. He uses *Magic Jack* to call me. These are the people who are invested in my life. But I also am connected with friends in Ecuador who keep me informed about the politics because media there are not a reliable source."

CULTURAL REPRODUCTION—HYBRID IMAGINATION OF THE WORLD LEFT BEHIND.

On the one hand, transnational ethnic media further a sense of proximity for diasporic populations. On the hand, media, with their continuous supply of content in real time also bring home the realization that the world left behind has transformed. The contemporary does not correspond with places in memory and this experience engenders new selective imaginings

---

2   Martha Gonzalez-Cortes is the current CEO of Hispanic Center of West Michigan (www.hispanic-center.org) a non-profit 510(c)(3)community based organization

of the old country, a transnational idea of the place in memory that transmutes the place of departure and the place of arrival (Beck, 2000). In this very construction media images play a role. In the 'Indian Culture' constructed in the festivals or cultural events in the city, there is a careful selection of cultural repertoire. The most available cultural products are Bollywood films, music and the vast variety of entertainment content that comes into the city via satellite TV, the Internet and CDs. The song and dance version of Bollywood seeps into a variety of celebrations in the city including weddings, traditional religious and seasonal festivals of India such as *Diwali, Holi* and *Pongal* and *Baisakhi*. As Suresh Bhargava describes:

> "In order to keep our heritage alive, we always have the Indian cultural event, a mix of Bollywood entertainment, a disco dancing time that uses old and Bollywood music. That's one way of keeping our culture alive."

These creative programs are media images, particularly fictional images, drawn from popular culture and are appropriated as 'traditional' culture. Popular culture in this way dominates the cultural discourse.

Similarly, in the rituals performed in places of worship and cultural festivals of Vietnamese, Chinese communities, there is a careful selection of what is beautiful, serene, worthy of preservation. In this selection, the darker aspects of the nation—of economic poverty, oppressive social hierarchy, corruption, are shaken off and only a celebratory imagination of the nation is preserved. These imaginations seldom correspond with the realities of the nation and yet they provide a sense of affirmation, a sense of community. This feeds into the nostalgia that allows for pride in national identity.

CONCLUSION

Diasporic accounts of transnational everyday life reveal a visceral need for connectivity to spaces of memory across borders as much as a drive for cultural reinvention in the new locales. There is an evident connection between language and national consciousness. Yet the 'nation' in the diasporic narrative is a space of memory and history and the need to be connected to these spaces alleviates the sense of displacement. Dispersed populations, whether forced or voluntary are a product of ruptures of modern times that engenders a need to experience continuity, need for a "narrative of identity" (Anderson, 1993).

The everyday accounts from transnational people reveal the texture of diasporic life and also point to how these aggregates of migrants transform into active transnational networks. The infrastructure of these networks are satellite and Internet technologies as well as the local physical networks the urban-local micro spheres of communicative practices: cultural events, celebrations such as Independence day- (of India, South Sudan), the church, poetry readings, musical events, community centers or clubs, political chats over a drink with friends, are as much part of diasporic communicative practices and media cultures. The variable geometry of relationship between the local and transnational networks; between media and horizontal communication; and the vibrant multidirectional flows of ethnic or language media across national borders has at once, expanded the global public sphere, and also rendered it fragmented. What then about the city and its transnational spaces? The most that can be said about this is that the urban locale evolves and transforms as it always has.

NOTES

i. Here we see the diasporic population as distinct from although they are a part of various transnational entities such as global business networks, village groups, epistemic communities that create global knowledge networks.

ii. In the 1920s a contingent of farm labor was brought from India for work on railroads and as farm hand in the fruit orchards in the North West US. This population until the 1960s consisted of only males who then married the local Hispanic women. Only after the Immigration and Nationality Act of 1965, Indian were able to enable acquire US visa for their family members to enter the country(see History of Indians in the U.S (http://www.shamit.org/Articales/history_of_indians_in_the_us.htm)

REFERENCES

Anderson, Benedict [1983] (1991) *Imagined Communities: Reflections on the origins and spread of nationalism.* London: Verso.

Appadurai, Arjun (1996) *Modernity at Large: Cultural dimensions of globalization.* Minneapolis and London: University of Minnesota Press.

Castells, Manuel (2002) *The Internet galaxy: Reflections on the Internet, Business and Society.* Oxford and New York: Oxford University Press.

Clifford, James (1994) 'Diasporas', *Cultural Anthropology,* 9 (3): 302–37

Corbett, Sarah, The Long Road from Sudan to America, *The New York Times* (archives) April 1, 2001.

Ethnic Atlas of West Michigan, Volume 1 (2005), Volume 2 (2006) Johnson Center for Philanthropy. Grand Valley State University. scholarworks.gvsu.edu/research/2

Faist, Thomas (2008) Migrants as Transnational Development Agents: An Inquiry into the newest round of the Migration-Development nexus. In *Population, Space and Place* (www.InterScience.Wiley.com)

Gilroy Paul (1995) Black identities as an outernational project, in H.W.Harris, Howard C. Blue and Ezra E.H. Griffin (eds.), *Racial and Ethnic Identity: Psychological development and creative expression.* London and New York: Routledge

Hall, Stuart (1990) Cultural Identity and Diaspora. In Jonathan Rutherford (ed.) *Identity, Community, Culture, Difference.* London: Lawrence and Wishart. Pp, 222–37

Harvey, David (1989) *The Condition of Postmodernity,* Oxford: Blackwell.

Hall, Stuart (1993) "Culture, Communication, Nation," *Cultural Studies* Vol 7, no. 3, pp 349–63.

Karim H. Karim (2003) *The media of diaspora.* London and New York: Routledge

Keane, John (1995) Structural Transformation of the Public Sphere, *Communication Review,* 1 (1) 1995: 8–22.

Ludden, Jennifer, 1965 Immigration law changed the face of America, *All Things Considered.* May 9, 2006. www.npr.org

Myria Georgiou and Roger Silverstone (2007) "Diasporas and Contra-Flows beyond Nation-Centrism, in *Media on the move: global flows and contra flows* pp 30–43. London, New York: Routledge.

Pries, Ludger (2001) The approach of transnational social spaces:Responding to new configurations of the social and the spatial. Ludger Pries (ed.) *New Transnational Social Spaces: International migration and transnational companies in the early 21st century.* London, New York: Routledge.

Sreberny, Annabelle (2000) Media and diasporic consciousness: An Exploration among Iranians in London, in Cottle Simon (ed.) *Ethnic Minorities and the media: Changing cultural boundaries.* Philadelphia: Open University Press.

BRAZIL AND THE GLOBALIZATION OF TELENOVELAS

By Cacilda M. Rêgo and Antonio C. La Pastina

There is a difference between the fascination a telenovela exerts in Brazil and abroad. In Brazil it is more popular because it is an open work, because it is unfinished. It is alive, the audience knows that the story he [sic] is watching is unfinished and therefore it has a special charm for him. The viewer has even the impression that his reaction will in some way affect the plot. The characters start to come to life; to be real citizens involved in the daily life when a telenovela is successful. And the viewer includes them in his life and shares in the uncertainties of their fate because the novel is in the process of being written as it is being produced. The art form is completely open. (Dias Gomes, 1990; telenovela scriptwriter)[1]

In the last few decades Brazilian and Mexican telenovelas, and to a lesser extent Venezuelan, Colombian and those produced in other Latin American countries, have been widely exported. Brazilian telenovelas have been aired—in dubbed and, sometimes, in edited versions—in more than 130 countries (Allen, 1995; Sinclair, 1996; Straubhaar, 1996). This international presence has challenged the traditional debate over cultural imperialism and the North-South flow of media products (Sinclair,

---

Antonio La Pastina and Calcilda M. Rego, "Brazil and the Globalization of Telenovelas," *Media on the Move: Global Flow and Contra Flow*, pp. 89-103. Copyright © 2007 by Taylor & Francis Group LLC. Reprinted with permission.

1996; 2003). Robert Evans has gone as far as to say that the export of telenovelas across the globe by Brazil can be viewed as an extension of cultural imperialism 'with Brazil surreptitiously spreading the United States culture to its audiences worldwide' (Evans, 2005).

Another way to look at the flow of the telenovela from Latin America is to consider its presence as a challenge to Hollywood's hegemony of cultural software exports. The Brazilian telenovela, for example, while adopting high production values and a star system not unlike the Hollywood standard, has strong local cultural roots. These serialized Brazilian melodramas discuss contemporary issues that cross national boundaries but also are firmly placed within the reality of a metropolis in the global South. In this chapter we will discuss the development of the telenovela genre and focus on the Brazilian telenovela, tracing its early history of borrowing and adapting from foreign sources to its insertion in the global market.

Primarily produced for the domestic market, Latin American telenovelas have been exported to Europe, Asia, Africa, the Middle East, and the United States since at least the late 1970s. Their worldwide success suggests that they are no longer a uniquely Latin American phenomenon, but a major global commercial force with extraordinary social and cultural importance. In this scenario, Brazil has cemented its place as one of the world's largest telenovela producers. Such recognition came in 2003 when TV Globo International was awarded two Latin ACE Awards for its telenovela *O Clone* [The Clone], the first ever to be sold abroad while it was still showing in Brazil. In the TV/ Dramatic Series category, Jayme Monjardim received the Latin ACE for Best Director, and Murilo Benício received the Best Actor award in the same telenovela. According to Helena Bernardi, director of marketing and sales for TV Globo International, *O Clone*, written by Glória Peres, 'is a continuation of Globo TV's tradition of excellence in telenovela programming, and the international success of this drama series shows that quality telenovelas possess a very strong appeal to viewers worldwide' (quoted in *Brazzil Magazine*, 2003). In 2004, TV Globo also received the Latin American award for the Best Telenovela Producer and Distributor worldwide (*Television Asia*, 2005). In the last 30 years TV Globo has produced more than 300 telenovelas, most of which sold in the international market in record numbers. *O Clone*, for example, was sold to more than 62 countries; *Laços de Família* [Family Ties] sold to 66 countries and *Terra Nostra* [Our Land] sold to 84. To this list one can also add past hits in the international market, such as *A Escrava Isaura* [The Slave Isaura], which was sold to 79 countries, and *Sinhá Moça* [Young Lady], which was shown in 62 countries (*TVMASNOVELAS*, 2005).

Globo's most important markets are Portugal, Russia, Romania, Hispanic United States, Chile, Peru, Uruguay, and Argentina. Although the key Asian markets, which include China, Indonesia, Malaysia, and the Philippines, have become increasingly important, they still represent a much smaller share of Globo's overseas sales, at only 0.5 per cent in 2003 (*Television Asia*, 2003; *Video Age*, 2005). Since the 1980s, Globo also has expanded its exports to the Middle East. In the past five years Globo has seen a growth of 70 per cent in program hours exported, totaling around 24,000 hours of programs every year. Such volumes of hours are due to the sale of telenovelas to over 50 countries, which account for 90 per cent of Globo's sales abroad. Movies and documentaries account for the remaining 10 per cent of sales in the international market (Mikevis, 2005). Understandably, Brazilian telenovelas—especially those produced by TV Globo—have maintained a near domination of the Portuguese market, which has served as a base for further expansion into the European market as well as the Portuguese-speaking African market, largely made up of former Portuguese colonies.

Despite its status as the fourth largest network in the world in terms of revenues and production capabilities, TV Globo is not the only influential telenovela producer in Brazil. The Sistema Brasileiro de Televisão (SBT), Brazil's second-largest television network, has consistently gained ground over its main competitor for the last two decades with telenovelas bought directly from Mexico's Televisa or with homemade remakes of telenovelas, especially from Argentina and Mexico. Like Globo, which has sold its highly polished telenovelas to more than 130 countries in the past 30 years, SBT—followed by other national telenovela producers such as Bandeirantes, Record, and Central Nacional de Televisão (CNT), which began telenovela co-production with Mexico's Televisa in 1996—has aimed to expand its exports beyond the lusophone market (*Variety*, 1997; Filipelli, 2004).

According to Bernardi, a key factor in the success of Globo telenovelas in the international market is their high production values.

> Buyers have come to expect quality. A good story is always the beginning of a case of success, but buyers now know that audiences would not settle for only that. They demand that a good story is not only told in a good way, but it also must 'look good' on the screen. They define a 'good product' referring not only to the plot or story, but by production values, such as lighting, wardrobe, scenery, good-looking talent, etc. Globo is constantly investing in technology, infrastructure and creative talent; our products present the highest production value in their category, with great stories about universal themes. (Bernardi, quoted in Carugati and Alvarado, 2005)

Other Brazilian networks have also learned that high production values ensure a competitive edge at home and abroad. The broadcaster Record, for example, invested $10 million in state-of-the-art recording equipment to consolidate its position as one of the main telenovela producers in the country.

Aside from high quality, other factors have contributed to the success of the genre worldwide, as Bernardi notes:

> Our telenovelas travel around the world successfully because they talk about universal themes, the feelings of viewers, things such as love, emotion, contemporary conflicts and issues that affect women, families and society as a whole. Globo's telenovelas are successful because of their formula that brings social issues, sometimes long forgotten, sometimes issues that society, for one reason or another, has chosen not to face. A good example was the discussion of cloning in *El Clon*, a telenovela that also discussed cultural differences

between Eastern and Western cultures and drug addiction. *Lazos de Familia* discussed leukemia and the lack of organ donors in the country, generating a nationwide campaign to increase that number, a campaign that was replicated by Telemundo in the United States. (Bernardi, quoted in Carugati and Alvarado, 2005)

Brazilian telenovelas have also experienced adaptations and changes to meet the tastes of international audiences. A rapidly rising trend, related to the expansion of the global telenovela market, is the sale of telenovela scripts by Brazilian writers to international broadcasters, who use their own actors, directors, and setting, with equal or greater success than imported telenovelas.

TELENOVELAS: LOCALLY PRODUCED, GLOBALLY CONSUMED

For the last 30 years telenovelas have dominated prime-time programming on Brazilian and most of Latin American television. Here Latin America refers to more than a geographic area. It entails a culturally constructed region that goes from the southern tip of South America to Canada and the United States, where the Hispanic community can watch daily telenovelas on several Spanish-language cable and satellite networks—namely, Telemundo, Gems Television (recently renamed MundoDos), TeleFutura, TV Azteca America, Univisión, and its affiliate channel, Galavisión.[2]

While telenovelas from Brazil and other Latin American countries cross national boundaries, and Latin American viewers pick and choose between Rio and Mexico City, glamor and down-to-earth ordinariness, fantasy and realism, it is becoming impossible to speak of the future of telenovelas except as part of the wider future of the new information and entertainment systems as they become globally interconnected. In the last decade, Latin America telenovela producers have confronted the advent of new technologies, the increasing neoliberalization of governments, and the opening of markets leading to greater competition from telenovela producers within and outside Latin America, such as Sony Pictures Television International (SPTI), Buena Vista International Television—a Walt Disney subsidiary—and Fremantle Media. Other strong competitors may soon be ABC, CBS, and Fox, three of the top English-language networks in the United States, which, after being outpaced by the Spanish-language networks in some major markets such as Miami and Los Angeles, announced in late 2005 their intention to create English-language versions of telenovelas in order to appeal to millions of younger second- and third-generation US Latinos/Latinas who speak English more frequently than Spanish (*New York Times*, 2006).

Some countries such as Germany, Romania, Portugal, Indonesia, Malaysia, China, and the Philippines, are also effectively venturing into local telenovela production, often in partnership with Latin American producers (Martinez, 2005; *Television Asia*, 2005). These local productions are now filling the prime-time slots that were once held by Latin American telenovelas (Jaspar, 2006).

The regional giants, Globo and Televisa, have had to deal with a more dynamic and diverse market in which their voices do not dominate the spectrum any longer, both within their own respective markets and in the broader regional market. According to Bernardi, 'the arrival of the majors [in the telenovela genre] makes it possible for new markets to open, markets where the telenovela genre is not that well accepted yet' (quoted in Carugati and Alvarado, 2005).

Of course, this can also work the other way around. Spurred by the success of Globo telenovelas abroad, especially in Eastern Europe, networks such as Romania's Acasa, which is entirely dedicated to telenovelas and other products from Latin America, have increasingly bought films produced by Globo solely on the strength of their cast, which include telenovela actors such as Giovanna Antonelli, Benício Murilo, Glória Pires, and Antonio Fagundes (de La Fuente, 2005). On the other hand, reality shows and game shows produced locally are considered the main competitors to Brazilian telenovelas in the international market, as they are generally low(er) budget productions. Even so, they are also thought to stimulate the habit of watching television and attracting potential viewers to those same telenovelas (*Television Asia*, 2005). As Bernardi says, what is important, in the final analysis, is that 'Globo's telenovelas are extremely ratings-oriented and are being perceived [by international broadcasters] as an important tool on the programming grid. In general, they occupy a strategic position in the afternoon, access and primetime grids' (quoted in Carugati and Alvarado, 2005).

While increasingly global, television remains primarily a national phenomenon and most television is still watched via national systems, despite the growth of transnational satellite systems. Further, unlike the situation observed in the early 1970s by Nordenstreng and Varis (1974), much of that television is also produced at the national level. However, most of this national programming is produced using regionalized or globalized genres or formats: Latin American telenovela is an example of the increasingly global commercial television reliance on soap opera. This contradiction echoes Robertson's (1995) idea that we are increasingly using globalized forms to produce the local, resulting in what he calls 'glocal' culture. TV Globo in Brazil and Televisa in Mexico are both far more powerful and important in their home markets than they were as partners in Sky Latin America, their Latin American regional broadcast joint venture with the very global Rupert Murdoch.

THE GENRE AND ITS ROOTS

English-language soaps in the United States, Britain, and Australia have a well-established research tradition (Cantor and Pingree, 1983; Allen, 1985, 1995; Geraghty, 1991; Brown, 1994; Brunsdon, 2000; Hobson, 2003; Spence, 2005). In the last few decades, in different parts of the world, the production of serialized television fiction has spread and so has the academic interest in its format and its role in society. Egypt developed its own local production more than two decades ago, winning over local audiences, slowly increasing its penetration in the regional market and exporting to other nations in the region (Abu-Lughod, 1993, 1995; Diase,

1996). China (Wang and Singhal, 1992) and India (Singhal and Rogers, 1988, 1989a, 1989b) have been gradually increasing such productions for their national markets in the last decade.

Distinct from United States soap operas, Latin American telenovelas are broadcast daily, 'have very definitive endings that permit narrative closure' normally after 180 to 200 episodes depending on their popularity, and are designied to attract a wide viewing audience of men, women, and children (Lopez, 1991:600). A teenage telenovela, *Malhação* (which can be roughly translated as 'Working out'), which began in 1995, is the longest-running telenovela in Brazil. Telenovela narratives are dominated by a leading couple of characters and rely on class conflict and the promotion of social mobility (Mazziotti, 1993). According to Aufderheide, 'Latin American television can be rich in wit, social relevance and national cultural style.' Brazilian *novelas* can tackle such issues as 'bureaucratic corruption, single motherhood and the environment; class differences are foregrounded in Mexican *novelas*', and Cuban *novelas* are bitingly topical as well as ideologically correct' (Aufderheide, 1993:583).

Telenovelas and soap operas have common roots, but over time they have developed as clearly different genres. Within Latin American production centers, these distinctions have been emphasized, creating particularities in theme, narrative style, and production values. For Lopez (1995), the Mexican telenovelas are the weepies—ahistorical telenovelas with no context provided. Colombians are comical and ironic with a greater concern for context. Venezuelans are more emotional, but they do not have the 'barroqueness' of Mexican sets. Brazilians are the most realistic, with historically based narratives that have a clear temporal and spatial contextualization. Hernández (2001) distinguishes telenovelas as *blandas* (soft) or *duras* (hard), placing the Mexicans and Venezuelans in the first category and the Brazilian and Colombian in the second.

Recently, however, these divergences in style have been challenged by increasing competition within the two largest markets, Brazil and Mexico, from new networks such as TV Azteca in Mexico and SBT in Brazil. TV Azteca, located in the industrial north, close to the border with the United States, has produced politically charged telenovelas with a contemporary bend to their narratives, undermining Televisa. By contrast in Brazil, the more weepy melodramatic Mexican telenovelas aired by SBT and CNT are, as mentioned earlier, challenging Globo's dominance.

Apart from their differing styles, telenovelas are faithful to the melodramatic roots of the genre. Lopez argues that melodrama in Europe and the United States was discriminated against primarily due to its association with female audiences, while in Latin America, melodrama was devalued due to its class association that placed it in the realm of the popular. In this context of class identification, she explains how melodrama pertains to telenovelas:

> The telenovela exploits personalization—the individualization of the social world—as an epistemology. It ceaselessly offers the audience dramas of recognition by locating social and political issues in personal and familial terms and thus making sense of an increasingly complex world. (Lopez, 1995:258)

Furthermore, Mazziotti argues that

> [telenovelas] allow for the viewers an emotional participation in a set of fictitious powers that play with elemental human questions: honour, goodness, love, badness, treason, life, death, virtue and sin, that in certain ways has something to do with the viewer. (Mazziotti, 1993:11)

MARKETING SOAP IN BRAZIL

Telenovelas have evolved in Latin America from the radio soap model developed in the United States by corporations such as Colgate-Palmolive, Proctor & Gamble, and Gessy-Lever. Seeing its success in reaching the female audience, the target consumer market for their products, these corporations invested in introducing the genre in Latin America, starting in Cuba and soon spreading to the rest of the continent. But it was in Havana in the 1930s that the Latin American version of the radionovela began its transition. In the next few decades, Cuba became the supplier of artists, technical personnel and, most importantly, the scripts for most of Latin America (*Ortiz et al.*, 1988).

The radionovela reached Brazil in 1941. The first to arrive was *A Predestinada* [The Predestined] on Radio São Paulo, after the artistic director of that station, Oduvaldo Viana, 'discovered' the genre while traveling in Argentina. This first radionovela, not surprisingly, was produced by Colgate-Palmolive. The success of the genre on Brazilian radio stations led to an increasing amount of time and resources devoted to radionovelas. The shows were produced and recorded in Rio de Janeiro and São Paulo and transmitted to the rest of Brazil. The leap from radio to television in Brazil took only a decade in the urban south, but in many rural areas the first TV set arrived in the late 1970s or 1980s.

Rede Tupi, the first TV station in the country, was inaugurated in São Paulo in 1950 and it aired the first telenovela, *Minha Vida Te Pertence* [My Life Belongs to You], in 1951 twice a week live from its studios (Klagsbrunn and Resende, 1991). Throughout the 1950s, television stations in the country, primarily in São Paulo and Rio de Janeiro, broadcast short serialized programs live. They were mostly adaptations of foreign literary works and followed the melodramatic formula established by the Cuban radionovelas. It was only in 1963, due to the development of videotape technology, that telenovelas were recorded and broadcast daily (Klagsbrunn and Resende, 1991). Nevertheless, radionovelas and the early serialized TV shows had a fundamental role in establishing the genre in Brazil. Scriptwriters were trained in the melodramatic conventions, and once the technology arrived, they were ready to embrace the new medium. Telenovelas, however, did not evolve only from the radio matrix; other traditions in serialized fiction impacted the development of the genre. From *the feuilletons* in France to the locally produced serialized romances from the beginning of the century (Ortiz *et al.*, 1988; Meyer, 1996) to the *cordel* literature in Brazil, the genre evolved in each country within Latin America with certain peculiarities (Martin-Barbero, 1993).

Early serial telenovelas were part of a line-up that included ballet, opera, and theater designed to attract the elite audience that consumed TV in the 1950s. For most of its first decades in Brazil, television remained an elitist medium. Assis Chateaubriand created the first TV station in 1950, bringing 300 TV sets into the country to sell to the local elite that would allow for the creation of a small audience. By 1960 less than 5 per cent of Brazilian households owned a television. After the military takeover in 1964 and Globo's inauguration in 1965, the number of sets in Brazil was still small and mainly in urban and upper-income households. By 1970, with the broadcasting of the soccer World Cup, 24 per cent of the households had television. Many larger communities in the interior of the country already had public television sets on which viewers could watch images beamed from the urban south, mostly from Rio de Janeiro.[3] The Brazilian military regime saw in television a medium ready to promote national integration. The national telecommunications company, Embratel, created in 1965, had as its motto: 'Communication is integration,' reiterating the regime's objectives. But the tool to achieve those goals turned out to be TV Globo (Mattos, 1982).

Globo was inaugurated in 1965, spearheaded by media tycoon Roberto Marinho, owner of the daily *O Globo*, the largest circulation newspaper in Rio de Janeiro. Globo established a sophisticated technological infrastructure with the financial and technical support of the United States media group Time-Life. In 1969, pressured by the government, Globo bought Time-Life's share, becoming a totally Brazilian-owned company (Mattos, 1982). For four years the military regime that had taken over only a year before Globo network came into existence, had overlooked Globo's foreign backing, disregarding the country's constitution, which at the time forbade even partial foreign ownership of any media in Brazil.

At the same time that Globo was establishing itself, the competing networks were pressured by federal regulations. Excelsior, the then-leader in terms of audience share, had its license withdrawn by the military regime. Tupi held on until the end of the 1970s with steadily declining ratings. It closed in 1979 and its stations' licenses were divided between two media groups to create two networks: Manchete and SBT.[4] By the 1970s, Globo had established itself as the leading network in the country, attaining the highest audience ratings and benefiting from the largest segment of the advertising market, which at this point was heavily reliant on state-owned corporations (Ortiz *et al.*, 1988). The main attractions at Globo remained the daily prime-time telenovelas and the evening newscast that came to be perceived as the official voice of the military regime (Lima, 1988; Mattos, 1982; Straubhaar, 1988).

Currently TV Globo's signal covers almost all the Brazilian territory (Amaral and Guimarães, 1994). In 30 years Globo became the main, if not the only, television voice available to all Brazilians. Several factors helped in this process. Embratel, following the military's goal of national unity, invested heavily in the development and expansion of the telecommunications infrastructure. Simultaneously, the production of TV sets in the country increased while consumer credit became available, leading to a boom in sales (Mattos, 1982). Finally, the government, through legislation and advertising support as well as favored use of the telecom infrastructure, allowed Globo to become a household presence in almost every corner of the nation. The Brazilian government also created the opportunities for Globo Network to become a vital player in the international media market and specially a leading voice in the lusophone market, filling the gap created by the end of the Portuguese colonial rule in Africa.

THE 'BRAZILIANIZATION' OF THE GENRE

Since the late 1960s and early 1970s the Brazilian telenovela has slowly evolved away from the general Latin American model. TV Globo, in particular, invested heavily in production values, increasing, for instance, the use of external shots that had been previously avoided due to production costs. The network also promoted a modernization of telenovela themes, including giving priority to texts produced by Brazilian writers. In this process, Globo created its own *'Padrão Globo de Qualidade'* or Global Pattern of Quality (Lopez, 1991).

Changes in style and format led Brazilian telenovelas to become more dynamic and closely associated with current events in the life of the nation (e.g. thematic inclusion of elections, strikes, and scandals that were happening in 'real' life). Events such as the killing of an actress by the actor who played her 'boyfriend' on the telenovela shocked the nation but also showed how reality and fiction blur in Brazilian life. Mattelart and Mattelart (1990) argue that Brazilian telenovelas are an 'open work' or an 'open genre'. During production, the telenovela's creators receive direct and indirect input from viewers and fans, theatrical productions, commercials, elite and popular press, institutional networks, audience and marketing research organizations, and other social forces in society, such as the Catholic church, the government, and civil society groups.

However, the genre was not so flexible in the early years of telenovelas. For several writers (Ortiz *et al.*, 1988; Mattelart and Mattelart, 1990; Mazziotti, 1993; Lopez, 1995), the landmark telenovela that started the redefinition of the genre in Brazil was *Beto Rockfeller* [Bob Rockfeller] aired by Rede Tupi in 1968–69. *Beto Rockfeller* escaped the traditional molds of the genre, presenting a telenovela in which artificial dramatic attitudes were abandoned and colloquial dialogue broke with the patterns of literary speech. But not only was the language different; the dramatic structure, narrative strategies, and production values were also modified.

Beto Rockfeller was the story of a middle-class young man who worked for a shoe store, but with charm and wit got himself mixed up with the upper class, passing himself off as a millionaire. To maintain his secret and status, he had to engage in many nefarious activities. The telenovela gained very high audience ratings, lasting for almost 13 months, much longer than the typical six to eight months (Fernandes, 1994). Globo, which up to that point had followed a traditional style of presenting telenovelas located in faraway places with exotic settings and plots, noticed the audience interest in *Beto Rockfeller* and took on this real style. In this process it reshaped the genre, distancing the Brazilian telenovela from the Latin American model.

However, according to officials from Mexico's Televisa, interviewed by *Variety*, Brazilian telenovelas did not truly reach the masses:

> Brazil's TV Globo produces esthetically better novelas but the content of Televisa's soaps is more understandable to the masses. Globo uses a lot of subplots and stories within stories, while our scripts are more direct and the themes more universal. Television is a mass communication medium. Cinema can be elitist but not television. (*Variety*, 1986:105)

The gap between the telenovela styles of Globo and Televisa is crudely summarized in the quote above, but it stretches beyond diversity of plot lines. Globo has included in its telenovelas the reality of the country, thus grabbing the attention of the majority of Brazilian households by incorporating contemporary social and political issues. During the military regime (1964–85), television became a space in which, even when censored, writers managed to stretch the limits of what was acceptable in the repressive atmosphere of the period, possibly also benefiting from the prevailing view that telenovelas were designed for a female audience. Telenovelas did not break completely with their melodramatic roots but rather incorporated a national voice. They introduced a popular language, using colloquialisms and characters rooted in the daily life of the Brazilian metropolis, not unlike what cinema, theater, and popular music were trying to do. But this process, unlike those of other media, was limited by what was perceived to be the targeted audience's expectations.

In the first 40 years, more than 400 telenovelas were produced by Globo and other networks in Brazil. The telenovelas produced in this period predominantly centered on Rio de Janeiro and dealt with an urban middle-class lifestyle. Beginning in the late 1980s and continuing through the 1990s, as a result of the political *abertura* (opening) that started with the transition of the power from the military to the civilian government, telenovela writers increased the visibility of their social agendas and included national political debates in their narratives. The commercial nature of telenovelas also evolved, increasing the opportunities through which these programs are used to sell not only products targeting housewives, but sports cars, services, and any other consumer products. The melodramatic glue that has maintained their popularity with audiences has evolved and has been modernized. Nevertheless, these melodramas remained loyal to traditional topics such as romantic desire and conflict, social mobility, and the expected happy ending.

GLOBAL PLAYER

In 2005 alone, more than 30 Globo telenovelas were aired in 20 Latin American countries, totaling more than 10,000 programming hours. According to Bernardi, Globo intends to continue strengthening its presence in the Latin American market, and increasing its presence on TV channels throughout the world (Sofley, 2006). About 90 per cent of Globo's exports are telenovelas and mini-series, reaching a value of $30 to $32 million in 1998, while the remaining 10 per cent account for documentaries (Cajueiro, 1998).

As to the pricing of Globo telenovelas in the international market, Bernardi says that

> they change according to the realities of new territories, and their local economies. As with any programming options, prices are closely associated with the advertising investment in a particular client's station, which in turn influences that client's buying power. All this is subject to competitive pressures as well. (*Brazzil Magazine*, 2003)

TV Globo is interested in having a presence in the international market even if it has to make concessions in markets with less capacity to pay higher prices for its telenovelas. Moreover, according to Carlos Castro, director of sales for Televisa International,

> Competition in Latin America is absolutely clear and transparent, as it is in the United States: forming alliances and agreements does not imply being disloyal. It is simply that commercial strategies have changed because times have changed, the audience changes and everything changes. The big players, Televisa, Venevision International, Coral, Tepuy and Globo, they all have a secure and deserved placed in the [telenovela] market. (Carlos Castro, quoted in Herman, 2002)

To break into new markets, such producers and distributors as Televisa, Comarex, Globo, Coral International, Telefe, and Venevision, decided in 2003 to create an association called Asotelenovela (Large and Kenny, 2004). The idea behind Asotelenovela is to promote telenovelas in markets where the genre does not have a presence yet, such as in Japan, the key Asian target for the group. Other markets include countries in Western Europe, particularly Scandinavia.

Ulises Aristides, international sales director of Sistema Brasileiro de Televisão (SBT) argued that, as with many other companies, 'we [at SBT] weren't going to a number of markets because of the language.' SBT, operating since 1983, has began to search for overseas markets only in the last few years. 'We have very good quality material and markets such as Asia are almost virgin territories as far as knowledge of our products is concerned' (Conde, 2001).

The internationalization of Brazilian television, and Globo Network in particular, increased in the 1980s when the import of television programs into Brazil declined (Straubhaar, 1988; 1996) while Brazilian exports of programming increased. Recognizing this new trend, Globo set up an international division to support the export of its telenovelas. In the process of expanding internationally, in 1985 it bought 90 per cent of Telemontecarlo in Italy and, later, in 1992, purchased 15 per cent of Sociedade Independente de Comunicação (SIC), one of the newly created private channels in Portugal (Sousa, 1996). Since the mid-1990s Globo network has increased coproductions with foreign companies, at the same time focusing on successful domestic narratives that will have a greater appeal to foreign markets.

Another of Globo network's concerns is to increase its penetration among the upper classes in the domestic market, an audience traditionally resistant to telenovelas. In *Patria Minha* [My Homeland] Globo dealt with the increasing migration from Brazil, primarily to the United States, due to the persistent economic crises and consequent lack of opportunities for the well-educated upper classes. Since then other telenovelas have used central narratives located in foreign contexts such as Morocco, Japan, France, Argentina, Russia, the Czech Republic, and currently Greece, which are among the reliable consumer markets of Brazilian telenovelas.

In the 2005 hit, *America*, one of the main plots dealt with the increasing presence of illegal immigrants from Brazil in the United States. The US press covered the telenovela with interest, linking the increased apprehension of undocumented Brazilians attempting to cross the Mexico-United States border to the telenovela's popularity (Chu, 2005). Another 2005 telenovela, *Começar de Novo* [A New Beginning], partly funded by Petrobrás, the Brazilian oil company, centered on a Russian oil magnate who discovers he was originally from Brazil. This telenovela presents a positive image of the oil industry as well as a non-judgmental image of Russia and the former Soviet Union (Khalip, 2004). By introducing such cross-cultural themes, Globo is trying to extend its appeal in an increasingly competitive international market. It realized early in its attempts to secure access to foreign markets that it would have to repackage some of its telenovelas. In many instances, local content was too specific for an international audience, many product placement references had to be deleted and, in a few cases, some footage of Brazil was included to increase the visual appeal of the narrative (Filipelli, 2004).

In recent years, Globo and other telenovela producers in Brazil and other Latin American countries, such as Mexico, Argentina, and Colombia, have done more than just sell their telenovelas to other countries. They are also showing these countries, especially in Europe, how to develop their own telenovela industries. In fact, as pointed out by Melo (1995), Sousa (1996), and Matelski (1999), Brazilians are specially keen to sell their telenovela formats (including scripts previously shown in the country, with scene and costume descriptions likely to be molded to particular cultural contexts), and Brazilian telenovela writers are being contracted by other countries to write scripts for local productions, or even for those destined for the international market at large. One such example was the telenovela *Manuela*, written by Manuel Carlos, which was co-produced by an Italian-American company and successfully distributed in the international market (Melo, 1995:9).

Traditionally, Brazilian telenovelas (except for those broadcast directly via satellite by TV Globo International) are dubbed into Spanish before they are aired in the United States and the rest of Spanish-speaking Latin America. *Vale Tudo* [Everything Goes], which was originally produced and broadcast in Brazil by TV Globo in 1988, was the first—and only, so far—Brazilian telenovela to be remade in Spanish (in a co-production with Telemundo) for the United States television market.

Between 2003 and 2005, the number of subscribers to TV Globo International jumped from 500 to 2 million. This is partly due to the fact that Globo started working with different time zones for different countries, motivating Brazilians who live abroad, especially in the United States and Europe, to sign up for the channel (*The Brazilians*, 2005:15E). Many satellite packages also include other Brazilian channels, like Record, among the international selections. Although no subscription data are available, Brazilians living abroad also now have the ability to stream Brazilian programming from Globo Network online through a subscription service. This increased availability, coupled with the growing presence of Brazilians abroad and the strengthening of Globo's position in the international market as a reference point for telenovelas, has guaranteed a certain level of globalization for the Brazilian industry.

Nevertheless, as we hope this chapter has demonstrated, the history of Brazilian telenovelas is far from a clear case of an indigenous product becoming a global commodity. Rather, it can better be seen as the transformation and hybridization of a genre into a product that can appeal to a broad range of consumers both domestically and globally.

NOTES

1. Dias Gomes, an already established playwright when telenovelas became popular, was influential in the development of the telenovela genre in Brazil. Quote from an interview with Dias Gomes conducted in 1990 by Klagsbrunn (Klagsbrunn and Resende, 1991, p. 23, authors' translation).
2. See Rodriguez (1999), for a discussion of the construction of a panamerican audience; Sinclair (1996), for an analysis of the Latin American cultural linguistic market; and La Pastina (1998) for the analysis of one specific case of a media product traveling within and between cultural linguistic markets.
3. For descriptions of communal viewing see Pace, 1993; Penacchioni, 1984.
4. Before closing its doors in the late 1990s, Manchete was owned by the Group Bloch, a family business that publishes magazines (specially *Manchete*) and owns radio stations. Silvio Santos who became a media tycoon due to the popularity of his day-long live Sunday variety show owns SBT.

REFERENCES

Abu-Lughod, L. (1993) 'Finding a place for Islam: Egyptian television serials and national interest', *Public Culture*, 5 (3):493–513.

Abu-Lughod, L. (1995) 'The objects of soap opera: Egyptian television and the cultural politics of modernity', in D.Miller (ed.), *Worlds Apart: Modernity through the Prism of the Local.* London: Routledge.

Allen, R. (1985) *Speaking of Soap Operas.* Chapel Hill: University of North Carolina Press.

Allen, R. (1995) *To Be Continued ... Soap Operas around the World*. New York: Routledge.

Amaral, R. and C.Guimarães (1994) 'Media monopoly in Brazil', *Journal of Communication*, 44 (4):26–38.

Aufderheide, P. (1993) 'Latin American grassroots video: beyond television', *Public Culture*, 5 (3):579–92.

The Brazilians (August 2005): 15E (English edition).

Brazzil Magazine (2003) 'Let's hear it for Brazil's Globo'. May. Accessed on 3 February 2006: http://brazzil.com/2003/html/news/articles/may03/p105may03.htm.

Brown, M.E. (1994) *Soap Opera and Women's Talk: the Pleasure of Resistance*. Thousand Oaks, CA: Sage.

Brunsdon, C. (2000) *The Feminist, the Housewife and the Soap Opera*. Oxford: Oxford University Press.

Cajueiro, M. (1998) 'Globo gets global in new genres', *Variety*, 372 (7):M40.

Cantor, M. and S.Pingree (1983) *The Soap Opera*. Beverly Hills, CA: Sage.

Carugati, A. and M.T.Alvarado (2005) 'The business of love', *WorldScreen.com*. June. Accessed on 27 January 2006: http://www.worldscreen.com/featurescurrent.php?filename=0605novelas.htm.

Chu, H. (2005) 'Rising tide of Brazilians trying to enter United States', *Los Angeles Times*, 5 July. Conde, P. (2001) 'The plot thickens', *Television Asia* (online). January. Accessed 27 January 2006: http://galenet.galegroup.com/servlet/BCRC?asl=telenovelas&ai2=KE&locID=ksstate_uka.

De La Fuente, A.M. (2005) 'Euro buyers lather up latino soaps', *Variety.Com* (online). 16 May. Accessed 7 January 2006: http://www.variety.com/article/VR1117922922?caterogyid=1443&cs=l.

Diase, M. (1996) 'Egyptian television serials, audiences, and the family house, a public health enter-educate serial'. Unpublished dissertation, University of Texas, Austin.

Evans, R. (2005) 'Research: TV Globo', *Media Matters* (online). Accessed 1 February 2006: http://journalism.cf.ac.uk/2005/MAJS/sjore/research1.html.

Fernandes, I. (1994) *Telenovela Brasileira: Memória*. São Paulo: Editora Brasiliense.

Filipelli, R. (2004) Responsible for Globo's exporting during the 1980s and 1990s. Personal interview.

Geraghty, C. (1991) *Women and Soap Opera: a Study of Prime Time Soaps*. Cambridge, MA: Basil Blackwell.

Herman, M. (2002) 'Telling tales', *Television Asia* (online). January-February. Accessed 27 January 2006: http://galenet.galegroup.com/servlet/BCRC?asl=telenovelas&ai2=KE&locID=ksstate_uka.

Hernández, O. (2001) 'A case of global love: telenovelas in transnational times'. PhD dissertation, University of Texas.

Hobson, D. (2003) *Soap Opera*. Malden, MA: Blackwell.

Jaspar, N. (2006) 'Falling in love ... all over again', *WorldScreen.com* (online). Accessed 7 January: http://www.worldscreen.com/featurearchive.php?filename=0603novelas.txt.

Khalip, A. (2004) 'Petrobrás financia novela da globo' [Petrobrás finances Globo telenovela]. Accessed 11 April 2005: http://www.midiaindependente.org/pt/blue/2004/08/289184.shtml.

Klagsbrunn, M. and B.Resende (1991) *Quase catálogo: A telenovela no Rio de Janeiro 1950–1963*. Rio de Janeiro: UFRJ, Escola de Comunicação CIEC.

La Pastina, A. (1998) 'Crossing cultural barriers with children's television programming: the case of Xuxa', *Children's Literature Quarterly Journal*, 23 (3):160–6.

Large K. and J.A.Kenny (2004) 'Latino soaps go global', *Television Business International* (online). Accessed 27 January 2006: http://galenet.galegroup.com/servlet/BCRC?asl=telenovelas&ai2=KE&locID=ksstate_uka.

Lima, V.A. (1988) 'The state, television, and political power in Brazil', *Critical Studies in Mass Communication*, 5:108–28.

Lopez, A.M. (1991) 'The melodrama in Latin America: films, telenovelas, and the currency of a popular form', in M.Landy (ed.), *Imitations of Life: a Reader on Film and Television Melodrama*. Detroit: Wayne State University Press, pp. 596–606.

Lopez, A.M. (1995) 'Our welcomed guests: telenovelas in Latin America', in R.Allen (ed.), *To Be Continued ... Soap Operas around the World*. New York: Routledge.

Martin-Barbero, J. (1993) *Communication, Culture and Hegemony: From the Media to the Mediations*, trans. E.Fox and R.White. Newbury Park, CA: Sage.

Martínez, I. (2005) 'Romancing the globe', *Foreign Policy* (online). November. Accessed 22 November 2005: http://yaleglobal.yale.edu/article.print?id=6442.

Matelski, M.J. (1999) *Soap Operas around the World: Cultural and Serial Realities*. Jefferson, NC: McFarland & Company.

Mattelart, M. and A.Mattelart (1990) *The Carnival of Images: Brazilian Television Fiction*. New York: Bergin & Garvey.

Mattos, S. (1982) *The Brazilian Military and Television*. Austin: The University of Texas Press.

Mazziotti, N. (1993) 'El estado de las investigaciones sobre telenovela lationo-americana', *Revista de ciencias de la informacion*, 8:45–59.

Melo, J.M. (1995) 'Development of the audiovisual industry in Brazil from importer to exporter of television programming', *Canadian Journal of Communications*, 20 (3). Online Issue. Accessed 7 January 2000: http://infor.wlu.ca/-wwwpress/jrls/cjc/BackIssues/20.3/demelo.html.

Meyer, M. (1996) *Folhetim: Uma História*. São Paulo: Companhia das Letras.

Mikevis, D. (2005) 'Brazil's Globo: a soap opera global empire', *Brazzil Magazine* (online). Accessed 30 January 2006: http://www.brazzil.com/content/view/8919/76/.

New York Times (2006) 'Networks see telenovelas as maybe the next salsa', 5 January: C6.

Nordenstreng, K. and T. Varis (1974) 'Television Traffic—A One-Way Street?', *Reports and Papers on Mass Communication,* 70. Paris: UNESCO.

Ortiz, R., S.H.Simoes Borelli and J.M.Ortiz (1988) *Telenovela: História e Producão.* São Paulo: Brasiliense.

Pace, R. (1993) *The Struggle for Amazon Town, Gurupá Revisited.* Boulder, CO: Lynne Rienner Publishers.

Penacchioni, I. (1984) 'The reception of popular television in northeast Brazil', *Media, Culture & Society,* 6:337–341.

Robertson, R. (1995) 'Glocalization: time-space and homogeneity-heterogeneity', in M.Featherstone, S.Lash and R.Robertson (eds), *Global Modernities.* Thousand Oaks, CA: Sage, pp. 25–44.

Rodriguez, A. (1999) *Making Latino News: Race, Language, Class.* Thousand Oaks, CA: Sage.

Sinclair, J. (1996) 'Mexico, Brazil, and the Latin world', in J.Sinclair, E.Jacka and S.Cunningham (eds), *New Patterns in Global Television: Peripheral Vision.* New York: Oxford University Press, pp. 33–66.

Sinclair, J. (2003) 'The Hollywood of Latin America. Miami as a regional center of television trade', *Television & New Media,* 4 (3):211–29.

Singhal, A. and E.M. Rogers (1988) 'Television soap operas for development in India', *Gazette,* 41:109–26.

Singhal, A. and E.M. Rogers (1989a) 'Educating through television', *Populi,* 16 (2): 38–47.

Singhal, A. and E.M. Rogers (1989b) 'Prosocial television for development in India', in R.Rice and C. Atkin (eds), *Public Communication Campaigns.* Newbury Park, CA: Sage.

Sofley, K. (2006) 'Globo brings new telenovelas to Natpe', *C21 Media.net* (online). Accessed 7 January 2006: http://www.c21media.net/news/detail.asp?area=1&article=28216).

Sousa, H. (1996) 'Portuguese television policy in the international context: an analysis of the links with the EU, Brazil and the US'. Accessed 7 January 2006: http://ubista.ubi.pt/-comum/sousahelena-portuguese-television-sydney.html.

Spence, L. (2005) *Watching Daytime Soap Operas: The Power of Pleasure.* Middleton, CT: Wesleyan University Press.

Straubhaar, J. (1988) 'The reflection of the Brazilian political opening in the telenovela 1974–1985', *Studies in Latin American Popular Culture,* 7:59–76.

Straubhaar, J. (1996) 'The electronic media in Brazil', in R.Cole (ed.), *Communication in Latin America: Journalism, Mass Media and Society.* Wilmington, DE: Scholarly Resources Inc. Imprint.

Television Asia (2003) 'As the story goes'. Accessed 27 January 2006: http://www.tvasia.com.sg/new/mag/03janfeb-teleoverview.html.

Television Asia (2005) 'Novela approaches: different novelas for different audiences'. Accessed 27 January 2006: http://galent.galegroup.com/servlet/BCRC?asl=telenovelas&ai2=KE&locID=ksstate.uka.

TVMASNOVELAS (2005) 'Globo shoots in exotic locations'. Accessed 30 January 2006: http://www.onlytelenovelas.com/Only_5_6_1_Telenovelalat.hp.

Variety (1986) 'Telenovela is something else', 142, March 12.

Variety (1997) 'Sudsers scoring sales with Latino neighbors: Televisa S.A.'s multipart expansion strategy in Central and South America', 369, 8 December.

Video Age (2005) 'Telenovelas face mature market and new challenges', *Video age*, December, 25 (7). Accessed 27 January 2006: http://www.videoageinternational.com/2005/articles/Dec/telenovelas.htm.

Wang, K. and A.Singhal (1992) '"Ke Wang", a Chinese television soap opera with a message', *Gazette*, 49:177–92.

ISSUES IN WORLD CINEMA

By Wimal Dissanayake

Dadasaheb Phalke, who is generally regarded by Indian film historians as the father of Indian cinema, relates an interesting anecdote (1970). His *Raja Harishchandra*, released on 3 May 1913, is highlighted by scholars as the first Indian feature film. Phalke tells us that he was inspired to make this film after seeing the movie *The Life of Christ* (USA, 1906) in the America-India Picture Palace in Bombay in 1910. As he was watching the film, he was overwhelmed by both a deep religiosity and an awareness of the potentialities of the art of cinematography. As he watched the life of Christ unfold before his eyes, he thought of the gods Krishna and Ramachandra and wondered how long it would be before Indians would be able to see Indian images of their divinities on screen. In fact, it was not long: three years later Phalke made the first Indian feature film based on the celebrated Indian epic the *Ramayana* (see Rajadhyaksha, Chapter 19). However, what this anecdote—and many similar ones by the early filmmakers in Asia, Latin America, and Africa—points to is a series of binaries that underpin the discourse of cinema in those continents: binaries of Westernization and indigenization, tradition and modernity, the local and the global.

Wimal Dissanayake, "Issues in World Cinema," *World Cinema: Critical Approaches*, ed. John Hill and Pamela Church Gibson, pp. 143-150. Copyright © 2000 by Oxford University Press. Reprinted with permission.

Any discussion of these cinemas, and the trajectories of their development, must necessarily address these crucial issues.

However, it is important that we do not lump these cinemas together indiscriminately as 'non-Western'. It is, of course, true that, geographically, they are from the non-Western world (with 'Western' here referring to North America and Europe), and that they share many interests and preoccupations. However, as the following chapters clearly demonstrate, while they may display commonalities of interest, each of the countries, because of its specific social formations and historical conjunctures, has its own distinctive trajectories of cinematic development and concerns.

In the same way, we must also avoid treating non-Western cinemas as expressive of some unchanging 'essence'. Instead, we must see them as sites of discursive contestations, or representational spaces, in which changing social and cultural meanings are generated and fought over. The discursive boundaries of the various societies that constitute the non-Western world are constantly expanding and cannot be accounted for in essentialist terms. Moreover, the filmmakers and film commentators (critics as well as scholars) who are at the leading edge of development of the film cultures of their respective societies have been exposed to, and in many cases trained in, Western countries so that their self-positioning in relation to the contours of their specific cultures is understandably complex and multifaceted (see Burton-Carvajal, Chapter 25).

The first Indian feature film, *Raja Harischandra* (1913)

The concept of Third Cinema, originally formulated by the Argentinian film directors Fernando Solanasand Octavio Getino (1973) and later expanded by film scholars such as Teshome H. Gabriel (1982), addresses a number of issues related to non-Westem cinemas. Put simply, one can say that First Cinema refers to mainstream Hollywood cinema, and Second Cinema to European 'art' cinema. In distinguishing it from First and Second Cinemas, proponents of Third Cinema see it as the articulation of a new culture and a vehicle of social transformation (see Burton-Carvajal). Paul Willemen (1989), however, suggests how the manifestos laying out the guiding ideas of Third Cinema give the impression that it was developed by Latin Americans for Latin America and that its wider applicability was added as an afterthought. He also argues that there is a danger in the concept of Third Cinema of homogenizing non-Westem cinema and not grappling sufficiently with questions of ethnic and gender divisions as well as the vexed relationship between cinema and nationhood. It is this complicated relationship between nationhood and cinema with which we shall begin.

> We must also avoid treating non-Western cinemas as expressive of some unchanging 'essence'. Instead, we must see them as sites of discursive contestations, or representational spaces, in which changing social and cultural meanings are generated and fought over.

NATIONHOOD AND CINEMA

Nationhood, as with all other forms of identity, revolves around the question of difference, with how the uniqueness of one nation differs from the uniqueness of other comparable nations. Benedict Anderson (1983) suggests that nationhood may be understood as an 'imagined community', and indicates how nationhood is a cultural artefact of a particular kind. It is imagined, because the members of even the smallest nation can never get to know, or even meet, most of their fellow members; yet in the imagination of each the notion of the nation persists. The nation is also imagined as a community because, regardless of the very real inequities and injustices that exist in society, it is always perceived as deep and horizontal comradeship. It is important, however, to note that Anderson employed the term 'imagined' and not 'imaginary'. 'Imaginary' signifies absence, or nothingness, while 'imagined' foregrounds a nice balance between the real and not the real. The critical weakness of Benedict Anderson's formulaton, however, is that it pays scant attention to materialities and underplays the discontinuities of history. It also minimizes the salience of the political character of nationhood and the role which ethnicity and religion have played in the construction of the nation. Any investigation into the ways in which cinema constructs nationhood, therefore, has to consider these thorny issues of ethnic loyalties, religious affinities, and local patriotism. It must also recognize that the nation also contains within itself diverse local narratives of resistance and memory and therefore take into account thefull force of these local and dissenting narratives which are embedded in the larger narrative of the nation.

It is evident that cinema is a very powerful cultural practice and institution which both reflects and inflects the discourse of nationhood. As a result, the concept of national cinema is at the base of many discussions of popular culture in Africa, Asia, the Middle East, and Latin America. It is generally analysed at two interrelated levels: the textual and the industrial (although see Crofts, Chapter 1, for a full discussion of the complexities involved in theorizing the concept of 'national cinema'). The textual level involves a focus upon the distinctiveness of a given cinema—whether it be Indonesian or Nigerian, Mexican or Senegalese—in terms of content, style, and indigenous aesthetics. The industrial level involves a focus upon the relationship between cinema and industry, the nature of film production, distribution, and consumption, and the ways ' in which the ever-present threats from Hollywood are met. However, it should also be noted that the concept of national cinema serves to privilege notions of coherence and unity and to stabilize cultural meanings linked to the perceived uniqueness of a given nation. As I have pointed out (Dissanayake 1994), it is implicated in national myth-making and ideological production and serves to delineate both otherness and legitimate selfhood.

How a nation tells its unifying and legitimizing story about itself to its citizens is crucial in the understanding of nationhood, and after the popularization of cinema as a medium of mass entertainment in Latin America, Asia, the Middle East, and Africa, the role of cinema in this endeavour has come to occupy a significant place (see Rajadhyaksha and Burton-Carvajal, Chapters 19 and 25 below). Benedict Anderson (1983) focused attention on the centrality of print capitalism in giving rise to the idea of the nation and the deep horizontal comradeship it promoted. He observed that newspapers and nationalistic novels were primarily responsible for the creation of a national consciousness. In social circumstances that were antecedent to the establishment of nationstates, newspapers, journals, and fiction served to co-ordinate time and space in a way that enabled the formation of the imagined community that is the nation. In the contemporary world, cinema has assumed the status of a dominant medium of communication, and its role in conjuring up the imagined community among both the literate and illiterate strata of society is both profound and far reaching. David Harvey (1989) suggests that the way in which cinema works to capture the complex and dynamic relationship between temporality and spatiality is not available to other media, and this becomes a significant issue for non-Westem cinemas.

The *topos* of nationhood becomes significant for another reason as well. Cinema in most countries in Africa, the Middle East, Asia, and Latin America is closely linked to the concept and functioning of the nation-state. Questions of economics—production, distribution, and exhibition—and control of content through overt and covert censorship have much to do with this. For most film producers in Latin American, African, and Asian countries that depend on the patronage of local audiences for returns on their investments, the assistance, intervention, and co-ordination of governments become extremely important (in the form of film corporations, training institutes, script boards, censorship panels, national festivals, and the honouring of filmmakers). It is evident, therefore, that the demands of the economics of film industries and the imperatives of the nation-state are interlinked in complex, and at times disconcertingly intrusive, ways.

Speaking in very broad terms, we can divide films made in Asia, Africa, and South America into three main groups: the popular, the artistic, and the experimental (again, see Crofts, Chapter 1, for a further elaboration of these categories). The popular films are commercial by nature and are designed to appeal to the vast mass of moviegoers and to secure the largest profit. The artistic films, while not immune to commercial pressures, are, none the less, driven by 'high art' concerns and tend to be showcased at international film festivals. The experimental films are much smaller in number and much less visible in the filmic landscape; they are committed to the creation of an oppositional cinema characterized by an audacious attempt to interrogate the Establishment and its values. Thus, if we take India as an example, filmmakers such as Raj Kapoor, Manmohan Desai, and Ramesh Sippy represent the popular tradition, directors such as Satyajit Ray and Adoor Gopalakrishnan belong to the 'art' tradition, while some of the work of Kumar Sahani and Mani Kaul may be categorized as experimental (see Rajadhyaksha, Chapter 19). What is of interest in terms of the relationship between the nation-state and cinema is that—again in general terms—while popular cinema generally upholds notions of a unified nation, the artistic cinema tends to offer critiques of the nation-state (and its associated economic, social, political, and cultural discourses and institutions) and the experimental cinema characteristically calls into question the hegemonic project of the nation-state and the privileged vocabularies of national narration. Thus, in a large country like India with its numerous languages and religions, films produced in regional languages like Bengali or Malayalam tend to valorize, directly or obliquely, the regional at the expense of the national, thereby revealing certain fissures and fault lines in the national discourse. The artistic and experimental filmmakers seek to draw attention to the ambiguous unities, silenced voices, emergent and oppositional discourses, that occupy the national space, and thereby instigate a de-totalizing project

For filmmakers in Asia, Africa, and Latin America, the cinematic representation of minorities presents a challenging problem, and this issue is inseparable from the dictates of the nation-state The putatively homogeneous nature of the nation-state and its legitimizing meta-narratives begin to come under scrutiny as filmmakers attempt to articulate the experiences and life-worlds of the minorities, whether they be ethnic, religious, linguistic, or caste, who inhabit the national space. Films that thematize the hardships of minorities create a representational space from where the hegemonic discourse of the state can be usefully subverted, and the idea of social and cultural difference emphasized. Indeed, one can see a wholly understandable tension between the idea of the unitary nation and cultural difference in many works of cinema produced in Asian, Latin American, and African countries. This tension is discernible in some of the works of internationally celebrated film directors like Nagisa Oshima of Japan, as well as in the creations of less well-known filmmakers such as Ji Qingchun (China), Park (Korea), and Euthana Mukdasnit (Thailand).

Artistic and experimental filmmakers seek to draw attention to the ambiguous unities, silenced voices, emergent and oppositional discourses, that occupy the national space, and thereby instigate a de-totalizing project.

Film commentators in Latin America and Africa also display such propensities to rethink issues and repose questions. For example, if we take Mexican cinema, we find that in the past the concept of *mexicanidad* (Mexicanness) was privileged in intellectual and aesthetic discussions, and was perceived as a leading topos guiding Mexican cinema. Distinguished writers, such as the Nobel laureate Octavio Paz, underlined its significance, and both filmmakers and film critics positively valorized it. However, modern commentators of Mexican cinema now highlight how *mexicanidad*, as it was formulated, was élitist, sexist, and class-bound, and privileged the *criollo* over the *mestizo* and the Indians. Through the interrogation of such concepts as 'Japaneseness' and 'Mexicanness' associated with filmic discourse, scholars are emphasizing the need for the reacquisition of subaltern agency and the repossessing of history. The discursive spaces that they are opening up can have profound consequences in examining afresh the cinemas of the non-West.

THE PUBLIC SPHERE

This discussion of the interconnections between cinema and nationhood leads to the importance of cinema in the public sphere. From the very beginning, cinemas in South America, Africa, and Asia were involved in the public sphere, addressing important questions related to tradition, Westernization, democracy, the caste system, and cultural identity. The pioneering work of the German social philosopher Jurgen Habermas (1991) has resulted in the widespread interest in the concept of the public sphere which has helped to foreground issues of democratization, public participation, and oppositionality. Others such as Oskar Negt and Alexander Kluge (1993) have built upon Habermas's work and discussed the ability of cinema to provide a site for the contestation of meaning in an increasingly technologically saturated public sphere, where democratic self-realization and community participation have become much more problematic. The question of the public sphere is particularly important in the case of the nations of Asia, Africa, and Latin America. In many of these countries, cinema has always been perceived as playing a social role and continues to be a significant form of mass communication, even in the face of the censorship which many countries—be it Indonesia or the Philippines or Nigeria—impose.

Many examples of the mutual animation of cinema and the public sphere may be provided. In the 1930s Indian filmmakers addressed the issue of untouchability, which continues to be extremely sensitive. In 1946 Akira Kurosawa made *No Regrets* for *Youth*, which had a profound impact on Japanese society, raising the whole issue of the democratization of society and leaving an indelible mark on later filmmakers such as Oshima, Kei Kumai, and

Kazuo Kuroki. Oshima, in his earlier films, made cinema a vital part of the public sphere by raising issues related to the plight of Korean minorities in Japan, capital punishment, and sexuality. The Indian film director Ritwik Ghatak, in his works, sought to focus on important issues related to the Indian public sphere such as the partitioning of India, the plight of the poor, the predicament of the artists, and the nature of mechanization. Many of the most interesting films made in Argentina after 1983, when the country returned to constitutional democracy, tex-tualize the nature, significance, and urgency of redemocratization and the sweeping-aside of fascistic tendencies. African filmmakers like Idrissa Ouedraogo have sought to make cinema a vital adjunct of the public sphere by raising questions concerning tradition, cultural identity, stereotypes, and misleading Western representations of African society.

However, it is in China where this relationship between cinema and the public sphere can be seen in its most vivid form. The work of the post-1980 group of filmmakers, generally referred to as the Fifth Generation of filmmakers, stirred up a great deal of interest both inside and ouside China (see Reynaud, Part 3, Chapter 20). Many of these films deal with the Cultural Revolution and seek to textualize directly or indirectly the phenomenon of the Cultural Revolution and its effects on the rural population, in particular, through an innovative filmmaking approach characterized by minimal narration, striking camera movements, a stress on spatiality, and disruptive montage. Films such as Chen Kaige's *Yellow Earth* (1984), *King of the Children* (1985), *The Big Parade* (1986), and *Farewell, my Concubine* (1993), Zhang Yimou's *Red Sorghum* (1988) and *To Live* (1994), Tian Zhuangzhuang's *The Horse Thief* (1986) and *The Blue Kite* (1991), to mention but a few titles, all bear testimony to a desire to make cinema an indispensable facet of the public sphere.

INTERTEXTUALLTY

As indicated at the start of this chapter, cinema was an imported art form that quickly became indigenized in the non-Western world. In a similar manner, European-American theories of cinema are impinging ever more strongly on the thought and sensibility of both filmmakers and film critics in Asian, African, and Latin American countnes. The impact of European-American film scholarship on the non-Western world raises some fundamental issues related to comparative film study.

Is it possible to broaden the European-American referents that guide Western film theories so as to accommodate the cinematic experiences of the non-Western world? Do those African, Asian, Middle Eastern, and Latin American intellectuals and film scholars who are vigorously antipathetic to these Western theories subscribe to a merely spurious notion of cultural authenticity and purity? What is the nature of the theoretical space from which Asian, Latin American, and African film scholars and theorists speak? Writing in the context of literature, African born Harvard professor Kwame Anthony Appiah (1992) argues against both the pseudo-universalism of Eurocentric theorizations which pose as universal and a 'nativism' which nostalgically appeals to an apparently 'pure' and 'authentic' indigenous culture. As Appiah points out, while 'nativism' may challenge Western norms, the way in which the contest is framed remains unchanged. 'The Western emperor has ordered the natives to exchange their robes for trousers: their act of defiance is to insist on tailoring them from homespun material. Given their arguments, plainly, the cultural nationalists do not go far enough; they are blind to the fact that their nativist demands inhabit a Western architecture' (1992: 60). These remarks also have a relevance for film theory.

It is clear that Eurocentric paradigms cannot take on the mantle of universal templates or they will hamper a deeper understanding and appreciation of cinemas in the non-Western world (see Ukadike, Chapter 24). During the last fifteen years or so, following a retheorization of such issues as the nature of cinematic representation, the role of ideology in cultural production, and the importance of female subjectivity in cinema, the genre of melodrama, for example, has been critically rehabilitated in Western film studies. However, melodramas produced in Latin America, Africa, and Asia—and the majority of films made in these regions have been melodramas—cannot be judged in terms of Western conceptualizations of melodrama. Melodrama functions differently in different cultural contexts and the melodramatic traditions evolved in these countries, especially in the theatre, have acquired highly distinctive characteristics. For example, in India, film melodramas bear the cultural inscriptions of folk theatre as well as the Parsee theatre of the nineteenth century. Other analytical tools developed by Western film scholars—such as those relating to point of view, the gaze, and textual subjectivity—may also be seen to have limited application. Paul Willemen (1994), for example, has perceptively demonstrated, in relation to the work of the Israeli filmmaker Amos Gitai, how in his cinema it is most decidedly not through point-of-view shots that we are mobilized, butthrough the differences between one point of view and another even within the one shot. The role of the aesthetic inter-texts and cultural contexts, in this respect, are crucial to the understanding of the various non-Western cinemas.

Film is not an isolated art form; it inhabits a common expressive culture fed by tradition, cultural memory, and indigenous modes of symbolic representation.

> It is dear that Eurocentric paradigms cannot take on the mantle of universal templates or they will hamper a deeper understanding and appreciation of cinemas in the non-Western world.

Therefore, films and other arts are mutually implicated in the production of meaning and pleasure, and this deserves to be examined more closely. In most African, Latin American, and Asian countries cinema, from the very beginning, has had a symbiotic relationship with the theatre, and continues to do so. Similarly with painting. The complex ways in which traditional arts inspire modern filmmaking would reward further exploration and are vitally connected to what Paul Willemen refers to as the 'orchestration of meaning' in cinema.

Let us, for example, consider the filmmaker Yasujiro Ozu. In his films, stillness and emptiness play a crucial role in the production of meaning. On the surface, if seen through Western eyes, nothing happens. But at a deeper level of emotional and cultural apprehension, much is going on in those stillnesses and emptinesses. This is, of course, connected with traditional Japanese aesthetics. For example, in Japanese manuals of painting it is remarked that emptiness does not occur until the first ink mark is inscribed on the paper, thereby calling attention to the vital interplay between emptiness and inscriptions as co-producers of meaning. In the same way, African filmmakers have made a conscious attempt to draw on the traditional African arts in filmmaking, especially the art of oral storytelling, and the use of dreams, fantasies, narrative detours, and parallelisms in the films of Ousmane Sembene, Haile Gerima, Souleymane Cissé, and Idrissa Ouedraogo demonstrate this link (see Ukadike, Chapter 24).

The interconnections between cinema and painting in most Asian countries is a fascinating one. Japanese, Chinese, and Korean filmmakers in the past have tapped the rich resources of painting in framing their shots, creating mise-en-scène, and organizing their visual material, and they continue to do so. For example, in the visual style of films such as Chen Kaige's *Yellow Earth*, one can see the impact of Taoism and traditional Chinese paintings of nature. The towering presence of hills and mountains and the diminutive human beings etched against them, the use of a limited range of colours, natural lighting, and the non-perspectival deployment of space, bear testimony to this fact. Similarly, in the work of Ritwik Ghatak, one perceives an attempt to use creatively and innovatively traditional Indian iconography associated with painting in order to communicate a cinematic experience that is anchored in the past but reaching out to the present.

However, we also need to bear in mind that this is not only a question of aesthetics; there is also an ideological and political aspect to it. For example, in *Yellow Earth*, the extreme long shots, the absence of depth, a nd the empty spaces that fill the frame can be read as a critique of the Cultural Revolution and its excesses. The supposedly apolitical visuals inscribed in the massive presence of nature therefore make a political statement. Going beyond this reading, as Rey Chow (1995) points out, we need to examine the film in terms of its material makings and rethink the cognitive value of emptiness and blankness. As she rightly observes, in order to make sense of 'space' the viewer would have to 'view' space from a position whose locality would 'see' non-signifying blankness in relation to the representational presence itself. Hence, in order to grasp the complexities of the enunciative positions and spectatorships that characterize non-Western cinemas, texts—and their inter-texts—must be analysed in terms of ideology and politics as well as artistic apprehension.

Any meaningful discussion of the cinemas of the non-Western world would compel usto confront issues of economics, politics, aesthetics, institutions, technology, and cultural discourse in general. What is the nature of the national film industry? What role do governments play, both positive and negative? How are the cinema industries located at the local and the global? How are they dealing with the hegemony of Hollywood? How do filmmakers seek to construct alternative histories and cultural identities? These, and similar issues that merit closer anlaysis, will be dealt with at length in the specific case-studies that follow. What I have sought to do in this introductory chapter is to raise some salient issues related to the cinemas of the non-Western world. As Paul Willemen (1989) observes, what the outstanding filmmakers from Asia, Africa, and Latin America have done is to start from a recognition of the multilayeredness of their own cultural-historical formations, with each layer being shaped by intricate linkages between local as well as international forces. As a consequence, these filmmakers suggest a way of inhabiting one's culture which is neither myopically nationalist nor evasively cosmopolitan. This is the ideal that stands before the filmmakers of the non-Western world.

> What the outstanding filmmakers from Asia, Africa, and Latin America have done is to start from a recognition of the multilayeredness of their own cultural-historical formations, with each layer being shaped by intricate linkages between local as well as international forces.

BIBLIOGRAPHY

Anderson, Benedict (1983), *Imagined Communities. Reflections on the Origin and Spread of Nationalism* (London: Verso).

Appiah, Kwame Anthony (1992), *In my Father's House: Africa in the Philosophy of Culture* (Oxford: Oxford University Press)

Chow, Rey (1995), *Primitive Passions: Visibility, Ethnography, and Contemporary Chinese Cinema* (New York: Columbia University Press).

Davis, Darrell William (1996). *Picturing Japaneseness: Monumental Style, National Identity, Japanese Films* (New York: Columbia University Press).

Dissanayake, Wimal (ed.) (1994), *Colonialism and Nationalism in Asian Cinema* (Bloomington: Indiana University Press).

Gabriel, Teshome K. (1982), *Third Cinema in the Third World* (Ann Arbor, Mi.: UMI Research Press)

Habermas, Jurgen (1991), *The Structural Transformation of the Public Sphere: An Inquiry into a Category of Bourgeois Society*, trans. Thomas Burger and Fredenck Lawrence (Cambridge, Mass : MIT Press).

Harvey, David (1989), *The Condition of Postmodernity. An Enquiry into the Origins of Cultural Change* (Oxford: Blackwell)

Negt, Oskar, and Alexander Kluge (1993), *Public Sphere and Experience: Towards an Analysis of the Bourgeois and Proletarian Public Sphere* (Minneapolis: University of Minnesota Press).

Phalke: Commemoration Souvenir (1970), (Bombay: Phalke Centenary Celebrations Committee).

Rajadhyaksha, Ashish (1985), 'The Phalke Era: Conflict of Traditional Forms and Modern Techology', *Journal of Arts and Ideas*, nos. 14–15.

Solanas, Fernando E., and Octavio Getino (1973), *Cine: cultura y descolonización* (Buenos Aires: Siglo XXI Argentino Editores).

*Willemen, Paul (ed.) (1989), *Questions oí Third Cinema* (Londorr British Film Institute).

— (1994), *Looks and Frictions: Essays in Cultural Studies and Film Theory* (Bloomington: Indiana University Press).

Part V

DISCONTENTS OF GLOBALISM AND NEW DIRECTIONS

Essays in this section examine problems and discontentment with globalization and also outline the patterns of resistance to globalization that signal new directions and innovative strategies to challenge control and dominance. Stiglitz's essay illustrates a long-standing conviction among International Communication scholars that economic globalization brought about by multinational corporations and supported by IMF and World Bank policies has been unjust to poorer nations. Stiglitz, former Chief Economist of World Bank speaks of this darker side of economic globalization and implicates global financial institutions for imposing unreasonable regulations that resulted in burdens and problems for developing countries beyond their capacity to manage.

Evans describes transnational social movements collectively known as global justice movements as evidence of resistance to neo-liberal or corporate globalization that has proved detrimental to labor, women in poor countries as well as to the environment.

Castells sees an active global public sphere constituted by the global communication infrastructure. He describes a global civil society of NGOs, social movements, and the movement of public opinion formed through diversified media systems and ad hoc mobilizations, such as against the military Junta in Myanmar in October 2007, that constitute this global public sphere. Castells' essay points to new directions and density of International Communication where the space of political decisions will, he suggests, increasingly take on a global dimension.

GLOBALISM'S DISCONTENTS

By Joseph Stiglitz

Few subjects have polarized people throughout the world as much as globalization. Some see it as the way of the future, bringing unprecedented prosperity to everyone, everywhere. Others, symbolized by the Seattle protestors of December 1999, fault globalization as the source of untold problems, from the destruction of native cultures to increasing poverty and immiseration. In this article, I want to sort out the different meanings of globalization. In many countries, globalization has brought huge benefits to a few with few benefits to the many. But in the case of a few countries, it has brought enormous benefit to the many. Why have there been these huge differences in experiences? The answer is that globalization has meant different things in different places.

The countries that have managed globalization on their own, such as those in East Asia, have, by and large, ensured that they reaped huge benefits and that those benefits were equitably shared; they were able substantially to control the terms on which they engaged with the global economy. By contrast, the countries that have, by and large, had globalization managed for them by the International Monetary Fund and other international economic institutions have not done so well. The problem is thus not with globalization but with how it has been managed.

Joseph Stiglitz, "Globalism's Discontents," *The American Prospect*, vol. 13, no. 1. Copyright © 2002 by The American Prospect. Reprinted with permission.

The international financial institutions have pushed a particular ideology—market fundamentalism—that is both bad economics and bad politics; it is based on premises concerning how markets work that do not hold even for developed countries, much less for developing countries. The IMF has pushed these economics policies without a broader vision of society or the role of economics within society. And it has pushed these policies in ways that have undermined emerging democracies.

More generally, globalization itself has been governed in ways that are undemocratic and have been disadvantageous to developing countries, especially the poor within those countries. The Seattle protestors pointed to the absence of democracy and of transparency, the governance of the international economic institutions by and for special corporate and financial interests, and the absence of countervailing democratic checks to ensure that these informal and public institutions serve a general interest. In these complaints, there is more than a grain of truth.

BENEFICIAL GLOBALIZATION

Of the countries of the world, those in East Asia have grown the fastest and done most to reduce poverty. And they have done so, emphatically, via "globalization." Their growth has been based on exports—by taking advantage of the global market for exports and by closing the technology gap. It was not just gaps in capital and other resources that separated the developed from the less-developed countries, but differences in knowledge. East Asian countries took advantage of the "globalization of knowledge" to reduce these disparities. But while some of the countries in the region grew by opening themselves up to multinational companies, others, such as Korea and Taiwan, grew by creating their own enterprises. Here is the key distinction: Each of the most successful globalizing countries determined its own pace of change; each made sure as it grew that the benefits were shared equitably; each rejected the basic tenets of the "Washington Consensus," which argued for a minimalist role for government and rapid privatization and liberalization.

In East Asia, government took an active role in managing the economy. The steel industry that the Korean government created was among the most efficient in the world—performing far better than its private-sector rivals in the United States (which, though private, are constantly turning to the government for protection and for subsidies). Financial markets were highly regulated. My research shows that those regulations promoted growth. It was only when these countries stripped away the regulations, under pressure from the U.S. Treasury and the IMF, that they encountered problems.

During the 1960s, 1970s, and 1980s, the East Asian economies not only grew rapidly but were remarkably stable. Two of the countries most touched by the 1997–1998 economic crisis had had in the preceding three decades not a single year of negative growth; two had only one year—a better performance than the United States or the other wealthy nations that make up the Organization for Economic Cooperation and Development (OECD). The single most important factor leading to the troubles that several of the East Asian countries encountered in the late 1990s—the East Asian crisis—was the rapid liberalization of financial and capital markets. In short, the countries of East Asia benefited from globalization because they made globalization work for them; it was when they succumbed to the pressures from the outside that they ran into problems that were beyond their own capacity to manage well.

Globalization can yield immense benefits. Elsewhere in the developing world, globalization of knowledge has brought improved health, with life spans increasing at a rapid pace. How can one put a price on these benefits of globalization? Globalization has brought still other benefits: Today there is the beginning of a globalized civil society that has begun to succeed with such reforms as the Mine Ban Treaty and debt forgiveness for the poorest highly indebted countries (the Jubilee movement). The globalization protest movement itself would not have been possible without globalization.

THE DARKER SIDE OF GLOBALIZATION

How then could a trend with the power to have so many benefits have produced such opposition? Simply because it has not only failed to live up to its potential but frequently has had very adverse effects. But this forces us to ask, why has it had such adverse effects? The answer can be seen by looking at each of the economic elements of globalization as pursued by the international financial institutions and especially by the IMF.

The most adverse effects have arisen from the liberalization of financial and capital markets—which has posed risks to developing countries without commensurate rewards. The liberalization has left them prey to hot money pouring into the country, an influx that has fueled speculative real-estate booms; just as suddenly, as investor sentiment changes, the money is pulled out, leaving in its wake economic devastation. Early on, the IMF said that these countries were being rightly punished for pursuing bad economic policies. But as the crisis spread from country to country, even those that the IMF had given high marks found themselves ravaged.

The IMF often speaks about the importance of the discipline provided by capital markets. In doing so, it exhibits a certain paternalism, a new form of the old colonial mentality: "We in the establishment, we in the North who run our capital markets, know best. Do what we tell you to do, and you will prosper." The arrogance is offensive, but the objection is more than just to style. The position is highly undemocratic: There is an implied assumption that democracy by itself does not provide sufficient discipline. But if one is to have an external disciplinarian, one should choose a good disciplinarian who knows what is good for growth, who shares one's values. One doesn't want an arbitrary and capricious taskmaster who one moment praises you for your virtues and the next screams at you for being rotten to the core.

But capital markets are just such a fickle taskmaster; even ardent advocates talk about their bouts of irrational exuberance followed by equally irrational pessimism.

LESSONS OF CRISIS

Nowhere was the fickleness more evident than in the last global financial crisis. Historically, most of the disturbances in capital flows into and out of a country are not the result of factors inside the country. Major disturbances arise, rather, from influences outside the country. When Argentina suddenly faced high interest rates in 1998, it wasn't because of what Argentina did but because of what happened in Russia. Argentina cannot be blamed for Russia's crisis.

Small developing countries find it virtually impossible to withstand this volatility. I have described capital-market liberalization with a simple metaphor: Small countries are like small boats. Liberalizing capital markets is like setting them loose on a rough sea. Even if the boats are well captained, even if the boats are sound, they are likely to be hit broadside by a big wave and capsize. But the IMF pushed for the boats to set forth into the roughest parts of the sea before they were seaworthy, with untrained captains and crews, and without life vests. No wonder matters turned out so badly!

To see why it is important to choose a disciplinarian who shares one's values, consider a world in which there were free mobility of skilled labor. Skilled labor would then provide discipline. Today, a country that does not treat capital well will find capital quickly withdrawing; in a world of free labor mobility, if a country did not treat skilled labor well, it too would withdraw. Workers would worry about the quality of their children's education and their family's health care, the quality of their environment and of their own wages and working conditions. They would say to the government: If you fail to provide these essentials, we will move elsewhere. That is a far cry from the kind of discipline that free-flowing capital provides.

The liberalization of capital markets has not brought growth: How can one build factories or create jobs with money that can come in and out of a country overnight? And it gets worse: Prudential behavior requires countries to set aside reserves equal to the amount of short-term lending; so if a firm in a poor country borrows $100 million at, say, 20 percent interest rates short-term from a bank in the United States, the government must set aside a corresponding amount. The reserves are typically held in U.S. Treasury bills—a safe, liquid asset. In effect, the country is borrowing $100 million from the United States and lending $100 million to the United States. But when it borrows, it pays a high interest rate, 20 percent; when it lends, it receives a low interest rate, around 4 percent. This may be great for the United States, but it can hardly help the growth of the poor country. There is also a high *opportunity* cost of the reserves; the money could have been much better spent on building rural roads or constructing schools or health clinics. But instead, the country is, in effect, forced to lend money to the United States.

Thailand illustrates the true ironies of such policies: There, the free market led to investments in empty office buildings, starving other sectors—such as education and transportation—of badly needed resources. Until the IMF and the U.S. Treasury came along, Thailand had restricted bank lending for speculative real estate. The Thais had seen the record: Such lending is an essential part of the boom-bust cycle that has characterized capitalism for 200 years. It wanted to be sure that the scarce capital went to create jobs. But the IMF nixed this intervention in the free market. If the free market said, "Build empty office buildings," so be it! The market knew better than any government bureaucrat who mistakenly might have thought it wiser to build schools or factories.

THE COSTS OF VOLATILITY

Capital-market liberalization is inevitably accompanied by huge volatility, and this volatility impedes growth and increases poverty. It increases the risks of investing in the country, and thus investors demand a risk premium in the form of higher-than-normal profits. Not only is growth not enhanced but poverty is increased through several channels. The high volatility increases the likelihood of recessions—and the poor always bear the brunt of such downturns. Even in developed countries, safety nets are weak or nonexistent among the self-employed and in the rural sector. But these are the dominant sectors in developing countries. Without adequate safety nets, the recessions that follow from capital-market liberalization lead to impoverishment. In the name of imposing budget discipline and reassuring investors, the IMF invariably demands expenditure reductions, which almost inevitably result in cuts in outlays for safety nets that are already threadbare.

But matters are even worse—for under the doctrines of the "discipline of the capital markets," if countries try to tax capital, capital flees. Thus, the IMF doctrines inevitably lead to an increase in tax burdens on the poor and the middle classes. Thus, while IMF bailouts enable the rich to take their money out of the country at more favorable terms (at the overvalued exchange rates), the burden of repaying the loans lies with the workers who remain behind.

The reason that I emphasize capital-market liberalization is that the case against it—and against the IMF's stance in pushing it—is so compelling. It illustrates what can go wrong with globalization. Even economists like Jagdish Bhagwati, strong advocates of free trade, see the folly in liberalizing capital markets. Belatedly, so too has the IMF—at least in its official rhetoric, though less so in its policy stances—but too late for all those countries that have suffered so much from following the IMF's prescriptions.

But while the case for trade liberalization—when properly done—is quite compelling, the way it has been pushed by the IMF has been far more problematic. The basic logic is simple: Trade liberalization is supposed to result in resources moving from inefficient protected sectors to more efficient export sectors. The problem is not only that job destruction comes before the job creation—so that unemployment and poverty result—but that the IMF's "structural adjustment programs" (designed in ways that allegedly would reassure global investors) make job creation almost impossible. For these programs are often accompanied by high interest rates that are often justified by a single-minded focus on inflation. Sometimes that concern is deserved; often, though, it is carried to an extreme. In the United States, we worry that small increases in the interest rate will discourage investment. The IMF has pushed for far higher interest rates in countries with a far less hospitable investment environment. The high interest rates mean that new jobs and enterprises are not created. What happens is that trade liberalization, rather than moving workers from low-productivity jobs to high-productivity ones, moves them from low-productivity jobs to unemployment. Rather than enhanced growth, the effect is increased poverty. To make matters even worse, the unfair trade-liberalization agenda forces poor countries to compete with highly subsidized American and European agriculture.

THE GOVERNANCE OF GLOBALIZATION

As the market economy has matured within countries, there has been increasing recognition of the importance of having rules to govern it. One hundred fifty years ago, in many parts of the world, there was a domestic process that was in some ways analogous to globalization. In the United States, government promoted the formation of the national economy, the building of the railroads, and the development of the telegraph—all of which reduced transportation and communication costs within the United States. As that process occurred, the democratically elected national government provided oversight: supervising and regulating, balancing interests, tempering crises, and limiting adverse consequences of this very large change in economic structure. So, for instance, in 1863 the U.S. government established the first financial-banking regulatory authority—the Office of the Comptroller of Currency—because it was important to have strong national banks, and that requires strong regulation.

The United States, among the least statist of the industrial democracies, adopted other policies. Agriculture, the central industry of the United States in the mid-nineteenth century, was supported by the 1862 Morrill Act, which established research, extension, and teaching programs. That system worked extremely well and is widely credited with playing a central role in the enormous increases in agricultural productivity over the last century and a half. We established an industrial policy for other fledgling industries, including radio and civil aviation. The beginning of the telecommunications industry, with the first telegraph line between Baltimore and Washington, D.C., was funded by the federal government. And it is a tradition that has continued, with the U.S. government's founding of the Internet.

By contrast, in the current process of globalization we have a system of what I call global governance without global government. International institutions like the World Trade Organization, the IMF, the World Bank, and others provide an ad hoc system of global governance, but it is a far cry from global government and lacks democratic accountability. Although it is perhaps better than not having any system of global governance, the system is structured not to serve general interests or assure equitable results. This not only raises issues of whether broader values are given short shrift; it does not even promote growth as much as an alternative might.

GOVERNANCE THROUGH IDEOLOGY

Consider the contrast between how economic decisions are made inside the United States and how they are made in the international economic institutions. In this country, economic decisions within the administration are undertaken largely by the National Economic Council, which includes the secretary of labor, the secretary of commerce, the chairman of the Council of Economic Advisers, the treasury secretary, the assistant attorney general for antitrust, and the U.S. trade representative. The Treasury is only one vote and often gets voted down. All of these officials, of course, are part of an administration that must face Congress and the democratic electorate. But in the international arena, only the voices of the financial community are heard. The IMF reports to the ministers of finance and the governors of the central banks, and one of the important items on its agenda is to make these central banks more independent—and less democratically accountable. It might make little difference if the IMF dealt only with matters of concern to the financial community, such as the clearance of checks; but in fact, its policies affect every aspect of life. It forces countries to have tight monetary and fiscal policies: It evaluates the trade-off between inflation and unemployment, and in that trade-off it always puts far more weight on inflation than on jobs.

The problem with having the rules of the game dictated by the IMF—and thus by the financial community—is not just a question of values (though that is important) but also a question of ideology. The financial community's view of the world predominates—even when there is little evidence in its support. Indeed, beliefs on key issues are held so strongly that theoretical and empirical support of the positions is viewed as hardly necessary.

Recall again the IMF's position on liberalizing capital markets. As noted, the IMF pushed a set of policies that exposed countries to serious risk. One might have thought, given the evidence of the costs, that the IMF could offer plenty of evidence that the policies also did some good. In fact, there was no such evidence; the evidence that was available suggested that there was little if any positive effect on growth. Ideology enabled IMF officials not only to ignore the absence of benefits but also to overlook the evidence of the huge costs imposed on countries.

AN UNFAIR TRADE AGENDA

The trade-liberalization agenda has been set by the North, or more accurately, by special interests in the North. Consequently, a disproportionate part of the gains has accrued to the advanced industrial countries, and in some cases the less-developed countries have actually been worse off. After the last round of trade negotiations, the Uruguay Round that ended in 1994, the World Bank calculated the gains and losses to each of the regions of the world. The United States and Europe gained enormously. But sub-Saharan Africa, the poorest region of the world, lost by about 2 percent because of terms-of-trade effects: The trade negotiations opened their markets to manufactured goods produced by the industrialized countries but did not open up the markets of Europe and the United States to the agricultural goods in which poor countries often have a comparative advantage. Nor did the trade agreements eliminate the subsidies to agriculture that make it so hard for the developing countries to compete.

The U.S. negotiations with China over its membership in the WTO displayed a double standard bordering on the surreal. The U.S. trade representative, the chief negotiator for the United States, began by insisting that China was a developed country. Under WTO rules, developing countries are allowed longer transition periods in which state subsidies and other departures from the WTO strictures are permitted. China certainly wishes it were a developed country, with Western-style per capita incomes. And since China has a lot of "capitas," it's possible to multiply a huge number of people by very small average incomes and conclude that the People's Republic is a big economy. But China is not only a developing economy; it is a low-income developing country. Yet the United States insisted that China be treated like a developed country! China went along with the fiction; the negotiations dragged on so long that China got some extra time to adjust. But the true hypocrisy was shown when U.S. negotiators asked, in effect, for developing-country status for the United States to get extra time to shelter the American textile industry.

Trade negotiations in the service industries also illustrate the unlevel nature of the playing field. Which service industries did the United States say were very important? Financial services—industries in which Wall Street has a comparative advantage. Construction industries and maritime services were not on the agenda, because the developing countries would have a comparative advantage in these sectors.

Consider also intellectual-property rights, which are important if innovators are to have incentives to innovate (though many of the corporate advocates of intellectual property exaggerate its importance and fail to note that much of the most important research, as in basic science and mathematics, is not patentable). Intellectual-property rights, such as patents and trademarks, need to balance the interests of producers with those of users—not only users in developing countries, but researchers in developed countries. If we underprice the profitability of innovation to the inventor, we deter invention. If we overprice its cost to the research community and the end user, we retard its diffusion and beneficial effects on living standards.

In the final stages of the Uruguay negotiations, both the White House Office of Science and Technology Policy and the Council of Economic Advisers worried that we had not got the balance right—that the agreement put producers' interests over users'. We worried that, with this imbalance, the rate of progress and innovation might actually be impeded. After all, knowledge is the most important input into research, and overly strong intellectual-property rights can, in effect, increase the price of this input. We were also concerned about the consequences of denying lifesaving medicines to the poor. This issue subsequently gained international attention in the context of the provision of AIDS medicines in South Africa [see "Medicine as a Luxury" by Merrill Goozner, on page A7]. The international outrage forced the drug companies to back down—and it appears that, going forward, the most adverse consequences will be circumscribed. But it is worth noting that initially, even the Democratic U.S. administration supported the pharmaceutical companies.

What we were not fully aware of was another danger—what has come to be called "biopiracy," which involves international drug companies patenting traditional medicines. Not only do they seek to make money from "resources" and knowledge that rightfully belong to the developing countries, but in doing so they squelch domestic firms who long provided these traditional medicines. While it is not clear whether these patents would hold up in court if they were effectively challenged, it is clear that the less-developed countries may not have the legal and financial resources required to mount such a challenge. The issue has become the source of enormous emotional, and potentially economic, concern throughout the developing world. This fall, while I was in Ecuador visiting a village in the high Andes, the Indian mayor railed against how globalization had led to biopiracy.

GLOBALIZATION AND SEPTEMBER 11

September 11 brought home a still darker side of globalization—it provided a global arena for terrorists. But the ensuing events and discussions highlighted broader aspects of the globalization debate. It made clear how untenable American unilateralist positions were. President Bush, who had unilaterally rejected the international agreement to address one of the long-term global risks perceived by countries around the world—global warming, in which the United States is the largest culprit—called for a global alliance against terrorism. The administration realized that success would require concerted action by all.

One of the ways to fight terrorists, Washington soon discovered, was to cut off their sources of funding. Ever since the East Asian crisis, global attention had focused on the secretive offshore banking centers. Discussions following that crisis focused on the importance of good information—transparency, or openness—but this was intended for the developing countries. As international discussions turned to the lack of transparency shown by the IMF and the offshore banking centers, the U.S. Treasury changed its tune. It is not because these secretive banking havens provide better services than those provided by banks in New York or London that billions have been put there; the secrecy serves a variety of nefarious purposes—including avoiding taxation and money laundering. These institutions could be shut down overnight—or forced to comply with international norms—if the United States and the other leading countries wanted. They continue to exist because they serve the interests of the financial community and the wealthy. Their continuing existence is no accident. Indeed, the OECD drafted an agreement to limit their scope—and before September 11, the Bush administration unilaterally walked away from this agreement too. How foolish this looks now in retrospect! Had it been embraced, we would have been further along the road to controlling the flow of money into the hands of the terrorists.

There is one more aspect to the aftermath of September 11 worth noting here. The United States was already in recession, but the attack made matters worse. It used to be said that when the United States sneezed, Mexico caught a cold. With globalization, when the United States sneezes, much of the rest of the world risks catching pneumonia. And the United States now has a bad case of the flu. With globalization, mismanaged macroeconomic policy in the United States—the failure to design an effective stimulus package—has global consequences. But around the world, anger at the traditional IMF policies is growing. The developing countries are saying to the industrialized nations: "When you face a slowdown, you follow the precepts that we are all taught in our economic courses: You adopt expansionary monetary and fiscal policies. But when we face a slowdown, you insist on contractionary policies. For you, deficits are okay; for us, they are impermissible—even if we can raise the funds through 'selling forward,' say, some natural resources." A heightened sense of inequity prevails, partly because the consequences of maintaining contractionary policies are so great.

GLOBAL SOCIAL JUSTICE

Today, in much of the developing world, globalization is being questioned. For instance, in Latin America, after a short burst of growth in the early 1990s, stagnation and recession have set in. The growth was not sustained—some might say, was not sustainable. Indeed, at this juncture, the growth record of the so-called post-reform era looks no better, and in some countries much worse, than in the widely criticized import-substitution period of the 1950s and 1960s when Latin countries tried to industrialize by discouraging imports. Indeed, reform critics point out that the burst of growth in the early 1990s was little more than a "catch-up" that did not even make up for the lost decade of the 1980s.

Throughout the region, people are asking: "Has reform failed or has globalization failed?" The distinction is perhaps artificial, for globalization was at the center of the reforms. Even in those countries that have managed to grow, such as Mexico, the benefits have accrued largely to the upper 30 percent and have been even more concentrated in the top 10 percent. Those at the bottom have gained little; many are even worse off. The reforms have exposed countries to greater risk, and the risks have been borne disproportionately by those least able to cope with them. Just as in many countries where the pacing and sequencing of reforms has resulted in job destruction outmatching job creation, so too has the exposure to risk outmatched the ability to create institutions for coping with risk, including effective safety nets.

In this bleak landscape, there are some positive signs. Those in the North have become more aware of the inequities of the global economic architecture. The agreement at Doha to hold a new round of trade negotiations—the "Development Round"—promises to rectify some of the imbalances of the past. There has been a marked change in the rhetoric of the international economic institutions—at least they talk about poverty. At the World Bank, there have been some real reforms; there has been some progress in translating the rhetoric into reality—in ensuring that the voices of the poor are heard and the concerns of the developing countries are listened to. But elsewhere, there is often a gap between the rhetoric and the reality. Serious reforms in governance, in who makes decisions and how they are made, are not on the table. If one of the problems at the IMF has been that the ideology, interests, and perspectives of the financial community in the advanced industrialized countries have been given disproportionate weight (in matters whose effects go well beyond finance), then the prospects for success in the current discussions of reform, in which the same parties continue to predominate, are bleak. They are more likely to result in slight changes in the shape of the table, not changes in who is at the table or what is on the agenda.

September 11 has resulted in a global alliance against terrorism. What we now need is not just an alliance against evil, but an alliance for something positive—a global alliance for reducing poverty and for creating a better environment, an alliance for creating a global society with more social justice.

Joseph E. Stiglitz, former chief economist at the World Bank and chairman of the Council of Economic Advisers under President Clinton, was recently awarded the Nobel Prize in Economic Science. He teaches economics at Columbia University.

COUNTERHEGEMONIC GLOBALIZATION

Transnational Social Movements in the Contemporary Political Economy

By Peter Evans

When people invoke "globalization," they usually mean the prevailing system of transnational domination, which is more accurately called "neoliberal globalization," "corporate globalization," or perhaps "neoliberal, corporate-dominated globalization." Sometimes they are referring to a more generic process—the shrinking of space and increased permeability of borders that result from falling costs of transportation and revolutionary changes in technologies of communication. Often the two are conflated.

Implicit in much of current discourse on globalization is the idea that the particular system of transnational domination that we experience today is the "natural" (indeed inevitable) consequence of exogenously determined generic changes in the means of transportation and communication. A growing body of social science literature and activist argumentation challenges this assumption. Arguing instead that the growth of transnational connections can potentially be harnessed to the construction of more equitable distributions of wealth and power and more socially and ecologically sustainable communities, this literature and argumentation raises the possibility of what I would like to call "counterhegemonic globalization." Activists pursuing this perspective have created a multifaceted set of transnational networks and ideological

Peter Evans, "Counterhegemonic Globalization: Transnational Social Movements in the Contemporary Political Economy," *The Handbook of Political Sociology: States, Civil Societies and Globalization*, pp. 655, 658-660, 662-668. Copyright © 2005 by Cambridge University Press. Reprinted with permission.

frames that stand in opposition to contemporary neoliberal globalization. Collectively they are referred to as the "global justice movement." For activists and theorists alike, these movements have become one of the most promising political antidotes to a system of domination that is increasingly seen as effectual only in its ability to maintain itself in power.

Although the growth of membership and political clout of transnational social movements is hard to measure, the burgeoning of their formal organizational reflections—transnational NGOs—is well-documented. Their numbers have doubled between 1973 and 1983 and doubled again between 1983 and 1993. Perhaps even more important than their quantitative growth has been their ability to seize oppositional imaginations. From the iconic images of Seattle to the universal diffusion of the World Social Forum's vision that "another world is possible," the cultural and ideological impact of these movements has begun to rival that of their corporate adversaries. [...]

THE NEW ORGANIZATIONAL FOUNDATIONS OF COUNTERHEGEMONIC GLOBALIZATION

Here I will focus on three broad families of transnational social movements aimed at counterhegemonic globalization: labor movements, women's movements, and environmental movements. Each of these movements confronts the dilemmas of using transnational networks to magnify the power of local movements without redefining local interests, of transcending the North–South divide, and of leveraging existing structures of global power without becoming complicit in them. Looking at the three movements together is useful because it highlights the ways in which surmounting these challenges might produce common strategies and possibilities for alliances among them. [...]

It is only a partial caricature to propose that the origins of the World Social Forum, which now arguably represents the largest single agglomeration of South-based organizations and activists, began as a sort of joint venture between ATTAC and the Brazilian Workers Party (Partido dos Trabalhadores or PT). Because the founding vision of the PT's organizers was of a classic Marxist socialist mobilizational party, the party's involvement in the World Social Forum is further confirmation of the extent to which "counterhegemonic globalization" has its roots in both quotidian struggles for dignity and economic security in the workplace and classic agendas of social protection in which the machinery of the nation-state is heavily implicated.

Even unsystematic participant observation of the meetings of the World Social Forum in Porto Alegre, Brazil confirms this hypothesis. The fact that the Workers Party controls the municipal administration of a major city and has (until the 2002 elections) controlled the state government as well has been essential to enabling the infrastructural investments that make a global meeting of thousands of participants and hundreds of oppositional groups from around the globe possible. At the same time, in part because of Workers Party sponsorship, both local and transnational trade unions play a major role in the WSF.

All of this suggests that counterhegemonic globalization is not as "postmodern" as its adherents (and detractors) sometimes argue. To the contrary, rescuing traditional social democratic agendas of social protection, which are otherwise in danger of disappearing below the tide of neoliberal globalization, is a significant part of the agenda of both ATTAC and the World Social Forum. At the same time, it would be a mistake to dismiss counterhegemonic globalization as simply "old wine in new bottles." [...]

LABOR AS A GLOBAL SOCIAL MOVEMENT

Emblematic of the contemporary global neoliberal regime is the effort to reconstruct employment as something closer to a spot market in which labor is bought and sold with only the most minimal expectations regarding a broader employment relationship. Around the globe—from Mumbai to Johannesburg, Shanghai to the Silicon Valley—jobs are being informalized, outsourced, and generally divorced from anything that might be considered a social contract between employer and employee.

Precisely because the attack on the idea of labor as a social contract is generalized across all regions of the world, it creates a powerful basis for generating global labor solidarity. I illustrate the point with two examples: the emerging relations of effective mutual support that join metalworkers in Brazil and Germany and the successful leveraging of transnational solidarity by the International Brotherhood of Teamsters (IBT) in the 1997 UPS strike. In addition to demonstrating again that the "geography of jobs" perspective cannot explain transnational relations among labor movements, these cases also further illustrate how the corporate structures that form the carapace of the global economy contain political opportunities as well as threats.

The long-term collaboration between IG Metal in Germany and the Brazilian Metalworkers affiliated with CUT (Central Unica dos Trabalhadores) provides a good example. In 2001, when IG Metal was starting its spring offensive in Germany, the members of the Brazilian Metalworkers union (CUT) working for Daimler-Chrysler sent their German counterparts a note affirming that they would not accept any increased work designed to replace lost production in Germany. This action grows out of a long-term alliance between the two unions that exploits transnational corporate organizational structures for counterhegemonic purposes and has proven to be of practical value to the Brazilian autoworkers in their struggle to maintain some semblance of a social contract in their employment relations. For example, in the previous year when workers at Volkswagen's biggest factory in Brazil went on strike trying to reverse job cuts, Luiz Marinho, president of CUT VW, was able to go to VW's world headquarters and negotiate directly with management there, bypassing the management of the Brazilian subsidiary, and producing an agreement that restored the jobs.

The successful 1997 UPS strike offers a North–North example of how transnational alliances can be built around the idea of social contract. One element in the victory was a very effective global strategy, one that took advantage of previously underexploited strengths in their own global organization—the International Transport Workers Federation (ITF). Through the ITF, a World Council of UPS unions was created—which decided to mount a "World Action Day" in 150 job actions or demonstrations around the world. A number of European unions took action in support of the US strikers.

Why were the Europeans so willing to take risks for the sake of solidarity with the IBT in the United States? The answer was summarized in one of the ITF's leaflets. "UPS: importing misery from America." UPS was seen as representing the intrusion of the "American Model" of aggressive antiunion behavior, coupled with the expansion of part-time and temporary jobs with low pay and benefits and the use of subcontracting. The Europeans also knew that they had a much better chance of reining in UPS operating in concert with the 185,000 unionized UPS workers in the United States than they would ever have alone. Solidarity made sense and the logic of competition based on the geography of jobs made no sense.

Although defending the idea of the employment relation as a social contract is a project that will draw broad sympathy, the actual organizational efforts remain largely internal to organized labor. Other global social movements may be ideologically supportive, but not likely to be mobilized. Given the fact that those who enjoy the privilege of a formal employment relationship with union representation is a shrinking minority of the global population, the success of labor as a global social movement depends on being able to complement "social contract" and "basic rights" campaigns with other strategies that have the potential of generating broad alliances with a range of other social movements. [...]

Building a Feminist Movement Without Borders

While the transnational women's movement also has a long history, global neoliberalism has brought issues of gender to the forefront of transnational social movement organizations in a dramatic way. Until there has been a revolutionary transformation of gender roles, the disadvantages of allocating resources purely on the basis of market logic will fall particularly harshly on women. The UNDP talks of a global "care deficit," pointing out that women spend most of their working hours on unpaid care work and adding that "the market gives almost no rewards for care." Others have pointed out the extent to which "structural adjustment" and other neo-liberal strategies for global governance contain a built-in, systematic gender bias. Consequently, it is almost impossible to imagine a movement for counterhegemonic globalization in which a transnational women's movement did not play a leading role.

At first glance, women's organizations have an advantage over transnational labor movements in that they do not have to transcend a zero-sum logic equivalent to that of the "geography of jobs" which would put the gendered interests of women in one region in conflict with those in another region. Perhaps for that reason, the transnational women's movement has been in the vanguard of transnational social movements in the attention that it has devoted to struggles over how to bridge the cultural and political aspects of the North–South divide and how to avoid the potential dangers of difference-erasing universalist agendas.

Like the labor movement, the women's movement's ideological foundations are rooted in a discourse of "human rights," but transnational feminism, much more than in the labor movement, has wrestled with the contradictions of building politics around the universalistic language of rights. Although no one can ignore the ways in which demanding recognition that "women's rights are human rights" has helped empower oppressed and abused women across an incredible gamut of geographic, cultural, and class locations, any earlier naïve assumptions that there was a single "one size fits all" global feminist agenda have been replaced by appreciation that the goal is much more complex.

On the one hand, the adoption of CEDAW (Convention on the Elimination of All Forms of Discrimination Against Women) by the UN might be considered the normative equivalent of the environmental movement's victories in the Montreal Accord to limit CFCs and the Kyoto Accord on global warming. On the other hand, critical feminists have examined UN activities like the 1995 Beijing World Conference on Women and accused them of perpetuating colonialist power relations under the guise of transnational unity. Mohanty summarizes the conundrum nicely: "The challenge is to see how differences allow us to explain the connections and border crossings better and more accurately, how specifying difference allows us to theorize universal concerns more fully." [...]

The numerically predominant situation of women in the global economy is one of precarious participation in the "informal economy"—a vast arena in which the traditional organizational tools of the transnational labor movement are least likely to be effective. Women in the informal sector experience the insecurity and lack of "social contract" that appear to be the neoliberal destiny of all but a small minority of the workforce, regardless of gender. If members of established transnational unions like the metalworkers are to succeed in building general political support for defending the "social contract" aspects of their employment relation, their struggles must be combined with an equally aggressive effort to expand the idea of the social contract into the informal sector. Insofar as the women's movement's campaigns around livelihood issues have focused particularly on the informal sector, it might be considered the vanguard of the labor movement as well as a leading strand in the movement for counterhegemonic globalization more generally.

One response to the challenge of the informal sector has been the diffusion of the "Self-employed Women's Association" (SEWA) as an organizational form, starting in India and spreading to South Africa, Turkey, and other countries in Latin America, Southeast Asia, and Africa, and eventually creating incipient international networks such as "Homenet" and "Streetnet." This is not only a novel form of labor organization. Because the archetypal site of informal sector employment is among the least-privileged women of the global South, it is simultaneously an organizational form that should help build the kind of "feminism without borders" that Mohanty argues is necessary to transcend the contradictions that have divided the international women's movement in the past.

Global and Local Environmentalism

Environmental stewardship is almost by definition a collective issue and therefore an issue that should lend itself to collective mobilization. Even neoclassical economic theory recognizes that environmental degradation is an externality that markets may not resolve, especially if the externalities are split across national political jurisdictions. Thus, environmental movements have advantages, both relative to mobilization around labor issues, which neoliberal ideology strongly claims must be resolved through market logic if welfare is to be maximized, and relative to women's movements, which are still bedeviled by claims that these issues are "private" and therefore not a appropriate target for collective political action (especially note collective political action that spills across national boundaries).

The obstacles to trying to build a global environmental movement are equally obvious. To begin with, there is the formidable gap that separates the South's "environmentalism of the poor," in which sustainability means above all else sustaining the ability of resource-dependent local communities to extract livelihoods from their natural surroundings, and the "conservationist" agenda of traditional Northern environmental groups, which favors the preservation of fauna and flora without much regard for how this conservation impacts the livelihoods of surrounding communities. The North–South divide in the global environmental movement may be less susceptible to being portrayed as "zero-sum" than in the "geography of jobs" perspective on the labor movement, but the logic of division appears more difficult to surmount than in the case of transnational feminism.

Even aside from the difficulties of superseding North–South divisions, integrating local and global concerns appears more daunting in the environmental arena. Some issues—such as global warming and the ozone layer—seem intrinsically global, whereas the politics of others, such as the health consequences of toxic dumps, can be intensely local. The challenges of building, a global organization that effectively integrates locally focused activities with global campaigns would seem particularly challenging in the case of the environmental movement.

Despite the structural challenges it faces, the global environmental movement is usually considered among the most successful of the transnational social movements. How do we explain the relative success of transnational movements with environmental agendas? The first point to be made is how strikingly parallel the political assets of the global environmental movement are to those of the labor and women's movements, despite the obvious differences among them. This is true both of ideological resources and institutional ones. Once again, we see a conterhegemonic movement leveraging the ideas and organizational structures implanted by hegemonic globalization.

As in the case of the labor and women's movements, political clout depends on the global diffusion of a universalistic ideology affirming the value of the movement's agenda. As the labor and women's movements are able to leverage the ideological power of abstract concepts like "human rights" and "democracy," environmentalists can claim an impeccable universal agenda of "saving the planet" and invoke "scientific analysis" as validating their positions. As in the other two cases, these ideological resources are worth little without organizational structures that can exploit them and without complementary mobilization around quotidian interests. Nonetheless, the point is that once again, hegemonic ideological propositions are not simply instruments of domination; they are also a "toolkit" that can be used in potentially powerful ways for "subversive" ends.

The possibility of using governance structures that are part of hegemonic globalization also applies in the case of the environmental movement. Even more than in the case of the women's movement, the UN system has proved an extremely valuable institutional resource. As in the case of the women's movement, global conferences organized by the UN have played a crucial role both in helping to solidify transnational networks and to promote and diffuse discursive positions. [...]

The intensive, widespread, decades-old debate over how to make sure that the women's movement fully reflects the perspectives and interests of its largest constituency (disprivileged women in the global South) rather than its most powerful members (elite women in the global North) appears to have a harder time getting traction in the transnational environmental movement.

The fact that the "scientific analysis" paradigm provides significant advantage to environmentalists in battles against degradation by corporate (and state) polluters may become a disadvantage when it comes to engaging in internal debates over competing visions within the transnational environmental movement, making it easier for Northern activists to assume that the solutions to environmental issues in the South can be "objectively" defined from afar rather than having to emerge out of debate and discussion with those immediately involved. None of this is to suggest that the environmental movement is doomed to go astray or end up fragmented. The point is that just as there is no "natural logic" that dictates the inevitability of a corporate neoliberal trajectory for globalization, even the most successful counterhegemonic movements have no functionalist guardian angels that will prevent them from undercutting their own potential. [...]

THE NEW PUBLIC SPHERE

Global Civil Society, Communication Networks, and Global Governance

By Manuel Castells

THE PUBLIC SPHERE AND THE CONSTITUTION OF SOCIETY

Between the state and society lies the public sphere, "a network for communicating information and points of view" (Habermas 1996, 360). The public sphere is an essential component of sociopolitical organization because it is the space where people come together as citizens and articulate their autonomous views to influence the political institutions of society. Civil society is the organized expression of these views; and the relationship between the state and civil society is the cornerstone of democracy. Without an effective civil society capable of structuring and channeling citizen debates over diverse ideas and conflicting interests, the state drifts away from its subjects. The state's interaction with its citizenry is reduced to election periods largely shaped by political marketing and special interest groups and characterized by choice within a narrow spectrum of political option.

The material expression of the public sphere varies with context, history, and technology, but in its current practice, it is certainly different from the ideal type of eighteenth-century bourgeois public sphere around which Habermas (1989) formulated his theory. Physical space—particularly public space in cities as well as

Manuel Castells, "The New Public Sphere: Global Civil Society, Communication Networks, and Global Governance," *The Annals of the American Academy of Political and Social Science*, vol. 616, no. 1, pp. 78-93. Copyright © 2008 by SAGE Publications. Reprinted with permission.

universities—cultural institutions, and informal networks of public opinion formation have always been important elements in shaping the development of the public sphere (Low and Smith 2006). And of course, as John Thompson (2000) has argued, media have become the major component of the public sphere in the industrial society. Furthermore, if communication networks of any kind form the public sphere, then our society, the network society (Castells 1996, 2004a), organizes its public sphere, more than any other historical form of organization, on the basis of media communication networks (Lull 2007; Cardoso 2006; Chester 2007). In the digital era, this includes the diversity of both the mass media and Internet and wireless communication networks (McChesney 2007).

However, if the concept of the public sphere has heuristic value, it is because it is inseparable from two other key dimensions of the institutional construction of modern societies: civil society and the state. The public sphere is not just the media or the sociospatial sites of public interaction. It is the cultural /informational repository of the ideas and projects that feed public debate. It is through the public sphere that diverse forms of civil society enact this public debate, ultimately influencing the decisions of the state (Stewart 2001). On the other hand, the political institutions of society set the constitutional rules by which the debate is kept orderly and organizationally productive. It is the interaction between citizens, civil society, and the state, communicating through the public sphere, that ensures that the balance between stability and social change is maintained in the conduct of public affairs. If citizens, civil society, or the state fail to fulfill the demands of this interaction, or if the channels of communication between two or more of the key components of the process are blocked, the whole system of representation and decision making comes to a stalemate. A crisis of legitimacy follows (Habermas 1976) because citizens do not recognize themselves in the institutions of society. This leads to a crisis of authority, which ultimately leads to a redefinition of power relationships embodied in the state (Sassen 2006).

As Habermas (1976) himself acknowledged, his theorization of democracy was in fact an idealized situation that never survived capitalism's penetration of the state. But the terms of the political equation he proposed remain a useful intellectual construct—a way of representing the contradictory relationships between the conflictive interests of social actors, the social construction of cultural meaning, and the institutions of the state. The notion of the public sphere as a neutral space for the production of meaning runs against all historical evidence (Mann 1986, 1993). But we can still emphasize the critical role of the cultural arena in which representations and opinions of society are formed, de-formed, and re-formed to provide the ideational materials that construct the basis upon which politics and policies operate (Giddens 1979).

Therefore, the issue that I would like to bring to the forefront of this analysis is that sociopolitical forms and processes are built upon cultural materials and that these materials are either unilaterally produced by political institutions as an expression of domination or, alternatively, are coproduced within the public sphere by individuals, interest groups, civic associations of various kinds (the civil society), and the state. How this public sphere is constituted and how it operates largely defines the structure and dynamics of any given polity.

Furthermore, it can be argued that there is a public sphere in the international arena (Volkmer 2003). It exists within the political/institutional space that is not subject to any particular sovereign power but, instead, is shaped by the variable geometry of relationships between states and global nonstate actors (Guidry, Kennedy, and Zald 2000). It is widely recognized that a variety of social interests express themselves in this international arena: multinational business, world religions, cultural creators, public intellectuals, and self-defined global cosmopolitans (Beck 2006). There is also a global civil society (Kaldor 2003), as I will try to argue below, and ad hoc forms of global governance enacted by international, conational, and supranational political institutions (Nye and Donahue 2000; Keohane 2002). For all these actors and institutions to interact in a nondisruptive manner, the same kind of common ideational ground that developed in the national public sphere should emerge. Otherwise, codestruction substitutes for cooperation, and sheer domination takes precedence over governance. However, the forms and processes of construction of the international public sphere are far from clear. This is because a number of simultaneous crises have blurred the relationships between national public spheres and the state, between states and civil society, between states and their citizens, and between the states themselves (Bauman 1999; Caputo 2004; Arsenault 2007). The crisis of the national public sphere makes the emergence of an international public sphere particularly relevant. Without a flourishing international public sphere, the global sociopolitical order becomes defined by the realpolitik of nation-states that cling to the illusion of sovereignty despite the realities wrought by globalization (Held 2004).

GLOBALIZATION AND THE NATION-STATE

We live in a world marked by globalization (Held et al. 1999; Giddens and Hutton 2000; Held and McGrew 2007). Globalization is the process that constitutes a social system with the capacity to work as a unit on a planetary scale in real or chosen time. *Capacity* refers to technological capacity, institutional capacity, and organizational capacity. New information and communication technologies, including rapid long-distance transportation and computer networks, allow global networks to selectively connect anyone and anything throughout the world. *Institutional capacity* refers to deregulation, liberalization, and privatization of the rules and procedures used by a nation-state to keep control over the activities within its territory. *Organizational capacity* refers to the ability to use networking as the flexible, interactive, borderless form of structuration of whatever activity in whatever domain. Not everything or everyone is globalized, but the global networks that structure the planet affect everything and everyone. This is because all the core economic, communicative, and cultural activities are globalized. That is, they are dependent on strategic nodes connected around the world. These include global financial markets; global production and distribution of goods and services; international trade; global networks of science and technology; a global skilled labor force; selective global integration of labor markets by migration of labor and direct foreign investment; global media; global interactive networks of communication, primarily the Internet, but also dedicated computer networks; and global cultures associated with the growth of diverse global cultural industries. Not everyone is globalized: networks connect and disconnect at the same time. They connect everything that is valuable, or that which could become valuable, according to the values programmed in the networks. They bypass and exclude anything or anyone that does not add value to the network and/or disorganizes the efficient processing of the network's programs. The social, economic, and cultural geography of our world follows the variable geometry of the global networks that embody the logic of multidimensional globalization (Beck 2000; Price 2002).

Furthermore, a number of issues faced by humankind are global in their manifestations and in their treatment (Jacquet, Pisani-Ferry, and Tubiana 2002). Among these issues are the management of the environment as a planetary issue characterized by the damage caused by unsustainable development (e.g., global warming) and the need to counter this deterioration with a global, long-term conservation strategy (Grundmann 2001); the globalization of human rights and the emergence of the issue of social justice for the planet at large (Forsythe 2000); and global security as a shared problem, including the proliferation of weapons of mass destruction, global terrorism, and the practice of the politics of fear under the pretext of fighting terrorism (Nye 2002).

Overall, as Ulrich Beck (2006) has analyzed in his book *Power in the Global Age*, the critical issues conditioning everyday life for people and their governments in every country are largely produced and shaped by globally interdependent processes that move beyond the realm of ostensibly sovereign state territories. In Beck's formulation, the meta-power of global business challenges the power of the state in the global age, and "accordingly, the state can no longer be seen as a pre-given political unit" (p. 51). State power is also undermined by the counterpower strategies of the global civil society that seek a redefinition of the global system. Thus,

> What we are witnessing in the global age is not the end of politics but rather its migration elsewhere. ... The structure of opportunities for political action is no longer defined by the national/international dualism but is now located in the "global" arena. Global politics have turned into global domestic politics, which rob national politics of their boundaries and foundations. (p. 249)

The growing gap between the space where the issues arise (global) and the space where the issues are managed (the nation-state) is at the source of four distinct, but interrelated, political crises that affect the institutions of governance:

1. *Crisis of efficiency:* Problems cannot be adequately managed (e.g., major environmental issues, such as global warming, regulation of financial markets, or counterterrorism intelligence; Nye and Donahue 2000; Soros 2006).

2. *Crisis of legitimacy:* Political representation based on democracy in the nation-state becomes simply a vote of confidence on the ability of the nation-state to manage the interests of the nation in the global web of policy making. Election to office no longer denotes a specific mandate, given the variable geometry of policy making and the unpredictability of the issues that must be dealt with. Thus, increasing distance and opacity between citizens and their representatives follows (Dalton 2005, 2006). This crisis of legitimacy is deepened by the practice of media politics and the politics of scandal, while image-making substitutes for issue deliberation as the privileged mechanism to access power (Thompson 2000). In the past decade, surveys of political attitudes around the world have revealed widespread and growing distrust of citizens vis-à-vis political parties, politicians, and the institutions of representative democracy (Caputo 2004; Catterberg and Moreno 2005; Arsenault 2007; Gallup International 2006).
3. *Crisis of identity:* As people see their nation and their culture increasingly disjointed from the mechanisms of political decision making in a global, multinational network, their claim of autonomy takes the form of resistance identity and cultural identity politics as opposed to their political identity as citizens (Barber 1995; Castells 2004b; Lull 2007).
4. *Crisis of equity:* The process of globalization led by market forces in the framework of deregulation often increases inequality between countries and between social groups within countries (Held and Kaya 2006). In the absence of a global regulatory environment that compensates for growing inequality, the demands of economic competition undermine existing welfare states. The shrinking of welfare states makes it increasingly difficult for national governments to compensate for structurally induced inequality because of the decreased capacity of national institutions to act as corrective mechanisms (Gilbert 2002).

As a result of these crises and the decreased ability of governments to mitigate them, non-governmental actors become the advocates of the needs, interests, and values of people at large, thus further undermining the role of governments in response to challenges posed by globalization and structural transformation.

THE GLOBAL CIVIL SOCIETY

The decreased ability of nationally based political systems to manage the world's problems on a global scale has induced the rise of a global civil society. However, the term *civil society* is a generic label that lumps together several disparate and often contradictory and competitive forms of organization and action. A distinction must be made between different types of organizations.

In every country, there are *local civil society actors* who defend local or sectoral interests, as well as specific values against or beyond the formal political process. Examples of this subset of civil society include grassroots organizations, community groups, labor unions, interest groups, religious groups, and civic associations. This is a very old social practice in all societies, and some analysts, particularly Putnam (2000), even argue that this form of civic engagement is on the decline, as individualism becomes the predominant culture of our societies. In fact, the health of these groups varies widely according to country and region. For instance, in almost every country of Latin America, community organizations have become a very important part of the social landscape (Calderón 2003). The difference between these groups in varying nations is that the sources of social organization are increasingly diversified: religion, for instance, plays a major role in Latin America, particularly non-Catholic Christian religious groups. Student movements remain an influential source of social change in East Asia, particularly in South Korea. In some cases, criminal organizations build their networks of support in the poor communities in exchange for patronage and forced protection. Elsewhere, people in the community, women's groups, ecologists, or ethnic groups, organize themselves to make their voices heard and to assert their identity. However, traditional forms of politics and ideological sources of voluntary associations seem to be on the decline almost everywhere, although the patronage system continues to exist around each major political party. Overall, this variegated process amounts to a shift from the institutional political system to informal and formal associations of interests and values as the source of collective action and sociopolitical influence. This empowers local civil society to face the social problems resulting from unfettered globalization. Properly speaking, this is not the global civil society, although it constitutes a milieu of organization, projects, and practices that nurtures the growth of the global civil society.

A second trend is represented by *the rise of nongovernmental organizations (NGOs) with a global or international frame of reference in their action and goals*. This is what most analysts refer to as "global civil society" (Kaldor 2003). These are private organizations (albeit often supported or partly financed by public institutions) that act outside government channels to address global problems. Often they affirm values that are universally recognized but politically manipulated in their own interest by political agencies, including governments. In other words, international NGOs claim to be the enforcers of unenforced human rights. A case in point is Amnesty International, whose influence comes from the fact that it is an equal-opportunity critic of all cases of political, ideological, or religious repression, regardless of the political interests at stake. These organizations typically espouse basic principles and/ or uncompromising values. For instance, torture is universally decried even as a means of combating greater "evils." The affirmation of human rights on a comprehensive, global scale gives birth to tens of thousands of NGOs that cover the entire span of the human experience, from poverty to illnesses, from hunger to epidemics, from women's rights to the defense of children, and from banning land mines to saving the whales. Examples of global civil society groups include Medecins Sans Frontieres, Oxfam, Greenpeace, and thousands of others. *The*

Global Civil Society Yearbook series, an annual report produced by the London School of Economics Centre for Global Governance and under the direction of Mary Kaldor, provides ample evidence of the quantitative importance and qualitative relevance of these global civil society actors and illustrates how they have already altered the social and political management of global and local issues around the world (e.g., Anheier, Glasius, and Kaldor 2004; Glasius, Kaldor, and Anheier 2005; Kaldor, Anheier, and Glasius 2006).

To understand the characteristics of the international NGOS, three features must be emphasized: In contrast to political parties, these NGOs have considerable popularity and legitimacy, and this translates into substantial funding both via donations and volunteerism. Their activity focuses on practical matters, specific cases, and concrete expressions of human solidarity: saving children from famine, freeing political prisoners, stopping the lapidation of women, and ameliorating the impact of unsustainable development on indigenous cultures. What is fundamental here is that the classical political argument of rationalizing decisions in terms of the overall context of politics is denied. Goals do not justify the means. The purpose is to undo evil or to do good in one specific instance. The positive output must be considered in itself, not as a way of moving in a positive direction. Because people have come to distrust the logic of instrumental politics, the method of direct action on direct outputs finds increasing support. Finally, the key tactics of NGOs to achieve results and build support for their causes is media politics (Dean, Anderson, and Lovink 2006; Gillmor 2004). It is through the media that these organizations reach the public and mobilize people in support of these causes. In so doing, they eventually put pressure on governments threatened by the voters or on corporations fearful of consumers' reactions. Thus, the media become the battleground for an NGO's campaign. Since these are global campaigns, global media are the key target. The globalization of communication leads to the globalization of media politics (Costanza-Chock 2006).

Social movements that aim to control the process of globalization constitute a third type of civil society actor. In attempting to shape the forces of globalization, these social movements build networks of action and organization to induce a global social movement for global justice (what the media labeled, incorrectly, as the antiglobalization movement) (Keck and Sikkink 1998; Juris forthcoming). The Zapatistas, for instance, formed a social movement opposed to the economic, social, and cultural effects of globalization (represented by NAFTA) on the Mexican Indians and on the Mexican people at large (Castells, Yawaza, and Kiselyova 1996). To survive and assert their rights, they called for global solidarity, and they ended up being one of the harbingers of the global network of indigenous movements, itself a component of the much broader global movement. The connection between many of these movements in a global network of debate and coordination of action and the formalization of some of these movements in a permanent network of social initiatives aimed at altering the processes of globalization, are processes that are redefining the sociopolitical landscape of the world. Yet the movement for global justice, inspired by the motto that "another world is possible," is not the sum of nationally bound struggles. It is a global network of opposition to the values and interests that are currently dominant in the globalization process (Juris 2004). Its nodes grow and shrink alternately, depending on the conditions under which each society relates to globalization and its political manifestations. This is a movement that, in spite of the attempts by some leaders to build a program for a new world order, is better described by what it opposes than by a unified ideology. It is essentially a democratic movement, a movement that calls for new forms of political representation of people's will and interests in the process of global governance. In spite of its extreme internal diversity, there is indeed a shared critique of the management of the world by international institutions made up exclusively of national governments. It is an expression of the crisis of legitimacy, transformed into oppositional political action.

There is a fourth type of expression of global civil society. This is *the movement of public opinion,* made up of turbulences of information in a diversified media system, and of the emergence of spontaneous, ad hoc mobilizations using horizontal, autonomous networks of communication. The implications of this phenomenon at the global level—that were first exemplified by the simultaneous peace demonstrations around the world on February 15, 2003, against the imminent Iraq war—are full of political meaning. Internet and wireless communication, by enacting a global, horizontal network of communication, provide both an organizing tool and a means for debate, dialogue, and collective decision making. Case studies of local sociopolitical mobilizations organized by means of the Internet and mobile communication in South Korea, the Philippines, Spain, Ukraine, Ecuador, Nepal, and Thailand, among many other countries, illustrate the new capacity of movements to organize and mobilize citizens in their country while calling for solidarity in the world at large (Castells et al. 2006). The mobilization against the military junta in Myanmar in October 2007 is a case in point (Mydans 2007). The first demonstrations, mainly led by students, were relatively small, but they were filmed with video cell phones and immediately uploaded on YouTube. The vision of the determination of the demonstrators and of the brutality of the military regime amplified the movement. It became a movement of the majority of society when the Buddhist monks took to the streets to express their moral outrage. The violent repression that followed was also filmed and distributed over the Internet because the ability to record and connect through wireless communication by simple devices in the hands of hundreds of people made it possible to record everything. Burmese people connected among themselves and to the world relentlessly, using short message service (SMS) and e-mails, posting daily blogs, notices on Facebook, and videos on YouTube. The mainstream media rebroadcast and repackaged these citizen journalists' reports, made from the front line, around the world. By the time the dictatorship closed down all Internet providers, cut off mobile phone operators, and confiscated video-recording devices found on the streets, the brutality of the Myanmar regime had been globally exposed. This exposure embarrassed their Chinese sponsors and induced the United States and the European Union to increase diplomatic pressure on the junta (although they refrained from suspending the lucrative oil and gas deals between the junta and European and American companies). In sum, the global civil society now has the technological means to exist independently from political institutions and from the mass media. However, the capacity of social movements to change the public mind still depends, to a large extent, on their ability to shape the debate in the public sphere. In this context, at this instance of human history, how is governance articulated in social practice and institutions?

GLOBAL GOVERNANCE AND THE NETWORK STATE

The increasing inability of nation-states to confront and manage the processes of globalization of the issues that are the object of their governance leads to ad hoc forms of global governance and, ultimately, to a new form of state. Nation-states, in spite of their multidimensional crisis, do not disappear; they transform themselves to adapt to the new context. Their pragmatic transformation is what really changes the contemporary landscape of politics and policy making. By *nation-states*, I mean the institutional set comprising the whole state (i.e., national governments, the parliament, the political party system, the judiciary, and the state bureaucracy). As a nation-state experiences crises wrought by globalization, this system transforms itself by three main mechanisms:

1. Nation-states associate with each other, forming networks of states. Some of these networks are multipurpose and constitutionally defined, such as the European Union; others focus on a set of issues, generally related to trade (e.g., Mercosur or NAFTA); while still others are spaces of coordination and debate (e.g., the Asia-Pacific Economic Cooperation or APEC and the Association of Southern Asian Nations known as ASEAN). In the strongest networks, participating states explicitly share sovereignty. In weaker networks, states cooperate via implicit or de facto sovereignty-sharing mechanisms.
2. States may build an increasingly dense network of international institutions and supranational organizations to deal with global issues—from general-purpose institutions (e.g., the United Nations), to specialized ones (e.g., the International Monetary Fund, World Bank, NATO, the European Security Conference, and the International Atomic Energy Agency). There are also ad hoc international agencies defined around a specific set of issues (e.g., environmental treaties).
3. States may also decentralize power and resources in an effort to increase legitimacy and/or attempt to tap other forms of cultural or political allegiance through the devolution of power to local or regional governments and to NGOs that extend the decision-making process in civil society.

From this multipronged process emerges a new form of state, the network state, which is characterized by shared sovereignty and responsibility, flexibility of procedures of governance, and greater diversity in the relationship between governments and citizens in terms of time and space. The whole system develops pragmatically via ad hoc decisions, ushering in sometimes contradictory rules and institutions and obscuring and removing the system of political representation from political control. In the network state, efficiency improves, but the ensuing gains in legitimacy by the nation-state deepen its crisis, although overall political legitimacy may improve if local and regional institutions play their role. Yet the growing autonomy of the local and regional state may bring the different levels of the state into competition against one another.

The practice of global goverance through ad hoc networks confronts a number of major problems that evolve out of the contradiction between the historically constructed nature of the institutions that come into the network and the new functions and mechanisms they have to assume to perform in the network while still relating to their nation-bound societies. The network state faces a *coordination problem* with three aspects: organizational, technical, and political. The state faces organizational problems because agencies that previously flourished via territoriality and authority vis-à-vis their societies cannot have the same structure, reward systems, and operational principles as agencies whose fundamental role is to find synergy with other agencies. Technical coordination problems take place because protocols of communication do not work. The introduction of the Internet and computer networks often disorganizes agencies rather than facilitating synergies. Agencies often resist networking technology. Political coordination problems evolve not only horizontally between agencies but also vertically because networking between agencies and supervisory bodies necessitates a loss of bureaucratic autonomy. Moreover, agencies must also network with their citizen constituencies, thus bringing pressure on the bureaucracies to be more responsive to the citizen-clients.

The development of the network state also needs to confront an ideological problem: coordinating a common policy means a common language and a set of shared values. Examples include opposition to market fundamentalism in the regulation of markets, acceptance of sustainable development in environmental policy, or the prioritization of human rights over the *raison d'etat* in security policy. More often than not, governments do not share the same principles or the same interpretation of common principles.

There is also a lingering geopolitical problem. Nation-states still see the networks of governance as a negotiating table upon which to impose their specific interests. There is a stalemate in the intergovernmental decision-making processes because the culture of cooperation is lacking. The overarching principles are the interests of the nation-state and the domination of the personal/political/social interests in service of each nation-state. Governments see the global state as an opportunity to maximize their own interests, rather than a new context in which political institutions have to govern together. In fact, the more the globalization process proceeds, the more contradictions it generates (e.g., identity crises, economic crises, and security crises), leading to a revival of nationalism and to the primacy of sovereignty. These tensions underlie the attempts by various governments to pursue unilateralism in their policies in spite of the objective multilateralism that results from global interdependence in our world (Nye 2002).

As long as these contradictions persist, it is difficult, if not impossible, for the world's geopolitical actors to shift from the practice of a pragmatic, ad hoc networking form of negotiated decision making to a system of constitutionally accepted networked global governance (Habermas 1998).

THE NEW PUBLIC SPHERE

The new political system in a globalized world emerges from the processes of the formation of a global civil society and a global network state that supersedes and integrates the preexisting nation-states without dissolving them into a global government. There is a process of the emergence of de facto global governance without a global government. The transition from these pragmatic forms of sociopolitical organization and decision making to a more elaborate global institutional system requires the coproduction of meaning and the sharing of values between global civil society and the global network state. This transformation is influenced and fought over by cultural/ideational materials through which the political and social interests work to enact the transformation of the state. In the last analysis, the will of the people emerges from people's minds. And people make up their minds on the issues that affect their lives, as well as the future of humankind, from the messages and debates that take place in the public sphere. The contemporary global public sphere is largely dependent on the global/local communication media system. This media system includes television, radio, and the print press, as well as a variety of multimedia and communications systems, among which the Internet and horizontal networks of communication now play a decisive role (Bennett 2004; Dahlgren 2005; Tremayne 2007). There is a shift from a public sphere anchored around the national institutions of territorially bound societies to a public sphere constituted around the media system (Volkmer 1999; El-Nawawy and Iskander 2002; Paterson and Sreberny 2004). This media system includes what I have conceptualized as mass self-communication, that is, networks of communication that relate many-to-many in the sending and receiving of messages in a multimodal form of communication that bypasses mass media and often escapes government control (Castells 2007).

The current media system is local and global at the same time. It is organized around a core formed by media business groups with global reach and their networks (Arsenault and Castells forthcoming). But at the same time, it is dependent on state regulations and focused on narrowcasting to specific audiences (Price 2002). By acting on the media system, particularly by creating events that send powerful images and messages, transnational activists induce a debate on the hows, whys, and whats of globalization and on related societal choices (Juris forthcoming). It is through the media, both mass media and horizontal networks of communication, that nonstate actors influence people's minds and foster social change. Ultimately, the transformation of consciousness does have consequences on political behavior, on voting patterns, and on the decisions of governments. It is at the level of media politics where it appears that societies can be moved in a direction that diverges from the values and interests institutionalized in the political system.

Thus, it is essential for state actors, and for intergovernmental institutions, such as the United Nations, to relate to civil society not only around institutional mechanisms and procedures of political representation but in public debates in the global public sphere. That global public sphere is built around the media communication system and Internet networks, particularly in the social spaces of the Web 2.0, as exemplified by YouTube, MySpace, Facebook, and the growing blogosphere that by mid-2007 counted 70 million blogs and was doubling in size every six months (Tremayne 2007). A series of major conferences was organized by the UN during the 1990s on issues pertinent to humankind (from the condition of women to environmental conservation). While not very effective in terms of designing policy, these conferences were essential in fostering a global dialogue, in raising public awareness, and in providing the platform on which the global civil society could move to the forefront of the policy debate. Therefore, stimulating, the consolidation of this communication-based public sphere is one key mechanism with which states and international institutions can engage with the demands and projects of the global civil society. This can take place by stimulating dialogue regarding specific initiatives and recording, on an ongoing basis, the contributions of this dialogue so that it can inform policy making in the international arena. To harness the power of the world's public opinion through global media and Internet networks is the most effective form of broadening political participation on a global scale, by inducing a fruitful, synergistic connection between the government-based international institutions and the global civil society. This multimodal communication space is what constitutes the new global public sphere.

CONCLUSION: PUBLIC DIPLOMACY AND THE GLOBAL PUBLIC SPHERE

Public diplomacy is not propaganda. And it is not government diplomacy. We do not need to use a new concept to designate the traditional practices of diplomacy. Public diplomacy is the diplomacy of the public, that is, the projection in the international arena of the values and ideas of the public. The public is not the government because it is not formalized in the institutions of the state. By *the public*, we usually mean what is common to a given social organization that transcends the private. The private is the domain of self-defined interests and values, while the public is the domain of the shared interests and values (Dewey 1954). The implicit project behind the idea of public diplomacy is not to assert the power of a state or of a social actor in the form of "soft power." It is, instead, to harness the dialogue between different social collectives and their cultures in the hope of sharing meaning and understanding. The aim of the practice of public diplomacy is not to convince but to communicate, not to declare but to listen. Public diplomacy seeks to build a public sphere in which diverse voices can be heard in spite of their various origins, distinct values, and often contradictory interests. The goal of public diplomacy, in contrast to government diplomacy, is not to assert power or to negotiate a rearrangement of power relationships. It is to induce a communication space in which a new, common language could emerge as a precondition for diplomacy, so that when the time for diplomacy comes, it reflects not only interests and power making but also meaning and sharing. In this sense, public diplomacy intervenes in the global space equivalent to what has been traditionally conceived as the public sphere in the national system. It is a terrain of cultural engagement in which ideational materials are produced and confronted by various social actors, creating the conditions under which different projects can be channeled by the global civil society and the political institutions of global governance toward an informed process of decision making that respects the differences and weighs policy alternatives.

Because we live in a globalized, interdependent world, the space of political codecision is necessarily global. And the choice that we face is either to construct the global political system as an expression of power relationships without cultural mediation or else to develop a global public sphere around the global networks of communication, from which the public debate could inform the emergence of a new form of consensual global governance. If the choice is the latter, public diplomacy, understood as networked communication and shared meaning, becomes a decisive tool for the attainment of a sustainable world order.

REFERENCES

Anheier, Helmut, Marlies Glasius, and Mary Kaldor, eds. 2004. *Global civil society 2004/5.* London: Sage.
Arsenault, Amelia, 2007. The international crisis of legitimacy. Unpublished working paper.
Arsenault, Amelia, and Manuel Castells. Forthcoming. Structure and dynamics of global multimedia business networks. *International Journal of Communication.*
Barber, Benjamin R. 1995. *Jihad vs. McWorld.* New York: Times Books.
Bauman, Zygmunt. 1999. *In search of politics.* Stanford, CA: Stanford University Press.
Beck, Ulrich. 2000. *What is globalization?* Malden, MA: Polity.
— . 2006. *Power in the global age.* Cambridge, UK: Polity.
Bennett, W. Lance. 2004. Global media and politics: Transnational communication regimes and civic cultures. *Annual Review of Political Science* 7 (1): 125–48.
Calderón, G., Fernando, ed. 2003. *Es sostenible la globalización en América Latina?* Santiago, Chile: Fondo de Cultura Económica PNUD-Bolivia.
Caputo, Dante, ed. 2004. *La democracia en América Latina.* Pograma de Naciones Unidas para el Desarrollo. Buenos Aires, Argentina: Aguilar, Altea, Alfaguara.
Cardoso, Gustavo. 2006. *The media in the network society.* Lisbon, Portugal: Center for Research and Studies in Sociology.
Castells, Manuel. 1996. *The rise of the network society.* Oxford, UK: Blackwell.
—. ed. 2004a. *The network society: A cross-cultural perspective.* Northampton, MA: Edward Elgar.
—. 2004b. *The power of identity.* Malden, MA: Blackwell.
—. 2007. Communication, power and counter-power in the network society. *International Journal of Communication* 1:238–66.
Castells, Manuel, Mireia Fernandez-Ardevol, Jack Linchuan Qui, and Araba Sey. 2006. *Mobile communication and society: A global perspective.* Cambridge, MA: MIT Press.

Castells, Manuel, Shujiro Yazawa, and Emma Kiselyova. 1996. Insurgents against the new global order: A comparative analysis of Mexico's Zapatistas, the American militia, and Japan's Aum Shinrikyo. *Berkeley Journal of Sociology* 40:21–59.

Catterberg, Gabriela, and Alejandro Moreno. 2005. The individual bases of political trust: Trends in new and established democracies. *International Journal of Public Opinion Research* 18 (1): 31–48. Chester, Jeff. 2007. *Digital destiny. New media and the future of democracy.* New York: New Press.

Costanza-Chock, Sasha. 2006. *Analytical note: Horizontal communication and social movements.* Los Angeles: Annenberg School of Communication.

Dahlgren, Peter. 2005. The Internet, public spheres, and political communication: Dispersion and deliberation. *Political Communication* 22:147–62.

Dalton, Russell J. 2005. The social transformation of trust in government. *International Review of Sociology* 15 (1): 133–54.

—. 2006. *Citizen politics: Public opinion and political parties in advanced industrial democracies.* Washington, DC: CQ Press.

Dean, Jodi, Jon W. Anderson, and Geert Lovink, eds. 2006. *Reformatting politics: Information technology and global civil society.* New York: Routledge.

Dewey, John. 1954. *The public and its problems.* Chicago: Swallow Press.

El-Nawawy, Mohammed, and Adel Iskander. 2002. *Al-jazeera: How the free Arab news network scooped the world and changed the Middle East.* Cambridge, MA: Westview.

Forsythe, David P. 2000. *Human rights in international relations.* Cambridge: Cambridge University Press.

Gallup International. 2006. The voice of the people. International survey conducted for the World Economic Forum. http://www.gallup-international.com/.

Giddens, Anthony. 1979. *Central problems in social theory: Action, structure, and contradiction in social analysis.* Berkeley: University of California Press.

Giddens, Anthony, and Will Hutton. 2000. *On the edge: Living with global capitalism.* London: Jonathan Cape.

Gilbert, Neil. 2002. *Transformation of the welfare state: The silent surrender of public responsibility.* Oxford: Oxford University Press.

Gillmor, Dan. 2004. *We the media. Grassroots journalism by the people for the people.* Sebastopol, CA: O'Reilly.

Glasius, Marlies, Mary Kaldor, and Helmut Anheier, eds. 2005. *Global civil society 2005/6.* London: Sage.

Grundmann, Reiner. 2001. *Transnational environmental policy: Reconstructing ozone.* London: Routledge.

Guidry, John A., Michael D. Kennedy, and Mayer N. Zald. 2000. *Globalizations and social movements: Culture, power, and the transnational public sphere.* Ann Arbor: University of Michigan Press.

Habermas, Jürgen. 1976. *Legitimation crisis.* London: Heinemann Educational Books.

—. 1989. *The structural transformation of the public sphere.* Cambridge, UK: Polity.
—. 1996. *Between facts and norms: Contributions to a discourse theory of law and democracy.* Cambridge, MA: MIT Press.
—. 1998. *Die postnationale konstellation: Politische essays.* Frankfurt am Main, Germany: Suhrkamp.
Held, David. 2004. *Global covenant: The social democratic alternative to the Washington consensus.* Malden, MA: Polity.
Held, David, and Ayse Kaya. 2006. *Global inequality: Patterns and explanations.* Cambridge, UK: Polity.
Held, David, and Anthony G. McGrew, eds. 2007. *Globalization theory: Approaches and controversies.* London: Polity.
Held, David, Anthony G. McGrew, David Goldblatt, and Jonathan Perraton, eds. 1999. *Global transformations: Politics, economics and culture.* Cambridge, UK: Polity.
Jacquet, Pierre, Jean Pisani-Ferry, and Laurence Tubiana, eds. 2002. *Gouvernance mondiale.* Paris: Documentation Française.
Juris, Jeffrey. 2004. Networked social movements: The movement against corporate globalization. In *The network society: A cross-cultural perspective,* ed. Manuel Castells, 341–62. Cheltenham, UK: Edward Elgar.
—. Forthcoming. *Networking futures: The movements against corporate globalization.* Durham, NC: Duke University Press.
Kaldor, Mary. 2003. *Global civil society: An answer to war.* Malden, MA: Polity.
Kaldor, Mary, Helmut Anheier, and Marlies Glasius, eds. 2006. *Global civil society 2006/7.* London: Sage.
Keck, Margaret E., and Kathryn Sikkink. 1998. *Activists beyond borders: Advocacy networks in international politics.* Ithaca, NY: Cornell University Press.
Keohane, Robert O. 2002. *Power and governance in a partially globalized world.* London: Routledge.
Low, Setha M., and Neil Smith, eds. 2006. *The politics of public space.* New York: Routledge.
Lull, James. 2007. *Culture-on-demand: Communication in a crisis world.* Malden, MA: Blackwell.
Mann, Michael. 1986. *The sources of social power,* vol. I, *A history of power from the beginning to A.D. 1760.* Cambridge: Cambridge University Press.
—. 1993. *The sources of social power,* vol. II, *The rise of classes and nation-states, 1760–1914.* Cambridge: Cambridge University Press.
McChesney, Robert Waterman. 2007. *Communication revolution: Critical junctures and the future of media.* New York: New Press.
Mydans, Seth. 2007. Myanmar comes face to face with a technology revolution. *International Herald Tribune,* October 3.
Nye, Joseph S. 2002. *The paradox of American power: Why the world's only superpower can't go it alone.* New York: Oxford University Press.

Nye, Joseph S., and John D. Donahue, eds. 2000. *Governance in a globalizing world.* Washington, DC: Brookings Institution Press.

Paterson, Chris A., and Annabelle Sreberny, eds. 2004. *International news in the 21st Century.* Eastleigh, UK: LIniversity of Luton Press.

Price, Monroe E. 2002. *Media and sovereignty: The global information revolution and its challenge to state power.* Cambridge, MA: MIT Press.

Putnam, Robert D. 2000. *Bowling alone: The collapse and revival of American community.* New York: Simon & Schuster.

Sassen, Saskia. 2006. *Territory authority, rights: From medieval to global assemblages.* Princeton, NJ: Princeton University Press.

Soros, George. 2006. *The age of fallibility: The consequences of the war on terror.* New York: Public Affairs.

Stewart, Angus. 2001. *Theories of power and domination: The politics of empowerment in late modernity.* London: Sage.

Thompson, John B. 2000. *Political scandal: Power and visibility in the media age.* Cambridge, UK: Polity. Tremayne, Mark, ed. 2007. *Blogging, citizenship, and the future of media.* London: Routledge.

Volkmer, Ingrid. 1999. *News in the global sphere: A study of CNN and its impact on global communication.* Eastleigh, UK: University of Luton Press.

—. 2003. The global network society and the global public sphere. *Journal of Development* 46 (4): 9–16.

CPSIA information can be obtained at www.ICGtesting.com
Printed in the USA
LVOW09s0740010915

452270LV00008B/44/P